THE HIGHLAND HOUSE TRʌ

THE HIGHLAND HOUSE TRANSFORMED

Architecture and Identity on the Edge of Britain,
1700–1850

Daniel Maudlin

Dundee University Press

First published in Great Britain in 2009 by
Dundee University Press

University of Dundee
Dundee DD1 4HN

http://www.dup.dundee.ac.uk/

ISBN: 978 1 84586 018 9

British Library Cataloguing-in-Publication Data
A catalogue record for this book is available
on request from the British Library

The publishers gratefully acknowledge the
support of the Scotland Inheritance Fund
towards the reproduction of illustrations
in this book.

Typeset by Mark Blackadder

Printed and bound in Britain
by Bell and Bain Ltd, Glasgow

Contents

Abreviations

MMA	Mull Museum Archive
NAS	National Archives of Scotland
NSA	New Statistical Account of Scotland
NSDTC	Nova Scotia Department of Tourism and Culture
PANS	Provincial Archives of Nova Scotia
PHC	Pictou Heritage Centre
RCAHMS	Royal Commission on Ancient and Historic Monuments of Scotland
SAS	Statistical Account of Scotland
SVBWG	Scottish Vernacular Building Working Group
WHC	Wick Heritage Centre

Illustrations

Preface

The dramatic landscape of the Scottish Highlands is punctuated by the well-ordered presence of hundreds of 'neat and regular' farmhouses and planned villages. *The Highland House Transformed* was born out of a desire to understand the distinct, and at times austere, character of the houses and villages that I repeatedly encountered in the Highlands over a ten-year period of study, work and travel: why are they there? Why are there so many? Why do they all look similar? What do they mean?

The architectural history that emerges is also the history of early modern agri-business. In the Highlands and Islands the construction of hundreds of new farmhouses, cottages and grid-plan villages through the late eighteenth and early nineteenth centuries was a key element in a revolutionary process of agricultural improvement that permanently transformed the landscape. Agricultural improvement initiated the mass clearances of thousands of traditional settlements. In their place a Highland building boom took place producing over 100 planned workers' villages, an unknown number of cottages and over 300 farmhouses; accounting for roughly three-quarters of all rural historic housing in the region today. This book follows the change in population of the Highlands' fertile straths and glens, from Gaelic communities to immigrant tenant farmers and sheep, through the transformation of the common Highland house from the indigenous turf-and-thatch 'blackhouse' into the white Georgian boxes of the improved farmhouse and the improved cottage. As the Highland Gaelic population were cleared from their lands many emigrated to North America. In the last chapter the houses of those Highlanders who crossed the Atlantic and built new homes in the New World are considered: the Highland house transformed again.

The reality of this 'architecture of improvement' stands at odds with the myths of Highland Romanticism that, since the early nineteenth century, have presented a highly misleading but resilient interpretation of Highland Scotland: kilted Highlanders living pastoral lives in thatched cottages. In the twentieth century, this romantic idea of the typical Highland house was used to promote a mythologised Scottish national identity. At the 1938 Empire Exhibition in Glasgow, alongside Modernist buildings by Jack Coia and Thomas Tait, Scotland presented to the world a highly imaginative recreation of a traditional Highland village: the Clachan (Fig. 1). Such was the power of this myth-making that later in 1953, on return from a tour of the Scottish Highlands in search of a suitable location for the musical *Brigadoon,* producer Arthur Freed commented that he could find 'nothing that looked like Scotland'. Freed went in search of the romantic Highland villages of the popular imagination. *The Highland House Transformed* is intended as an attempt to put romanticism and national mythologies to one side and to examine the distinctly unromantic but histori-cally and culturally significant houses that continue to define the Highland landscape.

1. The Clachan, Empire Exhibition, Scotland 1938 (National Museums of Scotland)

Acknowledgements

I would like to thank the following museums, archives and galleries for their assistance and suggestions: St Clair Prest at the Pictou Heritage Centre; Antigonish County Museum; Mull Museum, Tobermory; Wick Heritage Centre; Ullapool Museum; Provincial Archives of Nova Scotia, Halifax; Royal Commission on the Ancient and Historic Monuments of Scotland; National Archives of Scotland; Sheila Mackenzie, Joseph Marshall and Laragh Quinney of the National Library of Scotland; Dorothy Kidd of the National Museums of Scotland; Imogen Gibbon of the National Galleries of Scotland; Rachel Chisholm at the Highland Folk Museum, Kingussie; and Elizabeth Guthrie, Winterthur Museum and Library, Delaware.

Thank you to Carol Pope and John Tuckwell of Dundee University Press. Also, many thanks to Hazel Reid, editor, and Mairi Sutherland, project manager, with whom it has been a pleasure to work. The following also deserve my gratitude for their help and advice throughout the research and preparation of this book: Oliver Barratt; Elizabeth Beaton; Wayde Brown, University of Georgia; Kirsty Burrell; Martin Cherry; Jeffrey Cohen, Brynmawr College; John Crowley, Cynthia Neville and David Sutherland of Dalhousie University; Kitty Cruft; Randy and Ginny Donahue; Jane Geddes; Jeremy Gould, University of Plymouth; Elizabeth Hancock, University of Glasgow; Emma Howard; David Jones and John Frew, University of St Andrews; Judi Loach, University of Cardiff; James Lingard; Frank Matero, University of Pennsylvania; Deborah Mays, Ranald Macinnes and Aonghus Mackechnie of Historic Scotland; Mary Miers; Jason and Melanie O'Flynn, Milton Eonan, Glenlyon; Steven Parissien; Gareth Rees; Rosemary Sweet, University of Leicester; Iain Thornber; and Duncan Whitehead. And thank you most of all to Jane Campbell and my mother, Anna.

I would like to thank the Trustees of the National Library of Scotland, the National Museums of Scotland, National Galleries of Scotland, Royal Commission on the Ancient and Historic Monuments of Scotland, Winterthur Museum and Library, Delaware, and the Highland Folk Museum, Kingussie, for permission to reproduce images. The following institutions supported research for this book with grants and fellowships: Leverhulme Trust, Arts and Humanities Research Council (UK), Society of Architectural Historians of Great Britain, Royal Institute of British Architects, Winterthur Museum and Library, Delaware. Some of the material in this book has appeared in earlier forms in other publications, including *Proceedings of the Society of Antiquaries of Scotland* (vol. 133, 2003), *Architectural History* (vol. 50, 2007), *Urban History* (vol. 34, 2007), *Vernacular Architecture* (vol. 39, 2008).

Introduction

The neat and regular farmhouses, cottages and planned villages of the Scottish Highlands stand as monuments to the powerful social and economic forces that transformed the region through the long eighteenth century, *c.* 1700–1850. Although the landscape appears wild and untamed, what the twenty-first-century visitor to the Highlands experiences is a carefully managed, rational and well-ordered place. The present day Highland landscape dates from the agricultural revolution of the eighteenth and nineteenth centuries which saw the transformation of clan chieftains into commercial landowners and the clearance of indigenous communities to make way for single tenant sheep farms. A new breed of professional tenant farmers took root and built themselves modern British farmhouses. On the new sheep ranches numberless clusters of indigenous 'blackhouses' were replaced by 'modern' British farmhouses. Those indigenous Gaelic communities that chose not to emigrate out of the Highlands to the Lowlands or North America were faced with relocation to 'improved' cottages in the new industrial planned villages and a new way of life, or subsistence farming on the marginal lands of the crofting townships.

The Highland House Transformed is a study of the relationship between domestic architecture and social change and the powerful role architecture can play in forming and re-forming the physical character and identity of a place.[1] In terms of geography, the Scottish Highlands is the predominantly mountainous country of Northern Scotland that lies beyond the historic 'Highland Line', the notional boundary, which marks the geographic border between the Lowlands and the Highlands (Fig. 2).[2] In cultural terms, the geographic and geological boundaries of the Scottish Highlands broadly match those areas historically settled by Scotland's Gaelic-speaking population. The historic small-scale domestic architecture found in the Highlands today is the primary physical evidence of the commercial farming activities of the late eighteenth and early nineteenth centuries that permanently transformed the physical appearance, people and culture of the region. Besides numberless ruins, the total absence of historic indigenous Gaelic settlements and dwellings outside

2. Map of Scotland showing the 'Highland Line' (James Lingard)

of designated crofting areas is negative proof of the same activities.

The eighteenth-century Highland landscape saw the rapid replacement of one building tradition and settlement pattern with another. In strath and glen, the physical change from groups of indigenous blackhouses to a lone 'modern' eighteenth-century farmhouse meant a change in norms in architectural form, building materials and construction. The change in the type of houses commonly found in the Highlands was one manifestation of long-term social and economic changes ultimately resulting in a fundamental change in the ethnic population as new people built new houses. The farmhouses and cottages that stand today are artefacts of a material culture that emerged as the region's new commercial farmers engaged with a wider British culture and consumer society.

The white, two-storey symmetrical farmhouse standing alone against a mountainous landscape is an iconic image of the Scottish Highlands. These were the new homes of the new Highland middle class of tenant farmers built continuously from the mid-eighteenth through to the mid-nineteenth century (Fig. 3). The new farmhouses were highly visible symbols of agricultural improvement and agents in the creation of a 'modern' eighteenth-century landscape. The forty years between 1775 and 1815 were the peak years of a house building boom in the Highlands, which saw over 300 farmhouses built. The physical fabric of these houses is quantitative evidence of economic activity related to agricultural improvement. The Highland building boom started in Argyll and Bute in the middle of the eighteenth century under the modernising influence of the Dukes of Argyll. The boom did not spread evenly but developed in specific pockets of regional activity. The principal region of house building outside of Argyll was in the plains around Inverness but new houses were built throughout the

3. William Daniell, 'View of Cuniag, from Loch Inver', *A Voyage Round the Coast of Scotland and the Adjacent Islands*, 1814–1822 (National Library of Scotland)

Highlands, with smaller house building volumes in other parts of the Highlands often relating to the vast size of individual sheep farms, often of 70,000 acres or more, rather than an absence of agricultural reform.

The analysis of farmhouses can deepen our understanding of the lives and values of the farmers and landowners who built and occupied them. For instance, the high building costs involved demonstrate the importance placed upon the ownership of an improved farmhouse by improving farmers. A new farmhouse was a very expensive undertaking involving imported materials and components and the skills of migrant masons from Scotland's historic urban Masonic centres in the Lowlands. Why was a new farmhouse important? House building showed an ability to spend. But the design choices made by improving farmers when building a new house were also vitally important. The architectural uniformity of improved farmhouses in the Highlands indicates that improving farmers uniformly chose a plain classical style. In choosing to adopt a plain, everyday form of eighteenth century classicism (design dictated by the principles of symmetry, order and proportion), the typical farmer was making a deliberate statement that though they lived in the Highlands they belonged to a wider society informed by Scottish Enlightenment culture and British consumer values. In eighteenth-century Europe, the classical language of architecture was universally accepted as the socially acceptable language of good taste. By demonstrating good taste in matters of architecture and design, the farmer and his family demonstrated a certain social standing. The restrained use of classical ornament common to all improved farmhouses can be contrasted with the profusion of classical cornices, columns, pilasters and pediments that are characteristic of the smallest houses built by the humblest Highland landowners in the same period. Good taste required a sense of decorum, it would not have been socially or architecturally appropriate for a tenant farmer to mimic wholly the manners and ornament of his social superiors. Whilst draughty and difficult to heat, the new Highland farmhouse was valued as a complex display of messages about the social standing and cultural values of the farmer and his family who lived there. In contrast, the indigenous blackhouse kept you warm.

This new type of farmhouse also introduced new domestic spaces such as the parlour and drawing room to the modest Highland home. These rooms provided a stage for the social practices and rituals of Georgian British society. The dimly lit earth-walled interiors of the low blackhouse, where all life was based around an open central hearth, would have made a sharp contrast with the ordered and ornamented, multiple high-ceilinged rooms of the new farmhouses. The high ceilings, large windows, gable end fireplaces and exposed two-storey walls of a Georgian farmhouse combine to make the design exceptionally ill-suited to the Highland environment and climate. In contrast, the indigenous blackhouse evolved over centuries to be perfectly adapted, with every element of the plan, form and construction working to provide a warm and cosy interior domestic space. However, the primary function of the new farmhouse was social display not thermal efficiency.

British architectural and design history has largely ignored small everyday classical buildings, although this imbalance has been significantly redressed by Elizabeth McKellar and Barbara Arciszewska's *Articulating British Classicism*.[3] They are anonymous and uncomplicated buildings. This has been problematic for an art historical tradition centred upon the study of great works by known architects based upon archival evidence. However, when considered not as works of art but as artefacts of material culture, small buildings offer the opportunity to establish a new relationship between architecture and social and economic history; they can offer new perspectives in the analysis and interpretation of building practices, architectural form, style and the interaction between social practices, manners and rituals and designed spaces. Architecture can then be interpreted as an indicator of popular cultural values and social practices. A collation of physical evidence allows for the analysis of undocumented, ordinary, buildings in the same design context as well-documented works of architecture. A typical everyday building such as an improved farmhouse should not be judged negatively and dismissed as an ordinary, plain or even poor example of the art of architecture. An eighteenth-century farmhouse that exhibits formal and stylistic choices offers a fascinating architectural study when interpreted as a vehicle for the transmission of messages about social rank, social conformity and affiliation to distinct social groups.

The potential of design, and peoples' design choices, in advancing our understanding of peoples and cultures is a well-established concept in archaeology.[4] The question of design choice has also been the focus of North American 'folk studies' in the material culture of everyday undocumented lives but, with notable recent exceptions, it remains unfamiliar territory for British architectural history.[5] However, archaeology has also shown that caution must be taken when making inferences about social practices based upon the form of physical evidence and a tenable position must be taken between speculative guesswork and qualified objectivism.[6] The methodologies of socio-economic history, particularly quantitative analysis, can then provide architectural history with a new framework in which the formal and spatial trends of an entire region's building stock, incorporating hundreds of houses, can be understood. Although

4. An abandoned shepherd's bothy, Aberdeenshire (author)

little or nothing is known of the builders of the early modern farmhouses of the Scottish Highlands, quantitative formal analysis demonstrates that these buildings share a common design system. The sameness of eighteenth-century domestic architecture across the Highlands and Nova Scotia revealed by the quantitative data is remarkable and indicates a shared common culture despite their positions on the edge of Britain and the British Atlantic world.

The 'improved cottage' is the smaller relation of the improved farmhouse. It is the generic domestic housing type of the Highlands. Typically, it is a small, single-storey, two-room building but in all other formal respects it observes the same classical design rules of symmetry, order and proportion as the larger two-storey farmhouse (Fig. 4). However, the improved cottage occupies a very different social and economic position from that of the improved farmhouse. Improved cottages were built wherever the landlord or tenant farmer required their labourers to live. This could be a lone shepherd's bothy, a short terrace of cottages adjacent to a farmhouse and steadings, or in the urban environment of a planned estate village. The design of a new farmhouse expressed the choices and judgments of the tenant farmer who paid for it. The improved cottage was a didactic imposition upon the landless agricultural labourer: an expression of the landowner or tenant farmer's improving zeal and good taste. Forcibly removed from their indigenous blackhouse and resettled in a planned village, the ordinary Gael was obliged to build a new cottage according to building regulations set out by the landlord, which stipulated both design and building materials in order that a common neatness and regularity was maintained throughout a village or estate. They were not asked whether the improved cottage was actually a preferable place to live to a blackhouse. Whilst undoubtedly a dirty and therefore unhealthy environment, a winter passed inside a blackhouse was a much warmer and cosier experience than that provided by an improved cottage.

The nature of the typical Highland settlement also saw massive change with the eradication of indigenous Highland settlements in traditional farming areas and their replacement with planned villages established on unprofitable marginal land. The formal difference between the irregular cluster of homes that comprised the typical indigenous Highland *bailtean* or *clachan* and the grid-plan of the planned village is as marked as that between the blackhouse and the improved farmhouse and cottage. The planned village was the ultimate architectural manifestation of agricultural improvement (Fig. 5). It was an imposed alien form deliberately introduced into the Highland landscape to indicate that a new modern age of commercial estate management had begun. An entire urban environment was created in order to house and employ the population of an estate displaced by enclosures and new single tenant farms. Like the eighteenth-century farmhouse and cottage, the grid-plan of the typical Highland planned village is based upon the classical design principles of regularity and order.

A parallel development to the introduction of planned villages was the

5. James Maxwell, Sketch of the Village of Tobermory, 1791 (National Archives of Scotland)

emergence of the crofting system, through which displaced communities not settled in planned villages were relocated to strip-smallholdings on marginal land. Until the late nineteenth century, for the ordinary Gael crofting meant a chance to remain close to ancestral lands and a traditional way of life but it also meant the constant threat of starvation due to the infertility of the land and the constant possibility of eviction. Crofting was viewed by Highland landlords as a last resort: an unprofitable ghetto on the wasteland at the outer margins of the improved estate. Crofting townships were not subject to the same level of building control and regulation as planned villages, nor was there money available to build new modern cottages. Hence, within the boundaries of these communities the building tradition of the blackhouse persisted into the twentieth century whilst in all other areas of the Highlands it was systematically eradicated leaving only ruins.

In contrast, the planned village was a vigorously promoted cornerstone of improvement in the Highlands. The Highland planned village was conceived as a progressive industrial centre where the estate's population would live and, most importantly, work in the pursuit of a profitable industry such as weaving, spinning or fishing, as part of a new dual estate economy alongside the new single tenant farms. Planned villages were principally established by individual landowners; however, several governmental and quasi-governmental bodies encouraged the development of Highland planned villages through business loans, as in the case of the Board of Manufactures, or through active partici-pation, as with the villages of the Annexed Estates Commission and the British Fisheries Society. The planned villages established by these government-backed bodies were few in number but they were influential in establishing a planning model that was imitated repeatedly in private village schemes. The British Fisheries Society, founded in the late eighteenth century by a group of Highland landowners with strong government connections, established the model planned villages of Ullapool and Tobermory in the Western Highlands and the New Town of Pulteneytown as an adjunct to the old burgh of Wick in Caithness.

The prospect of employment in a planned village was also intended to act as a countermeasure to 'the evil of emigration'. Emigration to North America was a constant element in the history of agricultural improvement in the Highlands. In contrast to the terrible forced emigrations of the nineteenth century, the eighteenth-century improving landowner still placed a high value on their indigenous population and tried to prevent emigration. Despite their efforts, emigration from the Highlands to North America gained momentum through the eighteenth century. Following American Independence in 1783 immigration to North America meant Canada, particularly the coastal Atlantic province of Nova Scotia. Scottish Gaels settled in Nova Scotia in such numbers that the province maintains a strong Gaelic culture today. By the 1830s, out of approximately 39,000 immigrants in Nova Scotia some 20,000 were Scots, mostly Scottish Gaels.[7] The Gaels settled together creating new Gaelic communities, which dominated the ethnic population of northern Nova Scotia, notably Pictou and Antigonish Counties and Cape Breton.[8]

In Nova Scotia, the blackhouse was readily abandoned by Scottish Gaelic settlers in favour of timber-framed colonial farmhouses. A new environment brought new materials: an unfamiliar abundance of timber and related construction methods. However, the formal design and ornament of the colonial Highland house followed the same design rules of eighteenth-century classicism that defined the farmhouses built by their evictors in the Scottish Highlands (Fig. 6).[9] The eager adoption of fashionable tastes in classical architecture by Highland settlers in Canada, whilst retaining their Gaelic language, music, dance and poetry, indicates that emigrant Scottish Gaels held no great cultural attachment to the blackhouse and, given the choice, were quick to adopt the modern, comfortable house type of their colonial neighbours. The blackhouse provided excellent shelter as part of a subsistence existence; however, given land ownership and a small amount of money, Gaels were keen to become British consumers. The consistencies between the domestic architecture of Scottish

6. Early nineteenth-century farmhouse, Monk's Head, Antigonish County, Nova Scotia, Canada (author)

Gaels in Canada and British design of the period places them within the historic cultural sphere of the British Atlantic world. This was both a material and intellectual construct framed by the shores of the British Atlantic Empire which, maintained by transatlantic shipping, embraced the eastern seaboard of North America from Canada to Florida, the Caribbean, West Africa, Scotland, Ireland and England. The history of the British Atlantic has emerged as a distinct subject with recent works devoted to a British Atlantic perspective on diverse topics, from colonial legislation, chartered enterprises and cultural property to slavery, the fisheries and landscape painting.[10]

This book is an architectural history of the social and economic transformation of the Scottish Highlands and the region's engagement with early modern Britain. A new Highland population of improving tenant farmers, a mixture of tacksmen turned commercial farmers and strangers from the Lowlands, chose to replace the eminently practical indigenous Highland blackhouse with a new architecture informed by the stylistic rules of classicism and intended to convey the complex social messages of eighteenth-century British society.

CHAPTER I

The Highlands Transformed

Through the course of the eighteenth century, the landscape of the Scottish Highlands was permanently transformed by a series of economic land reforms described as 'agricultural improvements'. Agricultural improvements in the Highlands followed a process first established in the Lowlands, closely linked to the ideas and activities of the Scottish Enlightenment. The process principally involved the removal of indigenous small tenants to make way for large efficient and profitable, single tenant farms. For the most part the new farms in the Highlands were giant sheep ranches suited to the region's mountainous pastures. A new system of land use was introduced and a new type of tenant: business-minded improvers, modernisers and often 'strangers'.

For centuries, the common dwelling of the Scottish Highlands had been the turf and stone-walled indigenous 'blackhouse'. However, by the late eighteenth century there was a new Highland economy and a new population in need of houses suitable to their tastes and needs. Building a new modern farmhouse was an integral part of creating a profitable modern Highland farm. The transformation of Highland agriculture from traditional communal farming to large single-tenant farms was the catalyst for a 'rural building boom', which gained pace in the 1770s and lasted through to the 1830s.[1]

James Hunter's *Making of the Crofting Community*, of 1978, has for many years been considered the definitive history of the socio-economic transformation described in sources such as the Statistical Accounts. However, the history of the Scottish Highlands has also been the object of recent revision by historians such as T. M. Devine, Robert Dodghson, Allan Macinnes, and Chris Whately. A considered position is that Highland history of the eighteenth and nineteenth centuries needs to maintain a balance between the drama of the Jacobite Rebellions, the infamy of the Clearances and the practicalities of economic land reform.

Prior to the agricultural improvements of the eighteenth century, the Scottish Highlands were home to a Gaelic-speaking society based around the social structure of the clan. 'By its very nature, a kin-based society transformed physical space into a social space, one that was identified through and structured by the groups or clans that occupied it.'[2] The term 'Highlander' refers to a Scottish Gael as well as a resident of the Highlands. This dual, ethnic and geographic, definition of the term Highlander is critical when considering the nature of the Highland house in the eighteenth and nineteenth centuries: a change in building and design reporting a change in population in the fertile glens. Lowland farmers moved to new lives in the Highlands and Gaels moved away to new lives in the Lowlands and North America. Historically, a Highland clan was led by the clan chieftain, who was probably, but not necessarily, the principal landowner in the region associated with a particular clan. Some clan chieftains were also titled aristocrats, such as the Dukes of Argyll, the heads of clan Campbell, but this was not always the case and it did not necessarily follow that the title and status of chieftain in Gaelic society related to high rank within the British aristocracy. Below the chief and clan elite, or *fine*, the body of the clan consisted of ordinary clansmen and women who were loyal to the clan chief and lived and farmed on his lands, though they were not necessarily of the same name. However, clanship was not a straightforward economic relationship between a landowner and his tenants, it was a paternalistic, communal culture based upon the concept of *duthchas* or common heritage, i.e. the land traditionally held by a clan. In *Clanship to Crofters' Wars,* Tom Devine explains that *duthchas* was 'central to the social cohesion of the clan because it articulated the expectations of the masses that the ruling families had the responsibility to act as their protectors and guarantee secure possession of land in return for allegiance, military service, tribute and rental.'[3]

The small community groups of the Highlands lived in small settlements known as *bailtean* or *clachan* (hence the 'Clachan' at the Glasgow Empire Exhibition in 1938). Each clachan consisted of an irregular cluster of blackhouses. The blackhouses of *Baile Gean*, the bailtean built by the Highland Folk Museum at Kingussie, give a good indication of the appearance of an early eighteenth-century Highland house (Fig. 7). The blackhouse was built by the community using only immediately available 'found' materials. The term 'blackhouse' has been used by English speakers since the mid-nineteenth century to describe the indigenous dwellings of the Scottish Highlands. It is a mistranslation of the Gaelic word *tugadh*, which simply means thatch but which is phonetically similar to *tigh dubh* or 'black house'. The structure and site orientation of the blackhouse were developed to minimise the effects of the Highland environment and enclose a warm and dry living space.[4] The Scottish Vernacular Building Group describes blackhouses as 'integrated structures within the landscape . . .

7. Reconstruction of early eighteenth-century blackhouses, Highland Folk Museum (Highland Folk Museum)

the buildings' form, shape and colour merged naturally with the field.[5]

The single-storey, low walls of a blackhouse were typically constructed of field-cleared stones and turf, often in a double-wall construction with an insulated central core of in-filled earth. Earth and rubble walls could not support the weight of a roof. Therefore, the roof was supported by pairs of cruck frames, known as Highland couples, which were set in the ground and rose through the walls to meet overhead to form the apex of the roof. The cruck frames were the largest single components in the structure of a blackhouse and the most valuable in a largely treeless environment. In some communities the cruck frames were the property of the clan chief or other hereditary landowner. The roof was generally comprised of turfs covered with a thatch of heather or straw, the whole held in place by twisted heather ropes weighed down with stones. Regional variations in walling and roofing occurred across the Highlands, in particular, between the mainland and the Inner and Outer Hebrides.[6] The houses of the Western Isles, as can be seen in the case of 42 Arnol on the Isle of Lewis, are typically of longer and lower form and substantially thicker stone walls than those of the mainland Highlands where mud and wattle was also used (Fig. 8). In some parts of the Uists an earth-build of herring-bone-patterned turfs, known as 'fale-walling', can be found, whereas a higher proportion of timber was used in the wooded area of Speyside.[7]

8. 42 Arnol, Isle of Lewis (Historic Scotland)

A full description of a blackhouse from the 1780s is provided in the *Statistical Account of Scotland* entry for Lochcarron in Wester Ross:

> Of the houses, some are turf, but the greater part of stone frequently
> built with lime. The roof is covered over with turf, above which, there
> is a coat of heather or ferns. There is seldom a chimney to the houses.
> The fire is kindled alongside of the wall, or a stone in the centre of the
> room, and the smoke reeks its way out of the roof, or door, or
> windows. The windows generally consist of wooden shutters, made to
> open at pleasure and admit the fresh air. The floors are of clay and
> mud. In many houses the cattle are under the same roof, and even enter
> at the same door with the family, and are only separated from them by
> a partition of boards, wattles or stone, having a door in the middle. As
> will be readily imagined, the space between this partition and the outer
> door is sometimes so dirty, that it is difficult for him who enters to pick
> out a clean footing. The greater part of the people do certainly not
> enjoy the comforts of society.[8]

The walls and roof of the blackhouse provided the structure's primary function
of enclosing a well-insulated, warm and dry, living space. The orientation of the
blackhouse was also an important factor in the warmth of the interior: the
narrow gable end towards the prevailing wind and any openings such as the door

9. Interior of reconstructed blackhouse, Highland Folk Museum (author)

on the south-facing side towards the sun. As per the Gaelic proverb, '*An iar's an ear, an dachaigh as 'fhearr – cul ri gaoith, 's aghaidh ri grein*', or 'East to west, the house that's best – back to the wind and face to the sun'.[9]

The long, low rectangular form of the blackhouse provided an interior living space adapted to the social practices of Highland family life (Fig. 9). The space was heated by a peat fire lit in a simple stone hearth in the centre of the floor with the heavy peat smoke escaping slowly through the thatch. The central hearth was the focal point of Highland domestic life around which social gatherings, the *ceilidh*, took place. The interior was frequently partitioned to create a byre for livestock who shared the common entrance towards the centre. The excellent thermal properties of the blackhouse were noted by the travel writer Richard Ayton in 1815:

> These mud-huts, however, as they are called, in spite of the exceeding
> meanness of the exterior, are far superior in positive comfort to many
> stone-built cottages such as one sees in this country and in many parts
> of England too – cottages with a better name, and of a less wig-wamish
> appearance, but not half so warm and substantial . . . Mud-huts have
> the cardinal merit of being perfectly weather-proof.[10]

Descriptions of blackhouses were often written by 'gentlemen travellers' like Ayton; this was a region then considered as remote, wild and savage to the Lowland or English traveller as the African Congo was to the Victorian explorer. Eighteenth-century travellers to the Highlands were generally appalled by the living conditions they witnessed. Thomas Pennant's *A Tour in Scotland*, published in 1776, provides a rare description of the shielings. These were the temporary summer residences of Highland communities when grazing their livestock in the high summer pastures:

> Sheelins, the habitations of the peasants who attend the herds of milch
> cows. These formed a grotesque group; some were oblong, many conic,
> and so low that entrance is forbidden without creeping through the
> little opening, which has no other door than a faggot of birch twigs:
> they are constructed of branches of trees, covered with sods; the
> furniture a bed of heath placed on a bed of sod.

The ordinary Gael gave their ultimate loyalty to their clan chief; however, their direct dealings were with the chief's tacksmen. The tacksmen, or *fir-tacsa*, were the middle class of traditional Highland society. They were the lesser gentry and military captains of the clan structure as well as the large farm holders. The role and future of the tacksmen would lie at the heart of agricultural improvement in the eighteenth century. The tacksmen held their lands through tacks, a form of lease, granted by the clan chief in return for monetary rent and military service.[11]

The tacksman, in turn, sublet his often considerable holding to his numerous subtenants, the ordinary Highland Gaels. 'The overwhelming majority of the Highland population had no absolute right to land. They were either tenants whose rights were finite and limited by lease, so susceptible to rapid rent increases, or they belonged to the growing underclass of semi-landless cottars and servants who possessed no legal security of tenure whatsoever.'[12] Tacksmen were therefore extremely vulnerable when the landowners' priorities changed from that of clan chief to commercial landlord in the eighteenth century; an economic vulnerability compounded by the psychological disorientation brought on by the collapse of *duthchas*. The process of land reform was advanced throughout the Highlands by the 1750s but ordinary clansmen were largely insulated from its initial effects.

The typical house of the pre-improvement tacksman was as traditional as his role in the clan structure and was, for the most part, a house of similar build to that of his subtenants, although considerably larger and better furnished. John Macleod, minister for Morvern parish, described a traditional tacksman's house he remembered visiting in his youth, the home of Cameron of Glendessary, in the *New Statistical Account of Scotland,* 1843:

> He resided at Ach-a-charn and occupied a house of very peculiar construction; formed of oak beams placed at regular distances; the intervening spaces being closely interwoven with wicker work. The outside was wholly covered with heath, and the interior was divided into several apartments, and finished in a style of taste and elegance corresponding with the enlightened refinement of the occupants.[13]

The mixture of indigenous build and contemporary consumer goods in a tacksman's house was also noticed by Dr Johnson:

> There are huts, or dwellings of only one storey, inhabited by gentlemen, which have walls cemented with mortar, glass windows, and boarded floors . . . The houses and the furniture are not always nicely suited. We were driven, once, by missing a passage, to the hut of a gentleman, where, after a very liberal supper, when I was conducted to my chamber, I found an elegant bed of Indian cotton, spread with fine sheets. The accommodation was flattering; I undressed myself, and felt my feet in the mire. The bed stood upon the bare earth, which a long course of rain had softened to a puddle.[14]

The form and structure of the blackhouse dwelling type evolved in response to the cold and wet Highland climate and to the daily routines of subsistence farming. However, these conditions were not unique to the Highlands of Scotland. Similar traditional dwellings were built in other regions of Britain, particularly along the wet, treeless areas of Britain's uplands and western seaboard, such as Wales, Ireland, the Pennines and the South-west, giving us the Dartmoor Longhouse in Devon and the Pennine Laithe House.[15] The Highland blackhouse belongs to a wider architectural group of dwellings in Britain known as longhouses. The definition of a longhouse is 'a small house where farm animals and humans are housed within the same walls and under the same roof in an elongated rectangular building which has a cross-passage running behind the main hearth or fireplace in such a way that it is available for access for both humans and animals and for intercommunication between domestic and agricultural parts of the building.'[16] Outside Britain, variations on the longhouse can be found wherever similar environmental and social conditions were present, from the traditional Norse longhouse in areas of Scandinavia, whose influence is strongly present in the longhouses of the Western Isles, to the *barabara* of the Alaskan Unangan people.[17] The existence of similar longhouse traditions outside the Highlands illustrates how care must be taken not to assume that the form of the blackhouse is uniquely 'Highland', or that the eminently practical black-house represents Gaelic culture and identity.

Agricultural Improvement in the Highlands

The permanent transformation of rural Scotland began in the late seventeenth century with the 'Act anent Lands lying runrig' passed by the Scottish Parliament in 1695 which allowed landlords to instigate enclosures and remove traditional runrig or strip-farming systems. Enclosures meant the amalgamation of multiple small farms occupied by numerous tenant families into large single tenant farms, which were then 'enclosed' with ditches, hedges or walls to restrain stock and mark their boundaries. The pace of improvement increased after the Act of Union in 1707 as Scottish landowners came into closer and more regular contact with their southern English peers. However, agricultural improvement in Scotland was never simply imitative. Scottish agricultural improvement, and its vigorous promotion, was closely related to the ideas of the Scottish Enlightenment and its central figures: Lord Kames, David Hume, Adam Smith and Adam Fergusson. A central tenet of the European Enlightenment was that human progress could only be achieved through 'the exercise of autonomous reason'.[18] In the moral and philosophical terms of the Scottish Enlightenment, 'improvement' was a belief in progress and a belief that man possessed 'a wonderful capacity for improvement'.[19] Societal improvement marked 'a historical transition from rudeness to refinement or from barbarism to civilization'.[20] In eighteenth-century Scotland, the exercise of reason had a direct and immediate practical role in the improvement of Scottish society through the rationalisation of economic activities such as agricultural, transport, manufacturing and trade. These practical improvements were promoted through organisations such as the Edinburgh Society for the Encouragement of Arts, Science, Manufactures and Agriculture founded in 1755.

Agricultural experimentation began in the early eighteenth century on the Lowland estates of the major landowners particularly in the Lothians around Edinburgh. By the mid-century the spirit of improvement had extended to widespread enclosures amongst the great majority of Lowland landowners. However, it was not until the 1770s when the first experimental improved farms began to show profits that the improvement of tenant farms began on a wide scale. What ensued was an episode in Scottish history that has been described as 'a period of revolutionary change which laid the basis of the rural landscape of modern times'.[21] Crucial to this was Lord Montgomerie's Entail Act of 1770. Entail was 'a measure intended to perpetuate particular families, but which is very inimical to the improvement of its soil'.[22] By guaranteeing the landowner's non-alienable rights of ownership Entail encouraged landowners to set leases for extended periods, generally of 19 years, enabling tenant farmers to develop and invest in commercial farms for the first time without fear of eviction.[23] The circumstance of farms and farmers in Cockpen near Edinburgh was described in the 1790s:

> About 40 years ago, a number of small farmers cultivated the lands in the parish . . . at present, 7 families . . . occupy almost entirely the whole district. They discover a great spirit of enterprise and zeal for improvement, and live in a degree of affluence, unknown to their more humble predecessors.[24]

By the later eighteenth century, enclosures had changed the agricultural landscape of much of the Scottish Lowlands from Dumfries and Galloway through Lanarkshire to the Borders. In contrast to the arable farms of the Lothians, in the hill country of the Borders the emphasis was firmly upon sheep.

The minister for the parish of Bunkle and Preston in Berwickshire wrote:

> Our farmers pay as much attention to the breed of their sheep, as is paid to
> the highest breed of galloping horses in England; and I believe they bring
> much greater profit . . . Sheep is the great staple of this country in general.
> They are the English breed introduced by Mr Bakewell, and since carried
> on by . . . other eminent breeders, both in Northumberland, and this
> country. The criterion of their goodness and sort, is getting sooner and
> more easily fat . . . The whole parish under the Lammermuir Hills, as well
> as the whole low part of the country, are inclosed, principally with hedge
> and ditch.[25]

Such was the success of sheep farming in the Borders that the Rev. Douglas also
commented upon the increasingly high rents demanded for pasture land and the
pressure amongst sheep farmers for more land.[26] Border farmers turned their
attention to the possibilities of cheap rents and endless miles of open pasture that
were becoming available in the Highlands.

Agricultural improvement in the Highlands was, as in the Lowlands, driven
by the demands of landowners for higher rents from their estates.[27] Highland
landowners increased their rent by enclosing the fertile farming lands of the
straths and glens previously occupied by numerous *bailtean* communal farms
and letting them as vast single-tenant sheep farms, in some cases of 70,000 acres
or more, to the highest bidder. For the prospective tenant farmer the secure
tenancies offered by Highland landowners provided an opportunity to invest in
massive Highland farm holdings and improve them in a rational and profitable
manner. In Northern Argyll, the Rev. Mr Ludovick Grant reported for the
Statistical Account that:

> Short leases, and the promiscuous mode of letting farms to several
> tenants without assigning to each his due proportion of arable land
> throw a damp upon the efforts of industry and prevent the
> improvement which would otherwise be introduced . . . But it must
> be acknowledged that a remarkable alteration for the better, as to
> agriculture, has taken place within these few years . . . There are
> between 28,000 and 30,000 sheep of the larger breed brought some
> years ago from the south country . . . thousands are sold yearly to
> the low country . . . few farms are [now] let below L.60 and some
> pay more than L.200 . . . Farmers make a decent appearance; seem

to enjoy the comforts and conveniences of life suitable to their
station; and acknowledge that they have less difficulty than they had
30 years ago.[28]

A rent of £60 to £200 for a sheep farm in Argyll was very competitive compared
to the Rev. Douglas's estimate of £200 to £600 for a sheep farm in the Borders.
If the luminaries of the Scottish Enlightenment in Edinburgh viewed the 'nearby
and backward Highlands as a kind of sociological museum or laboratory', the
sheep farmers of the Scottish Borders saw the region as a business opportunity.[29]

The first Highland land reforms were aimed at removing the middlemen, the
traditional large tenants or tacksmen, not mass evictions.[30] The second Duke of
Argyll (1680–1743) was the first Highland landowner to mount an attack on the
tacksmen in the search for higher rental, when in the 1730s he attempted to
increase the return by letting directly to the subtenants and excluding tacksmen
altogether. However, it became apparent that large single-tenant farms, tenanted
to the highest bidder, whether they were a southern 'stranger' or native
tacksman, were more profitable and easier to manage than directly letting to
numerous small tenants. Widespread enclosures and evictions followed through
the late eighteenth and nineteenth centuries.

The change in the rural population from people to sheep meant that the
tacksmen's role as military captains and social leaders within the clan system was
moribund and the class faced extinction or adaptation.[31] Many tacksmen
adapted to this change to become wealthy tenant farmers themselves with more
in common, financially and culturally, with their new southern neighbours and
similar tenant farmers in the Lowlands or England than with the landless and
impoverished ordinary Gael. But many more were unable to adapt to the new
commercial order and were either evicted, fell into bankruptcy or emigrated to
North America. By the time of Samuel Johnson's tour of the Highlands in the
late eighteenth century, this negative view of the tacksmen had become received
opinion:

> Next in dignity to the Laird is the Tacksman; a large taker or lease-
> holder of land . . . These tacks have long been considered as hereditary,
> and the occupant was distinguished by the name of the place at which
> he resided. He held a middle station, by which the highest and the
> lowest orders were connected . . . This tenure still subsists, with its
> original operation, but not with the primitive stability . . . I have found
> in the hither parts of Scotland, men not defective in judgment or

general experience, who consider the Tacksman as a useless burden on the ground, as a drone who lives upon the product of an estate, without the right of property, or the merit of labour, and who impoverishes at once the landlord and the tenant. The land they say, is let to the Tacksman at six-pence an acre, and by him to the tenant at ten-pence.[32]

On the national political stage, improvement in the Highlands was vigorously promoted by influential public figures such as the fifth Duke of Argyll and Sir John Sinclair and by organisations such as the Highland Societies of Edinburgh and London.[33] The Dukes of Argyll, notably John, fifth Duke of Argyll (1723–1806), set the standard for improvement in the Highlands with a programme of wide-ranging and innovative improvements within their own massive estates and on the farms of Inveraray.[34] Even within a single Highland estate such as Inveraray, plans for improvement took many forms: in agriculture with field enclosures, the introduction of new crops, sheep and land drainage; to new enterprises in the textiles industry and fisheries; as well as road and bridge building and the founding of the new planned town of Inveraray.[35] The Dukes also exerted considerable political influence through a favoured position with successive Whig governments and the chairmanship of improving societies and government bodies.

Sir John Sinclair of Ulbster (1754–1835) was another important figure in the history of Highland improvement. Sinclair's improvements principally involved the enclosure of his lands into large-scale tenant sheep farms. The development of Thurso New Town, 1800–10, was the urban focus of much wider agricultural improvements across his 100,000-acre Caithness estates. However, he was also involved with the promotion of the Highlands on the national stage. In addition to representing Caithness at Westminster, he was also the founder and first President of the Board of Agriculture from 1793, and the founding editor of the *Statistical Account of Scotland*, published in twenty-one volumes, 1791–9. The *Statistical Account* was the first systematic attempt to compile social and economic data on every parish in Scotland and remains a resource of immense value to historians of eighteenth-century Scotland (frequently quoted in this book). Sinclair described the term statistical as, 'an enquiry into the state of the country, for the purpose of ascertaining the quantum of happiness enjoyed by its inhabitants, and the means of its future improvement'. It was a quintessential product of the Scottish Enlightenment.

The drive for higher rents by Highland landowners has often been depicted as a betrayal of Gaeldom and the sanctity of *duthchas,* the bonds of family, community and tradition, by Gaelic clan chiefs who squandered the revenue of their Highland estates on London-based lifestyles in order to gain status as British gentlemen and aristocrats. However, financially, enclosure was the only viable option available to most of the Highland landowning class in face of the inevitable changes heralded by the 'irresistible market pressures emanating from Lowland industrialisation and urbanisation'.[36] It is a common misunderstanding to view the pre-improvement Highland society of the seventeenth century as an unchanging timeless ancient world. The reality is that Gaelic society in the Scottish Highlands was a dynamic culture that underwent numerous historical, political, economic and social evolutions. Indeed, the 'traditional' clan system itself did not fully evolve until the sixteenth century and in some Highland regions was showing signs of imminent collapse as early as the mid-seventeenth century.[37] Equally, the social and economic transformation of the Highlands was not, as has often been argued, a straightforward and direct result of the political aftermath of the failed 1745 Jacobite Uprising in which those Highland clans loyal to the Stewart cause played such an important military role. It is true that the brutal 'pacification' of the Highlands by the Hanoverian government forces under the Duke of Cumberland, often indiscriminately razing areas held by Loyalist and Jacobite clans alike, and the proscription of many aspects of Highland culture, including the wearing of the plaid, accelerated the collapse of Scottish Gaelic culture. But the evolution from clan chief to commercial landlord had begun for many in the seventeenth century – long before the '45.[38] Nonetheless, many compassionate or tradition-minded Highland landlords were most reluctant to evict people and the intention of clearance was to relocate communities to less profitable marginal land and different employment, not to force complete removal from an estate.[39] In contrast to subsequent events in the nineteenth century, the modern improving Highland landowners of the eighteenth century were also firmly against total clearance and the 'evil of emigration' as a dangerous drain on a Highland population that was considered a valuable resource.[40] The process of economic change permanently transformed the structure of Highland society: the clan chieftain to commercial landlord and the ordinary clansman to landless labourer. A picture emerges of a period of rapid and large-scale population transmigration throughout the Highlands. There was an inward migration of farmers, shepherds, sheep dogs and sheep from the south. Many tacksmen turned into tenant farmers but for many, and for the indigenous population of small tenant farmers, change meant an outward migration towards planned villages or crofting townships on the coast or out of the Highlands altogether to the Lowlands and North America.

The Highland House Transformed

The economic and social transformation of the Highlands had a radical and permanent effect upon what can be termed the typical Highland house. Through the eighteenth century, the widespread building of new 'improved' farmhouses by new single tenant farmers where clusters of blackhouses had recently stood was an integral part of the process of agricultural improvement in the Highlands. The geographer David Turnock has observed, 'the results of [this] massive building programme are still clear for all to see'.[41]

In context of the British building industry as a whole, like the Agricultural Revolution itself, the Highland building boom was a counterpoint to the industrial revolution in southern central Scotland and the rapid growth of urban housing. Across Britain, house building changed from a process of gradual evolution and adaptation to one of rapid transformation; 'from the late eighteenth century new building construction and demolition throughout Britain began to change from a means of conserving a static building stock to become an agent of change in society'.[42] In the Lothians surrounding Edinburgh, where agricultural improvement in Scotland began, the minister for Kirkliston was able to state proudly in 1790 that, 'the farm houses in this parish are extremely commodious, and even elegant. They consist of two floors, besides garrets, are covered with blue and grey slates, and are in all respects superior to the generality'.[43] But, the Highlands were quickly catching up; at the same date a rapidly changing Highland landscape was also observed by George Fraser, minister for Monedie parish in Highland Perthshire:

10. 1 Colbost, Cuirnish, Skye, 1980 (Historic Scotland)

The lower farmers, who occupy only small farms build their own houses, [formerly] they built them of stone and soil, thatching with divot and straw; but now, when it is necessary to renew they employ masons to build them of stone and mortar, harling them on the outside with lime . . . These houses give the country a better and more cheerful look.[44]

The blackhouse disappeared from the farmlands of the Highlands but the building tradition persisted through to the twentieth century in the post-improvement crofting communities or townships. The history of crofting in the Highlands lies outside the contents of this book, however, it should be made clear that whilst the 'modern' farmhouse, cottage and planned village became the new architecture of the improved Highland estate, the blackhouse continued to be built, and to evolve, in the crofting townships. One such development was the introduction of the hanging 'lum', a flue box suspended over the hearth. The roof stack of a hanging lum can be seen protruding from the roof of the crofter's blackhouse at 1 Colbost, Cuirnish, Skye, photographed in the 1980s (Fig. 10).[45] As can be seen in the early twentieth century cottage interior preserved at the Highland Folk Museum, domestic comfort increased through the nineteenth century with the introduction of features such as timber plank panelling to the walls, flagstone floors, box beds, gable end fireplaces perhaps with a cast-iron range, glazed windows, and mass-produced furniture, kitchen implements and tableware (Fig. 11).[46]

11. Early twentieth-century cottage interior, Highland Folk Museum (author)

CHAPTER 2

The New Highland House

From the mid eighteenth century, a house building boom of unprecedented scale and speed took place in the Scottish Highlands (see Appendix 1, Chart 1). It is remarkable that 73 per cent of all extant houses built in the Highlands between 1600 and 1850 were built in the brief period between 1775 and 1815. It is even more remarkable that 78 per cent of those houses are improved farmhouses. The Highland building boom began with a handful of small country houses built for minor lairds in the late seventeenth century; extant houses are distributed throughout the Highlands. House building activity was dominated by landowners until the mid-to-late eighteenth century when estate improvements and their financial rewards extended to tenant farms. The Highland house transformed into a white two-storey farmhouse: the generic house type of eighteenth-century rural Scotland. These new farmhouses were built by the modernising tenant farmers who ran large and profitable single tenant sheep farms on lands recently occupied by thousands of ordinary Gaelic small tenants. Similar houses were also built by small, modest landowners and estate factors, by landowners, to serve as inns for travellers, and as parish manses.[1] The indigenous Highland blackhouse was displaced from the Highland landscape by a modern house type built with imported materials and imported skills and labour (Fig. 12). A building tradition based upon a direct response to the Highland environment was superseded by a house type, construction methods, materials and building skills imported from the Lowlands. The improved tenant farmhouse, the Highland house transformed, was a change in cultural practice within the historically settled areas of the Highlands brought about by a change in the house building population – or in the case of many tacksmen, a change in social and economic perspective. The new Highland house was an agent in the transformation of the Scottish Highlands which has been described by T. C. Smout as the 'great divide which meant the end of rural life as it had been lived since time immemorial and the beginning of rural life as it has been ever since'.[2] In direct relation to agricultural improvement itself, the Highland building boom gradually gained momentum through the eighteenth century reaching its peak

12. William Daniell, 'Liveras, near Broadford', *A Voyage Round the Coast of Scotland and the Adjacent Islands*, 1814–1822 (National Library of Scotland)

at the turn of the century and subsequently tailed off towards the middle of the nineteenth century.[3]

Form, Materials and Construction

Of the hundreds of new farmhouses built in the Scottish Highlands between the mid-eighteenth and mid-nineteenth centuries, over 300 stand today and are protected by Historic Scotland (see Appendix 1, Table 1).[4] They are remarkable buildings. The first and most striking feature of these houses is that, in comparison to the low, single-storey indigenous blackhouses they replaced, they are large and highly visible structures. Of overwhelmingly formal uniformity, the typical Highland farmhouse is a white two-storey building built on a rectangular plan, the whole appearing as a large white box placed upon the landscape. The walls are built of square-cut stone blocks laid in regular courses. The external walls are covered with a protective white harl.[5] The roof is covered with evenly sized slates. The high gable end walls are terminated by characteristic broad chimneystacks. The front of the house has a door to the centre with a rectangular window on either side. The upper storey has three windows placed directly above the ground floor windows and door. In some cases, the house has

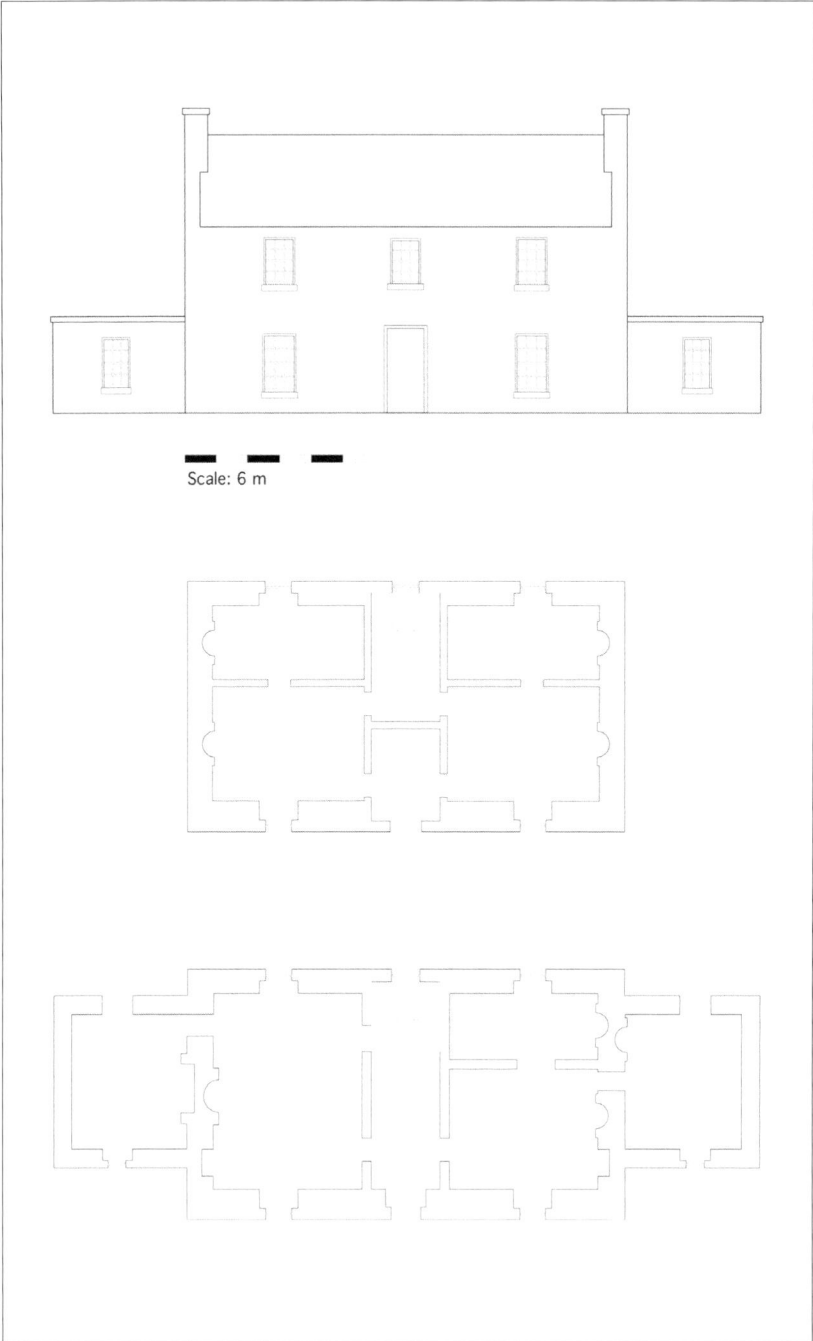

Scale: 6 m

13. Plan and elevation of a model late eighteenth-century Scottish farmhouse
(James Lingard)

matching single-storey wings to each side. Inside the typical farmhouse the three parts of the house front reflect the internal arrangement of the rooms on both floors, with a central passageway flanked by living rooms on the ground floor, such as the parlour and kitchen, and bedrooms upstairs (Fig. 13). All rooms are plastered and finished with simple architectural mouldings such as cornices.

The internal structure of the roof frame, floors, partition walls, skirting boards and stairs required large amounts of timber. In addition, the house contains any number of manufactured items that had to be bought, from nails to hinges, door handles, fireplaces, grates, window frames and glass. These buildings must have appeared most strange and alien to a local population accustomed to the natural forms and colours of the blackhouse. Almost a third of extant farmhouses have an additional third attic storey with dormer windows built into the roof (see Appendix 1, Table 2). This upper floor either consists of a small attic storey, requiring a few extra courses to the walls, or is simply located entirely within the roof space. The rectangular floor plan of the typical improved farmhouse is at least double the size of the typical blackhouse as the plan of the improved farmhouse is commonly two rooms deep, i.e. two to the front and two to the back with a central doorway. Although some houses, while appearing substantial from the front, are only one room deep. In addition, many

14. Menzies Mains farmhouse, Perthshire (author)

farmhouses, about 25 per cent, have extensions or additions to the sides and rear providing further space. These take many forms from two-storey wings to the rear, forming T-plan, U-plan, L-plan and M-gable houses, to single-storey additions to the sides.

The majority of stonework for walling in the Scottish Highlands uses sandstone. There are some regional variations depending on the local geology, such as the use of large, flat sandstone slabs in Caithness, granite in Eastern Inverness-shire towards Aberdeenshire, or whinstone in Argyll. As seen at Menzies Mains, Perthshire, the majority of houses in the Highlands are harled (Fig. 14).[6] Known to date from at least the medieval period, harling is a sacrificial coating of grit and lime applied to the exterior walls of buildings to protect the stonework and clay or lime mortar against the Scottish weather. Historically, many different regional harl mixes were used ranging from sand to seashells but this is difficult to detect under modern harls. Harling is often used to cover poorer quality walling constructed of random rubble bonded with clay mortar.[7] In most regions of the Highlands between 70 and 90 per cent of houses are completely harled. Accordingly, 96 per cent of houses are also built of random or squared rubble. Only 6 per cent of the highest-quality small houses are constructed of ashlar (finely cut stone blocks). These represent the relatively grander houses of the minor laird; fewer harled houses are found in Easter Ross and Inverness-shire due to the relatively higher number of larger country houses in the region, which are constructed entirely from ashlar or of ashlar frontages with harl covering cheaper rubble walls to the sides and rear. The windows and doors of harled Scottish houses are often picked out with a margin or surround of high quality squared or ashlar stonework. A raised stonework margin is an important constructional element for supporting a random rubble wall over doors and windows but it is also an aesthetic architectural feature highlighting the rhythm of the windows across a façade. In the Highlands just over half, 55 per cent, of houses have these architectural margins. However, this figure disguises distinct regional variations. The vast majority of houses in most areas of the Highlands feature margins, around 70 per cent, but a very low number of houses do in the Western Isles and Argyll and Bute, and only half in Western Inverness-shire including Skye. However, this does not amount to a direct east-west distinction as 73 per cent of houses in Wester Ross feature margins.

When put together, the form, building materials and construction methods of the typical 'modern' eighteenth-century farmhouse add up to a building that was completely inappropriate for life in the Scottish Highlands. The primary function of the indigenous blackhouse was to provide warmth and shelter. It was a building form evolved over centuries to meet the demands of the Highland environment extremely efficiently, using only locally available materials: a low, narrow structure was built of a combination of turf and field-cleared stones with walls and thatched roof set face into the wind for minimum wind resistance. The double-thickness walls and thatch enclosed and insulated a single living space heated by a single central hearth and by the warmth of the family milk cow. Unnecessary heat loss was restricted by a minimum number of openings, such as doors, chimney flues and windows. The most valuable part of the fabric in treeless regions was the cruck-roof frame made of highly prized Highland couples. In complete contrast, an improved farmhouse stands two storeys high with a surface area of exposed wall greater than that of the floor plan. The walls are of a single thickness of solid stone. The roof is a single covering of slate over a large un-insulated roof space. The fireplaces are located in the gable end walls losing heat through the external walls. There are also large expanses of single pane glass. The interior space is divided into numerous rooms requiring their own heat source and other spaces, such as the hall and landing, with no heat source. Furthermore, to build a house that was very difficult to heat and keep warm required a great deal of money to be spent importing the necessary materials, components and skilled labour. Why a tenant farmer would go to so much trouble to build such an impractical house is the subject of the next chapter.

Related Building Types

Farmhouses and small country houses were not the only new buildings that were introduced to the Highland landscape in relation to eighteenth-century improvements. Predominantly built adjacent to new farmhouses were new agricultural outbuildings in the form of, sometimes extensive, barn and byre complexes, or steadings. New inns to accommodate travellers were built in the new planned villages, at historic ferry crossings on lochs, and at the side of newly-laid roads as the Highland transport infrastructure was improved. Similarly related to planned villages, was the opening of new customs houses and storehouses to support the growing inshore herring industry in the Highlands. The Church, at both the national and parish level, also undertook extensive programmes of manse building. And, whilst not directly related to Improvement, mention should also be made of the British military's considerable Highland building programme and its impact upon the landscape.

Agricultural writers such as Lord Belhaven had recommended the combination of steadings and farm house in one complex as early as the late seventeenth century; however, the majority of steadings date from the later eighteenth
and early nineteenth century.[8] Steadings of this period are generally gabled,
stone-built buildings similar to the farmhouse in their regularity of plan and
elevation. Steadings were typically laid out in simple geometric plans from a
simple single range to L-plan, U-plan, E-plan or H-plan, and on to grander
semicircular or circular plans, such as Robert Mylne's half-built Maam Steadings
at Inveraray, 1786.[9] Mains of Arbuthnott, Kincardineshire, 1792, identified by
Bruce Walker, is an interesting example in which the farm house and steadings
are combined so that the house is flanked by adjoining steading ranges.[10] The
largest and most architecturally-accomplished steadings complexes are generally
connected to a landowner's country house and mains, or home farm, such as
Menzies Mains farmhouse and nineteenth-century circular steadings connected
to Castle Menzies, Perthshire (Fig. 15). In the Highlands large mains farm
steadings complexes also include the Duke of Argyll's estate at Inveraray; Daniel
Campbell of Shawfield's Islay Mains on Islay; Tongue Mains, Tongue,
Sutherland; and Mains of Newhall, Ross and Cromarty, a two-storey, nine-bay
rectangular courtyard steading with a doocot entrance-tower built in 1830 by
Colin Mackenzie of Newhall.[11] However, only 26 per cent of farmhouses in the
Highlands are recorded as having steadings. In part, this is because steadings are
not always included in the statutory listings but it also reflects the nature of

15. Menzies Mains farmhouse and steadings, Perthshire (author)

improved farming in the Highlands which was predominantly centred upon extensive sheep farming, which in contrast to cattle and arable farming does not require large steadings. Accordingly, by far the largest and most architecturally impressive steadings in Scotland are located in the wheat-growing belt of East Lothian.

Many improved farmhouses have related farm buildings that feature aspects of indigenous Highland construction and materials. For example, the improved farm of Risgary on Harris in the Western Isles has an eighteenth-century two-storey, stone-built barn which is thatched and covered with corrugated iron sheeting and a single-storey rubble-built byre with thatch secured with weighted ropes. The threshing barns at Applecross Mains and Kerrysdale House, Gairloch, Wester Ross, are noted for their low rubble walls, cruck-framed roof structures and thatch, also preserved under corrugated-iron sheeting and roofing felt. There are also many instances of smaller farms and crofts later in the nineteenth and early twentieth century, where the former indigenous house has simply been relegated to become the byre and stores when a new farmhouse or cottage was built. Although the process of transformation from one building tradition to another was dramatic, it was not always complete. Many examples of hybrid houses also survive, which are composed of both 'modern' eighteenth-century and indigenous Highland elements. Howlinn farmhouse on the Isle of Eigg is an example of a hybrid building. The roof was thatched until the late nineteenth century but the house was also celebrated locally as the first house 'of lime and glass' to be built on the island. The tenant farmer, Mackinnon, operated extensive sheep-walks on the island.[12] Unish House, Duirnish, is an early example on the Isle of Skye: a two-storey, late seventeenth-century laird's house which features putlocks, or protruding stones at the wallhead, originally used to hold down the thatch.[13]

Although both the manse and inn have their own distinct histories deserving of independent study, it is nonetheless the case that those built in the later improvement period tend to share the same 'neat and regular' architecture as the improved farmhouse: two-storey, three-bay, gabled buildings with symmetrical plan and elevation. This is a situation which was encouraged in part by the tendency of eighteenth-century architectural books, such as William Halfpenny's *Useful Architecture. Twenty Five New Designs . . . for erecting Parsonage-Houses, Farm houses and Inns,* to provide generic designs intended equally for all three building types. Furthermore, as with the effect of the Entail Act upon the building of new farmhouses, the building of both new manses and inns was encouraged by Acts of Parliament.

The mid-to-late eighteenth-century inn was a product of improvements to the national transport infrastructure. Following the 1751 Turnpike Act, landowners and government bodies, such as the Highland Roads and Bridges Commission, laid new roads capable of carrying carriages.[14] Inns fit for gentlemen travellers were much needed on these new roads, as travel by horse inevitably involved an overnight stay somewhere *en route*. Inns of this period generally share the same two-storey, three-bay symmetrical elevation and regular plan as the improved farmhouse. For instance, the roadside inn at Berrydale, Caithness, is a fine two-storey house with flanking pavilion wings, described by William Daniell (Fig. 16):

> One of the most pleasing changes of scene that occurred in this journey was the first sight of Berrydale, looking from the road down upon the two bridges; the inn with a finely wooded bank above it, and the summit of the hill crowned by the mansion belonging to Mr. Horn, which commands a fine view of the Moray frith [sic], which formerly belonged to the venerable Sir John Sinclair.[15]

16. William Daniell, 'Berrydale, Caithness', *A Voyage Round the Coast of Scotland and the Adjacent Islands*, 1814–1822 (National Library of Scotland)

New inns were also built at old ferry crossings such as the Kylerhea Inn, Isle of Sleat, and the Old Ferry Inn at Kylehea Ferry on the Glenelg side of the Sound of Sleat, Western Inverness-shire. This pair of ferry-houses was designed by James Gillespie Graham in 1801–2, who was engaged on estate works for Lord Macdonald on Skye, including Macdonald's chamberlain's house, Portree House.[16]

The inn at a newly-established planned village was not just a functional building; it was an architectural landmark, a statement of respectability, comfort and modernity, a deliberate and specific cultural indicator that the village, however remote, was an outpost of British society. The Badachro Inn, Badachro, Gairloch, Wester Ross, for example, was built in the early nineteenth century, in association with the neighbouring fish curing stations established by the local landowner, Sir Hector Mackenzie, to employ the cleared population of Gairloch.[17] The fifth Duke of Argyll believed that an inn was 'a building that ought to be very particularly studied and attended to . . . strangers will of course set the edge of their criticism [of a town] upon the Inn in the first place.'[18] This view was epitomised by the Argyll Arms Hotel, Inveraray, 1751–5, built by the contractor William Douglas to an amended John Adam plan.[19] At three storeys high and nine bays wide, it is the inn on a grand scale, described by Samuel Johnson as 'not only commodious but magnificent.'[20] In his role as Chairman of the British Fisheries Society, the fifth Duke of Argyll was also responsible for the Tobermory Inn, Mull, built in 1791 to a design by Robert Mylne, which, like the inn at Berrydale, featured flanking single storey wings (Fig. 17).[21] The establishment of planned fishing villages also introduced a number of new Customs Houses. Typically similar in construction and design to the improved farmhouse, Customs Houses were built to support the growing Highland fishing industry. New Customs Houses were built at Tobermory, Ullapool, Wick and Helmsdale.[22]

Like the improved farmhouse, the Church of Scotland manse is associated with the eighteenth-century rural landscape.[23] Indeed, until the 1770s, when tenant farmers began to feel the benefits of agricultural improvement, the manse was often the only substantial building in a rural parish, besides that of the landowner. The history of the manse dates back to a 1663 Edict of the Scottish Parliament, which obliged the landowners of a parish, the Heritors, to provide a 'competent manse'.[24] After Union, the Patronage Act of 1712 secured this obligation as one of the few remaining forms of direct patronage legally available to landowners. As a result, a well-built elegant manse became a matter of paternalist prestige for the landowning class and a new manse was often built as part

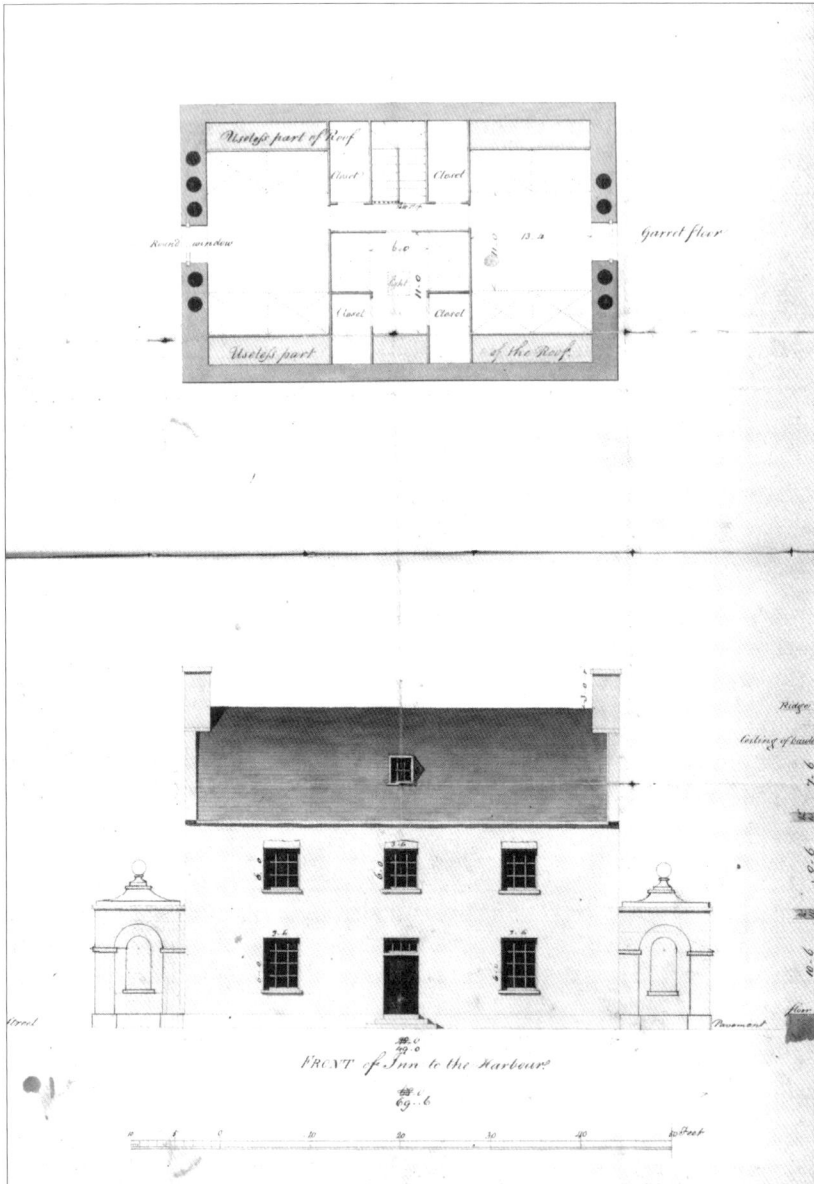

17. Robert Mylne, *Plan of an Inn at Tobermory*, 1790 (Reproduced Courtesy of RCAHMS)

of wider estate improvements.[25] Early-eighteenth-century manses were generally of two storeys and rectangular plan but varied in regularity of elevation and quality of construction, as at St Mungo Manse, Dumfries and Galloway, 1704, a rubble-built manse with heather thatch.[26] However, the two-storey, three-bay,

18. Kirklands of Coull, Aberdeenshire (author)

stone-built and slated, improved manse emerged in the Scottish Lowlands by the 1730s. Kirklands of Coull, a model manse in Highland Aberdeenshire, was built in the early nineteenth century (Fig. 18).[27] Similar manses can be found throughout the Highlands, for example: Tongue Manse in Sutherland, 1841; or Arngask Manse, Gelnfarg, Perthshire, which is an example of a typical improved manse in the Central Highlands; whilst Kinlochspeluie Manse and Salen Manse are both good examples from Mull, Argyll, in the West Highlands.[28] On Skye, Upper Ostaig Manse and Duirnish Manse both feature hipped roofs as a slightly more refined alternative to the predominant gabled roof.[29]

In the central and western Highlands, the plans of individual landowners were augmented in the late eighteenth and early nineteenth century by a Church of Scotland programme of manse building to attract 'civilising' ministers to remote Highland parishes.[30] In 1826 Thomas Telford was commissioned to design a standard manse building to install Church of Scotland ministers in remote parishes, notably Western Inverness-shire and Wester Ross, that did not have an established Church of Scotland presence, for example, Kilmallie House, Corpach, Western Inverness-shire, or Kinlochluichart Manse, Contin, 1825 (Fig. 19).[31] Many parishes, particularly in the eastern Highlands, also have a Free Church Manse. These were built in direct competition to the established Church of Scotland parish church and manse after the ministers of the Free Church split from the Church of Scotland in 1843. Although the Free Church

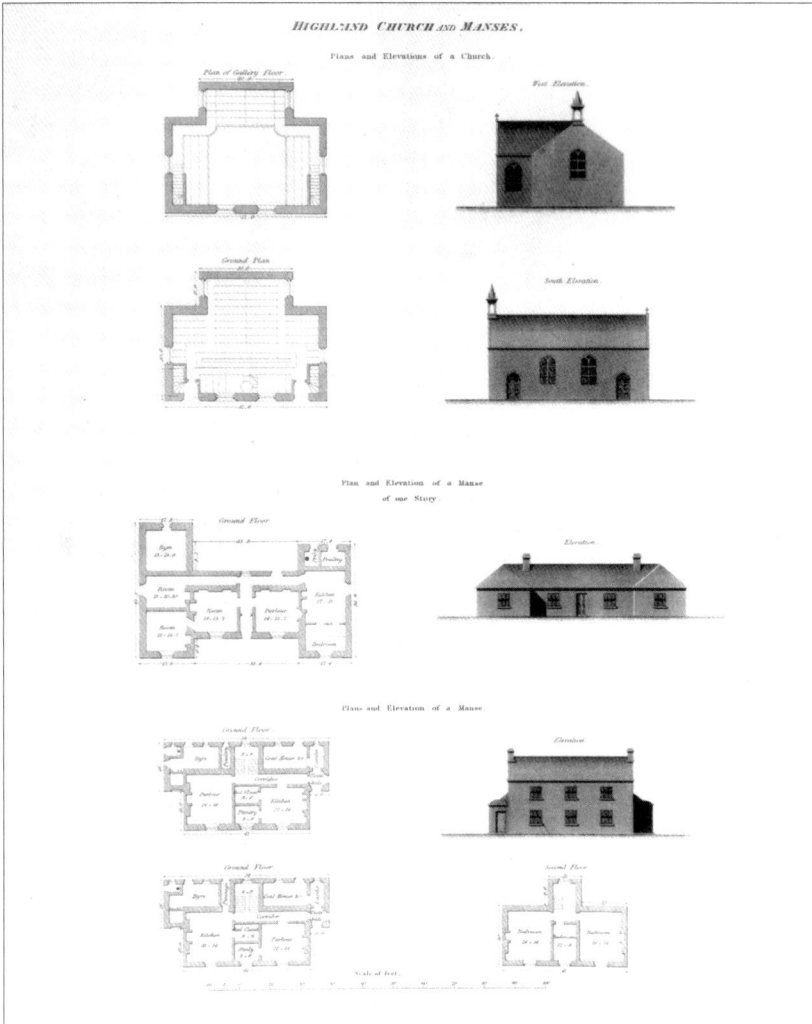

19. Thomas Telford, 'Highland Church and Manse', *A Biographical Atlas to the Life of Thomas Telford by Himself,* 1838, plate 59 (Crown Copyright: RCAHMS)

offices in Edinburgh were designed in an overtly historicist Seventeenth-Century Revival style to embody the spirit of the Covenanters, Free Church manses are for the most part of similar plain design to those of the Church of Scotland.

The two Jacobite Uprisings of 1715 and 1745 ensured that, for the first half of the eighteenth century, Highland history was in part one of military campaigns followed by building programmes to ensure the long term pacification of the region. Several rest-houses and office lodgings were built in conjunction with

George, Lieutenant General Wade's road building programme in the aftermath of the first Uprising of 1715. Wade's roads brought many remote Highland regions within reach of the British army. However, in terms of improvement they were not of great long-term value as the routes taken were frequently too precipitous and the surfaces too uneven for the use of goods or passenger transport.[32] Englishton House, Kirkhill, Ross and Cromarty, is an early eighteenth-century house named after its most famous resident, General Wade, who was billeted at the house during the 1720s. Wade's Inspector of Roads, William Caulfield, lived at Cradlehall House, Inverness and Bonar, from 1732–67. Caulfield planned and laid over 800 miles of roads in the Highlands, later becoming Deputy Governor of Inverness Castle. Cradlehall, is a model two-storey symmetrical house with single-storey flanking wings. The house was reputedly named after the cradle that was used to hoist drunken guests to their beds. Ruthven Barracks, 1719–21, stands on a prominent hilltop site near Kingussie, Inverness-shire. The square, high-walled enclosure housing symmetrical three-storey barrack blocks is a highly visible reminder of the British military presence in the Highlands on the approach to Inverness from the south.[33]

The grandest military building work in the Highlands undertaken by the British government in the eighteenth century was the military fort and barracks of Fort George at Ardersier, Inverness-shire: a triangular fortified complex covering 42 acres of a spit of land extending into the Moray Firth. Designed by William Skinner in 1747 and contracted to William Adam, Fort George was constructed to replace the first Fort George in Inverness, which had been damaged in the 1745 Uprising. The buildings within the fortified bastion walls of Fort George consist of three-storey regular blocks geometrically arranged around a central square or parade ground. Although obsolete by the time it was completed, Fort George was built to be the base for a permanent British military presence in the Highlands and a highly visible deterrent against any further uprisings or military support from France or Spain arriving by sea.

The Logistics of Building in the Highlands

With the total cost ranging from £400 to £800, equivalent to several years' farm rent, building a house in the Highlands was a very expensive undertaking requiring an array of imported building materials, manufactured components and skilled labour.[34] The construction process of the typical improved farmhouse required a large number of building materials that were simply not available in the Highlands outside towns such as Inverness, Dingwall or Stornoway. These items had to be transported to the building site, including roof slates, roofing lead, timber for floor boards, internal framing of partition walls and lathes for plastering, highly unstable lime for lime mortar and exterior render, and oil paint for the woodwork. The most valuable component of the thatched roof structure of a Highland blackhouse was the cruck-frame 'couples'. As discussed in the previous chapter, these were the largest and most valuable parts, as timber in the Highlands was scarce and therefore very expensive. The roof of an improved farmhouse is a much larger A-frame structure made of multiple lengths of sawn timber: timber for the A-frames, the joists, rafters and other parts of the roof structure. High quality pine lumber, or deal, was imported from the Baltic by merchants in ports such as Glasgow and Aberdeen. The deal was then purchased by building contractors who had to arrange for the transportation of the deal to the building site where it would have to be measured, sawn and assembled by a skilled wright. All improved farmhouses in the Highlands are covered with slates. Roofing slates also had to be ordered and transported, often shipped from Highland quarries such as Ballachulish and Easdale. In addition, there was any number of manufactured components required: nails, hinges, door handles, locks, keys, escutcheon plates, weights and pulleys for window casements, grates for fireplaces, window glass, window casements and sash frames, panelled doors, and moulds for interior plasterwork mouldings.

Who built the new stone and slate houses of the Scottish Highlands? Overall, building a modern farmhouse in the Highlands involved a very substantial expenditure; however, the above list of supplies does not include the skilled craftsmen required to assemble all the imported materials and components. The highly skilled work required to build an improved house could not be found in a region still dominated by indigenous self-build traditions. A master mason-contractor was required to oversee the design of the house and the building works. Masons were required to select a quarry, quarry the stone, cut the stone, mix the lime mortar, lay the foundations, build the walls, and finish the mouldings and surfaces of the walls and ceilings. Wrights were required to construct the roof frame, lay the floorboards and fit the doors and windows. Craftsmen migrated from regional urban centres with established guild systems, such as Inverness, Stornoway, Tain, Dingwall or larger Lowland centres such as Perth, Edinburgh, Glasgow, Dundee and Aberdeen. So, for example, Cuier Manse on Barra in the Western Isles was built, in 1816, by John Loban of Stornoway.[35] Or, Newhall in Ross and Cromarty, 1805, was built by James Smith of Inverness for Donald Mackenzie of Newhall.[36] The late eighteenth and early nineteenth-century Highland landscape was peppered with parcels of migrant masons and wrights working for one or two seasons on new house builds and then moving on to the next contract. It was this economic migration of masons, dispersed from Scotland's regional Masonic centres to all parts of the Highlands, which accounts for the similarity of materials, components and build found in the new houses of the Highland building boom.

Throughout the seventeenth century, the Scottish Masonic lodges produced highly trained masons capable of finely balanced work that was based upon geometric proportion and the workings of the classical orders.[37] This was later codified by the influence of classicism in the eighteenth century.[38] In 1710, there were 25 Masonic lodges in the Lowlands and North East. Their members were divided into operative masons and non-operative members, often gentlemen attracted by the rituals and sophisticated mathematical beliefs of freemasonry.[39] Apprentice masons were bound to serve seven years, substantially longer than that required by most trades, and joined a lodge two or three years into their apprenticeship.[40] In order to prove their knowledge and ability, apprentices had to produce an Assay piece. John Hamilton, for example, was admitted to the Lodge of St Mary's Chapel, Edinburgh in 1686 upon completion of an Assay piece:

> ane house of ane hundred and twentie footes of length and twentie-four
> footes over the walls, with ane large scaill stair for ane entrie, with ane
> turnpike in the back syd. The house is to consist in three story hight,
> ten footes betwixt floore and floore, with doores, windowes and
> chimneys conveniently placed.[41]

The typical improved farmhouse in the Highlands is a plain, harled building with windows and doorways picked out with plain stone margins, covered with a slate roof. This specific combination of building elements emerged in the medieval period in the construction of laird's houses. By the seventeenth century it was a well-established formula which continued in the urban domestic architecture of the expanding Scottish cities and burghs. In terms of construction, the eighteenth-century farmhouses of the Highlands were therefore an extension of Scottish Masonic practices to a new building type in a new geographic region by economic-migrant masons.

Who paid for the new farmhouses of the Scottish Highlands? Different estates made different arrangements for the cost of building a new farmhouse. In some cases, such as the Sutherland Estates, tenant farmhouses were built and

paid for by the estate. However, in the majority of cases an agreement was made
between landlord and tenant to share the costs of improvement, generally in the
form of a fixed term of reduced rent. The typical arrangement between landlord
and tenant farmer regarding the building and maintenance of new farm
buildings in Caithness was outlined by Captain John Henderson in *A General
View of the Agriculture of the County of Caithness,* 1812:

> In all bargains betwixt landlord and tenant, the latter is bound to repair
> the dwelling house and farm offices which he receives on the farm at his
> entry . . . In cases where a tenant takes a tract of land formerly
> occupied by small tenants . . . the farmer stipulates that he is to be
> allowed the first one, two or three year's rent for building a house and
> offices, he being bound to leave the house on the land at the expiration
> of his lease . . . In no cases so far as I could discover does the proprietor
> build houses etc for the farmer.[42]

How did a tenant farmer keen to build a new farmhouse in a remote glen of the
Highlands find a building contractor? Tenders for house building contracts were
advertised in newspapers such as the *Inverness Courier* or even the *Edinburgh
Evening Courant.* For example, the contract for Akernish House, South Uist, was
advertised in the *Inverness Courier,* 25 March 1835. Culrain Mains, Kincardine,
Ross and Cromarty, a plain, two-storey house was built in 1821 by John Rose, a
mason from Cromarty and Nicholas Vass, a wright from Tain; both craftsmen
responded to an advertisement for tenders in the *Inverness Courier,* 27 August
1819.

Documentary evidence of a typical working mason's career is rare. Given the
extraordinarily large number of farmhouses that were built by these itinerant
craftsmen, and the high quality of their work, it is remarkable how the vast
majority remain anonymous with no documentation, signed architectural
drawings or architectural reputation to survive them. By contrast, for the smaller
number of eighteenth-century minor laird's houses in the Highlands there is a
higher number of houses by known masons. This is because the higher wealth
and social status of the minor landowner attracted the architect-mason. The
architect-mason was a trained operative mason with claim to a reputation for
architectural design. Several celebrated Scottish architects of the eighteenth
century were in fact architect-masons. William Adam (1689–1748) was an
architect-mason who paid for his sons Robert and James Adam to become two
of Scotland's first professional architects by sending them on the Grand Tour to

Italy. The same is true of Robert Mylne (1733–1811) of the Mylne dynasty of Edinburgh master masons. Thomas Telford (1757–1834) also trained as an apprentice mason working in the Edinburgh New Town. However, there were many other lesser-known house designers who stood at the architect-mason, professional-artisan threshold. In the Highlands, William Robertson of Elgin (1786–1841) stands out for the number of minor landowners' houses he designed in the Inverness region towards the middle of the nineteenth century.[43] In Argyll and Bute, Rossdhu House, Luss, built in 1772 for Sir James Colquhoun, is an important house in terms of architectural history as the design was the result of a collaboration between the architect-mason John Baxter (d. *c.* 1770) and a key figure of the Scottish Enlightenment, Sir John Clerk of Penicuik, who also collaborated with William Adam in the design of his own house, Mavisbank, Midlothian.[44]

20. Herman Moll, *Scotland Divided into its Shires*, 1745 (National Library of Scotland)

CHAPTER 3

Regional House Building Patterns in the Highlands

The strong relationship between building houses and agricultural improvement in the Highlands can be seen in the geographic distribution of farmhouses built in the eighteenth and early nineteenth centuries. The distribution of small-scale houses, incorporating both farmhouses and minor country houses, reveals the different types of tenant farmer, landowner, and their business relationships, that were active in the different regions of the Highlands (Fig. 20). The regional relationships between the house building activities of landowners and their tenant farmers is an important consideration as it demonstrates their financial interdependence during the process of land improvement. The Highland building boom falls into distinct areas of development (see Appendix 1, Table 1). The greatest numbers of houses, both farmhouse and smaller country house, were built in the arable, topographically low, areas of Eastern Inverness-shire and Easter Ross centred on the urban centre of Inverness. This was a historically prosperous agricultural area, well connected to local markets and regional transport routes, characterised by numerous small to medium-scale estates and related tenant farms; a region dominated by smaller landowners, successful local tenant farmers and a small intake of 'strangers' from the Lothians.

The second largest area of growth was the Campbell-dominated western coastal and central Highland region from the Isle of Bute, through mainland Argyll and northwest Perthshire to the Isle of Mull and the Morvern peninsula. A region where improvement and its related building programmes was directly related to the influence of those zealous advocates of improvement, the Dukes of Argyll, Earls of Breadalbane and related cadet families. In Argyll, the improving tenant farmers were also predominantly Campbells with preference given by Campbell landowners to modernising Campbell farmers over southern strangers. Sutherland was also a distinct area of building activity. From Assynt in the northwest to Golspie on the southeast coast, across the county the near total dominance of the Sutherland Estates of the Duke and Duchess of Sutherland allowed a single well-managed programme of tenant farm and estate factor house building to be undertaken in the early nineteenth century.

The remaining regions of low or uneven building activity and agricultural improvement fall together as a final group. The regions in this group have the shared characteristics of geographic remoteness, poor overland connections to southern markets and a lack of a dominant landowner: Caithness, the Western Isles, Wester Ross and Western Inverness-shire. Another contributing factor to the low number of individual farmhouses was the vast size of some individual tenant sheep farms in the north west.

Eastern Inverness-shire and Easter Ross and Cromarty

The region is characterised by a higher than average number of small landowners than in other Highland regions, which were dominated by great estates. The relatively high number of landowners with fairly small estates translates to a relatively higher number of tenant farmers with farms smaller than the Highland average. It is an area of high-density farming, which does not necessarily equate to a high number of successful tenant farmers with the money to build new houses. The answer is localised mixed arable farming. While the more westerly and hilly parishes turned to sheep farming, the success of so many tenant farmers and minor landowners, notably Mackenzies, in the low lands of the Highlands was grounded in the ability of mixed arable farms to supply produce, particularly wheat and cattle, to the urban centres of Inverness, Tain, Dingwall and Nairn, as well as barley to the distilleries. This was in contrast to the dominance of sheep ranches suited to the upland pastures and boggy, lower ground found elsewhere in the Highlands. This, highly regional, economic interrelationship between town and country was possible because of manageable transportation distances and good roads. It is a situation that is comparable to the economic relationship between Edinburgh and the Lothians established in the early to mid-eighteenth century. In the late eighteenth century Avoch on the Black Isle was described as having a poor, mixed agriculture, with the large tenantry variously producing black cattle, sheep, goats and barley for the distilleries, and the tenants still removing each year to the upland summer shielings. By the 1830s, it was boasted that 'a field of wheat on the estates of Avoch might have vied in luxuriance and quality with any field in the Lothians.'[1] A not unrealistic claim for a region, which included Tarrel Farm House, Tarbat, built by a farmer who migrated from East Lothian in 1798 for a 19-year lease.[2]

The minor landowners of Easter Ross and Cromarty were frequently cadet branches of Highland families long established in the area, such as the Munros,

Frasers and Mackenzies. For example, Teaninich House, Alness, Ross and Cromarty, a modest five-bay mansion, has a datestone inscribed, 'Seat of Captain Hugh Munro of Teaninich . . . 1797 and the estate much improved by him'.[3] Coul House, Contin, Ross and Cromarty, 1821, seat of the Mackenzies of Coul, was described as 'handsome and commodious . . . surrounding grounds, tastefully laid out, garden . . . of superior style'.[4] The high number of tenant farms in Contin parish relates to the Mackenzies of Coul, such as Kinellan Farm, advertised in the Elgin Courier in January 1832, 'To let Kinellan Farm by Coul. New dwelling house very commodious . . . complete set of offices and excellent threshing mill.' The widespread estate improvements by the small-scale landowners of the region, including 32 new minor country houses, in turn led to a regional building boom amongst their new tenant arable farmers; 108 farmhouses were built in the combined region of Easter Ross and Cromarty and Easter Inverness-shire between 1700 and 1825, the highest number of houses built in any Highland region. A remarkable 75 per cent were built in a brief period of fifty years between 1775 and 1825. Cadboll House, Fearn, for example, was a modest, early eighteenth-century farmhouse remodelled in the late eighteenth century when the lease was taken by Crawford Ross. A memorial stone reads 'Crawford Ross Tacksman of Cadboll for 50 years who died there in 1862'. Bellfield Farmhouse, North Kessock, 1834, is described in the New Statistical Account as 'a most complete set of offices, and a handsome dwelling house . . . newly built and commodious'. Bellfield was one of several mains farms built by the improving Colin Mackenzie of Kilcoy who also offered his tenants five pounds per acre for reclaiming waste ground.[5]

Campbell Country: Argyll and Bute

Across Argyll and Bute, 115 small-scale houses were built between 1700 and 1850. Of those, 79 per cent were farmhouses and 21 per cent small country houses. The high number of both smaller country houses and tenant farmhouses relates to the presence of the numerous, improving and wealthy cadet branches of the Campbells and the success of their tenant farmers. Of the 52 houses in Northern Argyll (including Mull) built between 1600 and 1850, 36, or 69 per cent, were built in the period 1775–1825. Of those houses, 43, or 83 per cent, are farmhouses, whilst nine, or 17 per cent, are small country seats. Nine houses are recorded as built in the early to mid-eighteenth century and five in the mid-century. This shows that the Highland building boom gained momentum at least twenty years earlier in Northern Argyll than elsewhere in the Highlands. The cadet branches of the clan Campbell built themselves new country seats. For example, Airds House, Port Appin, the seat of the Campbells of Airds built 1738. Barbreck House, Craignish, Northern Argyll, principal seat of the Campbells of Barbreck, dated 1790, was built for Major John Campbell of Barbreck. Or, Strachur House, Northern Argyll, 1770, built for General John Campbell of Strachur. Many minor Campbell lairds brought wealth back to the region from imperial service overseas. The British Empire was an economic lifeline offering overseas employment in the armed forces, professions, trade and colonial government.[6] Indeed, British military service was so extensive amongst Highlanders that it is considered by the historian Andrew Mackillop, 'as perhaps the most obvious symptom of the region's increasingly British status'.[7]

Campbell landowners had a notably paternalistic approach towards agricultural improvement and the encouragement of their tenant farmers. The Earl of Breadalbane's establishment of the Kilbrandon Agricultural Society, with prizes for best produce, was typical of the Campbells in Argyll, especially when other Campbells were the beneficiaries:

> Farms whose tenements consist chiefly of arable ground, detached and scattered, without sufficient enclosures, found it in their interest to quit them, except for a few, whose farms are more extensive . . . The state of husbandry in this part of the country has been greatly improved of later years . . . [the] Marquis of Breadalbane gives great encouragement to his tenants improving their lands by draining , ditching, and the work is done at the mutual expense of landlord and tenants.[8]

 The Earl of Breadalbane also showed preference to Campbell tenants and re-set their rents at a lower value than that offered to 'strangers'.[9] Campbell tenants who built new farmhouses included the Campbells of Ballieveclan, tacksmen to the Campbells of Barcaldine, who built Ballieveolon House, Druimavuic in the mid eighteenth century. Or, Glenure House, Ardchattan, built on a tack granted to Colin Campbell of Glenure in 1738. On the islands, Island House, Heylipol, 1748, was built for the Duke of Argyll's factor on Tiree.[10] However, Campbell patronage did not extend to all social ranks and the widespread eviction of small tenants:

> It appears that this district was better peopled a few years ago than it is at present. Within these two year 140 persons emigrated from hence to

America; and this year more are preparing to follow, being much encouraged by the flattering accounts of the former emigrants. The principal cause of the decrease of population is the engrossing and uniting of several farms, and turning them into sheep walks. Farms that formerly supported 8 or 9 families are now occupied by only 2 or 3, and in some places solely by the shepherd.[11]

In Southern Argyll and Bute, including Islay and Jura, 66 farmhouses and 16 minor country houses were built between 1700 and 1850 of which 54, or 82 per cent, were built from 1775 to 1825: a slower start than in Northern Argyll. However, Southern Argyll and Bute has the second largest number of both new farmhouses and smaller country houses after Easter Ross and Cromarty. Northern Argyll comes closely behind Eastern Inverness-shire. Besides the success of the Campbells, the high number of smaller country houses or villas in Southern Argyll was a symptom of the region coming within the outer suburban reaches of Glasgow where wealthy Glasgow merchants were beginning to build their villas. Ardenconnel House, Rhu, for instance, was designed by the architect David Hamilton for the Glasgow merchant Andrew Buchanan.[12] The presence of the suburban villa in Southern Argyll informs the narrative of agriculture improvement as it highlights the critical interdependent relationship between rural and urban growth.

As in the north, southern Argyll and Bute is punctuated with farmhouses built by improving Campbell tacksmen turned tenant farmers. Ardnave House, Kilchoman, Southern Argyll, is an early Campbell tacksman's house built in 1750 by Duncan Campbell, tacksman of Ardnave.[13] Barr House, Killean and Kilchenzie, Southern Argyll, is a mid to late eighteenth-century farmhouse built by the Campbells of Barbeck. Carse House, South Knapdale, dated 1828, was built by the Campbells of Carse, whilst Druimdrishaig Farmhouse, South Knapdale, is a late eighteenth-century farmhouse built by the Campbells of Druimdrishaig. And, Ardpatrick House, also in South Knapdale, is a mid-eighteenth-century house built by the Campbells of Ardpatrick.

Minor Campbell lairds also prospered on the new rents received from their improving tenants, with many family seats remodelled or entirely rebuilt. On Islay, many improvements were undertaken by Daniel Campbell of Shawfield and Woodhall, who purchased the island in 1726, including the remodelling of seventeenth-century Islay House in 1737, the extensive steadings complex of Islay Mains Farm and the planned village of Bowmore.[14] Kilmun House, Dunoon and Kilmun, is another early eighteenth-century house built around the core of a late sixteenth-century house. The house was built by the Campbells of Finab who purchased the estate from the Campbells of Kilmun. The house and estate was let to the Campbells of Ballochyle from 1778 when Robert Campbell of Finab succeeded to the Perthshire estate of Monzie.[15] New houses built from the later eighteenth century include, Foreland House, Kilchoman, built in 1820 for Captain Walter Campbell of Foreland and Sunderland.[16] Like many Campbells, Walter Campbell embraced the new modern Britain and made his fortune in the service of the British Empire, in this instance the East India Company, before returning to Argyll to improve his estate. Others are Lochgair House, Kilmichael Glassary, built by the Campbells of Asknish, or, Saddell House, Saddell and Skipness, of 1774, the seat of Campbells of Glen Saddell.

The Argyll Morvern Estates

From Lochaline following the Sound of Mull westward to the headland at Drimnin and returning eastward along Loch Sunart, the fertile foreshore of Morvern is punctuated by a series of farmhouses dating from the mid-to-late eighteenth century (Fig. 21). Neatly slated and harled, regular and symmetrical, these houses, built by the Dukes of Argyll's Morvern tacksmen, form an architectural group that embodies the spirit of late eighteenth-century improvement. Between 1754 (when the Morvern tacks were reset by the third Duke of Argyll)

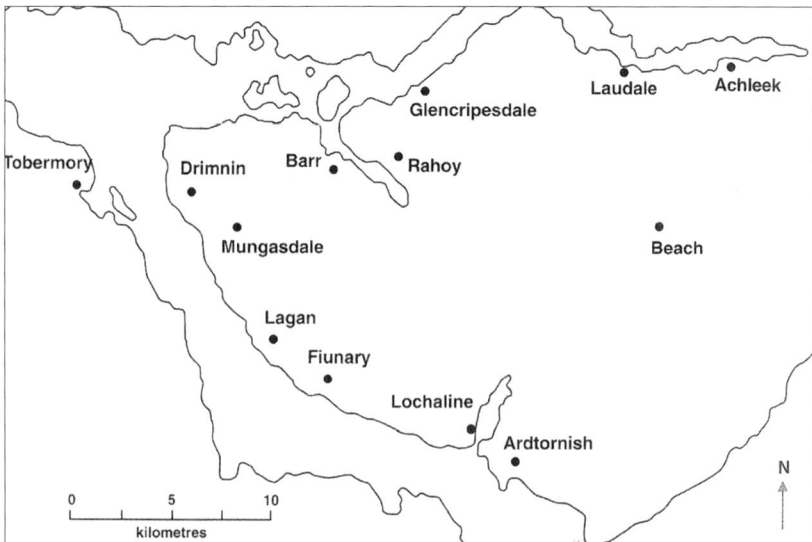

21. Map of Morvern showing farmhouses built by Argyll tacksmen (author)

and the Argyll sales of 1819 a new generation of entrepreneurial improving tacksmen reorganised their Morvern farms into profitable sheep and cattle farms.[17]

Being remote from Inveraray, improvement came late to Morvern in comparison to the rest of the Argyll estates (though still ahead of much of the Western Highlands) but the pattern was established and the issue of tacks, as ever, was central to reform.[18] A late addition to the Campbell empire, only being annexed in the late seventeenth century, Morvern was remote, untamed and in the mid-eighteenth century still very much unimproved. The House of Argyll was, by its own standards at least, slow to turn its attention and improving zeal to this outermost region and it was not until 1754 that the first agricultural reforms were carried out by Archibald, third Duke of Argyll (1682–1761) with the resetting of tacks. The old hereditary tacksmen were removed and the new tacksmen, men willing to adapt, were rewarded with vast tacks, often comprising several adjoining farms, in return for previously inconceivable rentals, their success being confirmed when their tacks were, for the most part, renewed in 1773–5 by John the fifth Duke (1723–1806), 'recognised as one of the great exponents of highland affairs'.[19] The principal tacks in Morvern, those over one thousand acres, comprised: Ardtornish, the largest of the group with 9,965 acres, set to Donald Campbell of Airds, stretching southward along the shore of the Sound of Mull from Lochaline round to Loch Linnhe; Glencripesdale, 7,834 acres set to Duguld MacLachlane, on Loch Sunart on the northern shore of the peninsula, reset to Duncan Campbell of Glenure in 1775; Liddesdale, 7,508 acres set to Lieutenant Colin Campbell, later subdivided in 1807 into Liddesdale, set to John Campbell, and East Liddesdale, or Achleek, set to Allan MacDougall; Laudale, 7,284 acres, set to John Campbell of Ardslignish; Barr, 4,224 acres set to Duncan Campbell; Rahoy, 3,059 acres, facing the small inlet of Loch Teacuis, set to Archibald Campbell; Beach, 2,645 acres, in the central fertile strip of Glen Geal bordering Ardgour, set to Ewen McFie; Lagan, 2,681 acres, set to John Campbell; and Mungasdale, 1,459 acres of land set to John Beatton bordering the Drimnin peninsula, which was still held by the Macleans of Drimnin.[20]

Amongst the various improvements carried out by these new tacksmen, and their only lasting testament when even the sheep pastures have declined, was the building of large, modern farm houses.[21] The houses these tacksmen built were purposefully, and without exception, archetypal late-eighteenth-century 'improved' farm houses 'of neat modern fabrick'.[22] All the houses faced the sea, whether on the north or south side of the peninsula. Of the major Argyll tacks in Morvern, four improvement-era houses survive today: Glencripesdale House,

Laudale House, Mungasdale House and Achleek House. The largest of the group, Donald Campbell of Airds' house at Ardtornish, was demolished in 1907 to avoid tax on unoccupied property by the then proprietor, Valentine Smith.[23] This was particularly unfortunate as it was the keystone of the whole group. Although of the same basic design, Ardtornish was larger and grander in proportion than all the others, representing the top end of the scale, a position fitting to the size and potential wealth of the tack and of Campbell of Airds' additional position as the Duke of Argyll's Morvern factor. Built between 1755 and 1770, significantly by 'a parcel of Low Country masons', it was described as 'a handsome mansion house': two storeys, harled white with three broad symmetrical bays to the front elevation and a large, M-gabled wing to the rear, some three bays deep.[24] It was a building that not only reflected the status of its owner but set the example for the other tack holders to emulate.[25]

Laudale House is the largest surviving house of the group, although the tack itself had slightly fewer acres than Glencripesdale (Fig. 22). A settlement has been recorded at Laudale since the fifteenth century but the present house was built by John Campbell of Ardslignish between 1755 and 1790.[26] Glencripesdale House is next to Laudale in scale. Glencripesdale House, although the largest tack after Ardtornish, is a half-storey smaller than Laudale and not as well balanced architecturally, having only one oversized, pavilion wing. The farm of Glencripesdale is shown on a 1733 military survey map of Loch Sunart but the present house, like Laudale, dates from the late eighteenth century and was built

22. Laudale House, Morvern, 1930s (Iain Thornber)

by Duncan Campbell of Glenure, *c.* 1775.[27] Typically harled and slated, Glencripesdale House has three broad bays to the north-east-facing front elevation and stands two-and-a-half storeys high with a row of four small, neatly-gabled dormers punctuating the roof. These are set perfectly to the larger proportions of the three windows to the first floor below; the windows to the ground floor flank a gabled entrance porch. A large one-and-a-half-storey, gable-roofed pavilion adjoins the house to the south-east gable end, with two roof dormers and an additional cross-bay to the gable end forming an overall T-plan. The interior is based on the same symmetrical standardised plan as Laudale but slightly trimmed, with the central cross passage terminating in an internal staircase to the rear and with apartments to left and right, front and back.

Little is known about Mungasdale other than it was a small-to-medium-size tack at 1,459 acres, leased to a Lowland farmer, John Beatton, when first reset in 1754 and later packaged together with several other smaller tacks at the Morvern sales in 1824. Like the other houses in the group, Mungasdale House probably dates from between 1755 and 1770. Of similar design to Laudale and Glencripesdale, it provides an example of the medium-size farmhouse, reflecting the size and revenue of the tack (Fig. 23). Typically two storeys high and three broad bays wide, harled and slated, south-west-facing Mungasdale has a rectangular porch to centre, with piended roof and slightly smaller windows to the upper storey. There is a single-storey pavilion wing with lean-to pitched roof to the south-east gable end. The roof is the only one in this group of houses to

23. Mungasdale House, Morvern (Iain Thornber)

feature raised skews to the gable ends, which suggests the work of different masons, possibly from the Lothians.[28] The original house for the large 1754 tack of Liddesdale was converted from an existing storehouse, built by the short-lived Morvern Mining Company in the 1730s, now a ruin of rectangular-plan foundations and one gable end. However, Achleek House, further along Loch Sunart to the east, has survived.[29]

Achleek House was built by Allan MacDougall, *c.* 1807, when the Liddesdale tack was split into West and East Liddesdale, of which Achleek was the principal farm. North-facing across Loch Sunart, Achleek House is the last and smallest of the Morvern group and, accordingly, also the simplest. It is, typically, harled white and slated, with broad gable-end chimneystacks, two storeys high, three symmetrical bays and a central doorway reached by four modern concrete steps. The most distinctive feature is that the smaller size of Achleek sees the proportions of the windows differ from the larger houses, being smaller in dimension on the ground floor and having square, not rectangular, upper-storey windows, but all still house the original four pane sash-and-case frames. Both gable ends are blank, as would be expected, with only two windows and an upper-storey central stair window to the rear. The wall to the west of the front elevation suggests the former presence of a small single-storey pavilion or an enclosed yard. The slightly overhanging eaves and exposed rafters of the roof at the gable ends reflect the beginning of changes in house design in the early nineteenth century.

Of the other houses belonging to the large Argyll tacks, those that have been lost include Barr House built in the late eighteenth century by Duncan Campbell and demolished in 1930, Archibald Campbell's Rahoy House, demolished in the mid-nineteenth century, and Beach House, demolished *c.* 1870.[30] Elsewhere in Morvern, the model was repeated on the neighbouring Achranich estate with the erection of a new farmhouse by Macdonald of Borrodale, *c.* 1815, similar in scale to Mungasdale House.[31] Another lost improvement-era house in Morvern was Fiunary Manse, built in 1779 for Norman Macleod, father of John Macleod, the Presbyterian minister installed by the fifth Duke of Argyll to improve the religion of the largely Episcopalian population of Morvern. The architectural significance of the Argyll Morvern farmhouses lies in their uniformity. Taken together, the houses form a coherent architectural group of buildings that represented the arrival of the modern world in Morvern. The tacksmen knew they were on the northern frontline of agricultural improvement in Scotland, bringing new innovative farming methods from the south and introducing them to the unimproved wilds of Morvern, and their houses needed to reflect this self-image.[32]

The Sutherland Estates

> It is a marked feature in its character, since the succession of the
> Duke of Sutherland, that new farm-houses and inns have
> displaced the old – introducing a new era in this district . . . .
> The interior was let to sheep-farmers and the Tenantry moved
> to the coast.[33]

A series of tenant farmers' and factors' farmhouses were built across Sutherland
by the Sutherland Estates following the succession of the Duke of Sutherland in
the early nineteenth century. The new Duke of Sutherland undertook a county-
wide programme of enclosures, re-setting of rents and purchase of any pockets
of land that could be bought, such as the Mackay estate at Tongue in northwest
Sutherland which included Tongue House built in 1678 by Donald Mackay,
Master of Reay, and later remodelled in 1750.[34] On his tour of Scotland William
Daniell stayed at the recently completed house of Mr. Gunn, factor to the
Sutherland Estates at Fillire in northwest Sutherland.[35] Prior to the Sutherland
Estates' improvements, farming in Sutherland followed the long-established
patterns of runrig subsistence farming, producing a mixture of black cattle,
sheep and some crops 'in favourable years'. For example, the tenants of Kildonan
in southeast Sutherland, population 1440, collectively kept an estimated 2,497
head of cattle and 5,041 sheep, but their crops frequently failed and their pastures
were over-grazed, resulting in the Duchess of Sutherland often having to provide
'foreign victual'.[36] However, by 1831 the population of Kildonan had decreased
to 257:

> The decrease is accounted for by the change that occurred in the
> rural economy of the parish, by the substitution of the Cheviot
> sheep for Highland cattle; between the years 1811 and 1821. The
> system of small holdings and subletting; previously common in the
> parish, was thereby altered; and no part of the parish being adapted
> for new settlements, the bulk of the population was settled in the
> coast-side parishes; and in particular they resorted to the village of
> Helmsdale . . . Almost the whole of the parish is occupied as sheep
> farms. The number of sheep grazed . . . is estimated at 18,000 head,
> and they are divided amongst six tenants of separate farms. The
> Cheviot stocks occupy whole pasture grounds of the parish – and
> the shepherd's dog must not be omitted, for without this faithful

and tractable animal, it would be impossible to conduct sheep
farming in the successful manner now done. The first of the dogs
was obtained from the Borders.[37]

The Rev. James Campbell's enthusiastic account of the Sutherland Estates'
improvements and the managed depopulation of Kildonan for the *New
Statistical Account* did not mention that these activities were overseen by the
popular villain of the Clearances, the Duke of Sutherland's factor, Patrick Sellar.
Sellar has been criticised for the violence employed by his men in the forcible
remove of the indigenous tenantry and the burning of highly-valued roof frames:
serious action for a people adapted to an evolved building tradition that in a
treeless region depended upon locally-available materials. The historian Eric
Richards judges Sellar as having been overzealous, insensitive and clumsy but not
intentionally wicked nor exceptional in his work as an improving estate factor.[38]
Sellars and Kildonan form the most infamous example of the Sutherland Estates'
systematic transformation of the region's settlement patterns.

In terms of architecture, even within the standards of the Highlands, the
houses of the Sutherland Estates form a uniform architectural group: plain two-
storey, rectangular-plan houses with few if any additions or ornament. All
Sutherland houses feature a framed Sutherland Arms above the central doorway.
Fifty-six new farmhouses were built in Sutherland between 1800 and 1850
distributed fairly evenly between the northwest and south-eastern parts of the
county. In northwest Sutherland these include: Ard Neackie, Durness; Leirinbeg
House, Durness; Scourie House, Eddrachillis, an estate factor's house; Bettyhill
House, Farr; Ivy Cottage, Farr; and Melness House, Tongue, which was a sheep
farm of over 70,000 acres. Similar Sutherland Estates tenant houses in southeast
Sutherland include Rhives House, 'an excellent house has been built . . . with
apartment for clerks', and Morvich Lodge, Golspie, let to Patrick Sellar.[39] In 1844
Sellar bought the Ardtornish estate on Morvern, including Ardtornish House,
formerly the residence of the Duke of Argyll's Morvern factor, Donald Campbell
of Airds.

The Western Isles, Caithness and the North West

The regions of the Western Isles, Caithness, Western Inverness-shire and Wester
Ross are considered together as a group because they were the farthest areas
geographically from the twin-engines of agricultural improvement and industrial

revolution originating in the Lowlands. These regions saw the fewest new houses built. This is partly because without the energetic land improvement programme of the Duke of Sutherland, which extended to the most north-westerly points of mainland Scotland, there were fewer improvements, concentrated in small pockets of activity, until the mid to late nineteenth century. It is also partly because the sheep farms that were enclosed were of such a vast size that fewer farmhouses were required.

In the Western Isles, a relatively low number of new houses, 17, were built. The overall trend, however, echoes building activity in the mainland Highlands with a vast majority of new build being tenant farmhouses and the peak period of building activity falling in the period, 1775–1825. As would be expected in the Outer Hebrides, there is a dominance of small landowner's houses related to Clanranald and the Macleans. For example, Ormaclett House, South Uist, built in the early nineteenth century, and Balranald House, North Uist, architect Alexander Mackenzie of Portree, 1832, are both Clanranald houses. While Lochmaddy Mansion, North Uist, dated 1852, was built for the Macleans of Boreray. Howlin Farm built by Lachlan Mackinnon, 'who built the present farmhouse', on the Isle of Eigg was one of eight farms on Eigg leased to Clanranald tacksmen in the 1770s.[40]

In Caithness 33 houses were built between 1750 and 1825 of which 22 were tenant farmhouses. The pattern of improvements undertaken by Caithness landowners was one of extensive single-tenant farms and, more than in any other region of the Highlands, the establishment of coastal fishing stations and new villages to profit from the herring fishery. A focus of improving activities, such as the extensive buildings of Ulbster Mains near Wick, was the estates of the Scottish Enlightenment luminary, advocate of agricultural improvement and instigator of the *Statistical Account of Scotland*: Sir John Sinclair.

In Western Inverness-shire only 28 farmhouses were built but that figure represents 82 per cent of all houses built in the region, 1700–1850. There was a distinct pocket of building activity related to Lord MacDonald's estates on Skye. William Daniell describes how in 'Glenvargle bridge, near Portree', 'the latter place is to be recognised by the distant cluster of houses near an elevated neck of land toward the centre. The detached mansion on the left is that of Mr. Macpherson, the factor of Lord Macdonald' (Fig. 24).[41] The 'cluster of houses' depicted shows a flurry of recent building activity including three tenant farmhouses in addition to Mr. Macpherson's pedimented mansion. The new enclosed sheep farms of Western Inverness-shire were noted for their scale and the prosperity of the tenants. The *New Statistical Account* records that:

24. William Daniell, 'Glenvargle bridge, near Portree, Skye', *A Voyage Round the Coast of Scotland and the Adjacent Islands*, 1814–1822 (National Library of Scotland)

> In Knoydart and Glenelg proper, there are several large and comfortable houses, occupied by extensive sheep-farmers. Of these the principal are at Barrisdale, Beolary and Ellanreach. The last especially is commodious, well finished, and finely situated near the sea.'[42]

As such, outwith the Macdonald estates, the actual number of new farmhouses built on the glen floors and sea loch foreshores of this remote part of the Highlands was relatively low.

The total number of houses built in Wester Ross was also relatively low, only 26, however it is notable that six farmhouses and two small country houses are in the one parish of Gairloch. This is the highest concentration of new build for any individual parish outside of Easter Ross and Cromarty and Western Inverness-shire. The highly localised grouping evident in Gairloch is related to improvements by the Mackenzies of Gairloch and a handful of cadet Mackenzie families. Flowerdale House, Gairloch, Wester Ross, 1738, the seat of the Mackenzies of Gairloch, was described by Daniell as, 'the seat of Sir Hector Mackenzie, Lord Lieutenant of Inverness-shire, situated amidst very picturesque scenery, and surrounded by mountains abundantly wooded. It is a most delightful summer residence, and deserves a more dignified title than that which is jocosely given to it by its hospitable owner, who calls it his *shieling*' (Fig. 25).[43]

25. William Daniell, 'The Gair-loch in Rosshire', *A Voyage Round the Coast of Scotland and the Adjacent Islands*, 1814–1822 (National Library of Scotland)

It is a double-pile classical country house distinguished by its *piano nobile*, or first floor, main entrance reached via a flight of stairs, central pediment with traditionally Scottish crowstepped gables typical of the earlier eighteenth century.[44] Closely related to Flowerdale is Urdigle House, Gairloch, a smaller house built by a cadet branch of the Mackenzies, 1745–56, which has similar panelling, doors and chimneypieces.[45]

By the 1790s much of the parish of Lochcarron had already been enclosed and new long leases of 25 years had been set followed by a 'spirit of industry and improvement' amongst the new tenant farmers, 'They [the farmers] are now building comfortable houses, and turning their lands to the best advantage.'[46] However, improvement had still not reached many other parts of Wester Ross by the end of the eighteenth century. Glenshiel in the 1790s was reported as having, '17 farms, each of which is occupied by a number of tenants so that each forms a village. The tenants graze their cattle promiscuously, each restricting himself to a number of heads; and the arable ground they occupy in like manner.'[47] This contrasts sharply with a description of Glenshiel in 1834:

> Two new farmhouses built . . . substantial and comfortable though
> small . . . The climate and pasture were perfectly congenial to the sheep.
> The rearing of the black cattle was by degrees abandoned, and there is

at present no farm in the parish . . . of which the staple commodities do not consist of wool and mutton. But though the change now described produced an amazing increase of rent, the advance in some instances of mountain pasture amounting to from 1000 to 6000 per cent, in the course of single generation, the effect upon the population was not so favourable.[48]

In the 1790s Kintail was still dominated by Macrae smallholders and agriculture meant the rearing and droving of black cattle: 'The natives of Kintail . . . are generous and hospitable, and if they are sometimes peevish to strangers, it is by reason of encroachments on their grazings and hill pastures.'[49] The natives of Kintail were right to have been peevish. By the 1830s all the native people had been removed to the coast at Dornie to 'pursue the fishery' and the rest of the country was, 'almost exclusively directed to the sheep stock, which has of late years been greatly improved – which has been attended with the happiest results as sheep from this parish generally fetch the first prices at southern markets'.[50]

The regional distribution of farmhouses and minor country houses built in the Highlands through the eighteenth and early nineteenth centuries shows a varied pattern of agricultural improvement and its related building activity with distinct regional narratives emerging: the proliferation of new tenant farmhouses and minor country houses in the low, arable farm lands around Inverness; the dominance and early economic success of the Campbells in Argyll; the sweeping programme of enclosures undertaken by the Sutherland Estates in Sutherland; and, a slower process and chequered pattern of improvement and house building in the remote regions of the North West, Western Isles and Caithness.

CHAPTER 4

Modern Homes for Modern People

Unlike the low, streamlined and well-insulated indigenous blackhouse, the improved farmhouse is not well-suited to the adverse weather of the Scottish Highlands. Indeed, in terms of heating and insulation the typical improved farmhouse is one of the worst possible designs for its location. Improved farmhouses have tall, relatively thin stone walls which expose the structure to the full force of the weather and offer very poor insulation. This is exacerbated by large areas of glazing and an un-insulated roof space covered with a single layer of slates. The heating itself is equally impractical. Whereas the fireplace in the eighteenth-century blackhouse was located in the centre of the living space for maximum heat efficiency, the fireplaces of the improved farmhouse are built into the gable end walls losing heat through the flue and external wall. The flow of air and the spread of warmth through the house are then restricted by the division of the interior into multiple high-ceilinged rooms and unheated passageways. However, these practical considerations were of secondary importance to the improving tenant farmer when choosing the design of a new house. The primary function of the new Highland house was not thermal efficiency but to act as a highly visible, three-dimensional, social statement: a change in priority from practicality to style. The appearance of the house conveyed specific social messages about the house's occupants to a specific audience (principally other tenant farmers). The new Highland house told visitors that despite their remote location the tenant farmer and his family who lived there were not 'primitive Gaels' but affluent members of modern British society.

As we have seen, the number and distribution of improved farmhouses built during the long eighteenth century provides clear statistical evidence of a Highland building boom and contributes a new perspective to the socio-economic history of agricultural improvement in Scotland. However, these farmhouses become a much richer resource when they are also viewed as individual cultural artefacts. Each house is a record of eighteenth-century culture and its values, in which 'the artefact plays the role that known individuals have in documentary history.'[1] The many considered choices made by the improving tenant farmer and his family in the design of their new farmhouse, from walls to wallpaper, revealed themselves and their view of themselves to their social group in the eighteenth century, and, through the physical fabric of the building, to us today. The contrast between the blackhouse and the improved farmhouse is the victory of 'form over substance or manner against content' for specific social purposes.[2]

The Farmhouse as Social Statement

The typical farmhouse was not just a functional shelter but a rhetorical construct of social statements commonly understood within eighteenth century British society. The internal space of the house was subdivided into rooms created for the performances of daily life; the exterior, the superficial face of the house, was the householder's public statement to the rest of the world. The different rooms of a house were decorated and ornamented according to their function but also as indicators of the household's identity. The internal spaces of any house are a constant interplay between the occupants and the rooms, each room becoming an active agent in the formation and maintenance of its occupants' social actions and practices, 'the correlation between one's position in society and one's place in physical space' both articulated and framed by the architecture of the home.[3]

As seen in the previous chapters, the first and most significant observation about eighteenth-century farmhouses in the Scottish Highlands is the overwhelming uniformity, or sameness, of their design. Glassingall, Perthshire, is a good example of the two-storey, three-bay symmetrical elevation and rectangular plan common throughout the Highlands (Fig. 26). Uniform buildings suggest conformity in the architectural choices made by improving tenant farmers. What this tells us about eighteenth-century tenant farmers has been neatly expressed by the architectural historian Nicholas Cooper writing about English houses of the same period: 'in building uniform houses . . . which conformed to architectural norms . . . members of eighteenth-century [society] expressed their standing and their sense of community'.

Conformity in the context of eighteenth-century British society can be explained as a product of that society's obsession with the social and aesthetic rules of taste. The ability to demonstrate good taste was central to a family's social standing within eighteenth-century British society. Beyond financial wealth, the ability to demonstrate good taste, one's education and refinement, was a statement of your social rank (or that to which you and your family

26. Glassingall, Perthshire (author)

aspired). Therefore, there was a lot riding on the question of good taste; the result of which was considerable social pressure, particularly amongst the socially insecure 'middling sorts', such as the tenant farmer. The ready solution to social anxiety was social conformity. The requirement to demonstrate good taste inevitably led to social anxiety at the possibility of demonstrating bad taste. This could be avoided by strict conformity in one's design choices. The combination of individual social anxiety and collective social pride produced over three hundred farmhouses across the Highlands that are much the same in appearance.

To have good taste meant to have the capacity to make discerning judgements on beauty. This implied that one had the leisure time and resources to acquire a suitable education in the arts. An artistic eye was therefore an indicator of social status.[4] Taste was also a sign of moral virtue as a person with good taste avoided crassness and excess in art as in life. Taste patrolled the boundary between wealth and display, virtue and morality. However, the average tenant farmer and his wife were more likely simply concerned with getting it right within their immediate social world.[5] The role of the home, and the architectural and design choices made, was a critical tool for sending out the right messages.

The main elevation, or façade, is inherently superficial, the face of the building, but it is this superficiality that gives the façade its importance in terms of social display. The well-ordered, symmetrical, three-bay façade visually maintained the household's standing within the community: a statement of modernity and wealth, social aspiration and social conformity. There is a marked contrast between the improved farmhouse and the Highland blackhouse, where little value was placed upon external display; all elements of that building, including its external walls, were subservient to its primary and practical function, that of creating a warm, dry interior.

The visual signs of good taste also dominated the interiors of the improved farmhouse and the eighteenth-century farmhouse interior centred upon the parlour. The parlour is denoted on eighteenth-century house plans as one of the large, ground floor, rectangular rooms to the front of the house. On entering from the central passageway the first impression would be of a light and airy room with high ceilings, a large expanse of glass window and a fireplace with its mantelpiece immediately opposite. The parlour at Glassingall, today the living room, is typical (Fig. 27). An eighteenth-century Scottish builder's dictionary describes the parlour as 'a fair . . . room, designed for the entertainment of company'. The parlour was the primary public space of the 'polite' British home: a space carefully created and maintained for the social theatre of eighteenth-century manners and etiquette. Thus, the physical movements and postures of the social rituals that took place in the parlour, such as afternoon tea, connected the actors to the physical space of the parlour, the shape and size of the room, to its decoration and to the objects that filled the room. The tea ritual in particular was the focus point of eighteenth-century social life. Tea was a display of wealth and taste, which incorporated an array of expensive and tasteful products, from the tea itself, to bone china, silverware, textiles and the tea table. These fashionable objects provided a material focus for the 'social imagination': the individual's sense of belonging to a social group.[6]

It is clear from the architectural choices made that the typical improved farmhouse would not have been furnished with the traditional Highland vernacular furniture found in a blackhouse – homemade pieces adapted to life in a low-roofed, smoky, central living space. However, in the absence of known documented inventories or domestic interior paintings of tenant farmhouses in the Highlands from the eighteenth century, it must be inferred that these interiors were suitably furnished to match the mouldings and fireplaces. As observed in Argyll, farmers 'seem to enjoy the comforts and conveniences of life . . . and acknowledge that they have less difficulty than they had 30 years ago'

27. The parlour, Glassingall, Perthshire (author)

(though the typical eighteenth-century interior was sparsely furnished in comparison to our rooms today, with perhaps only a few select quality items in the parlour such as a bookcase, a table and a few chairs).[7]

The contrast between the light, plastered and painted interior of the parlour of a farmhouse such as Glassingall and the dark, smoky, peat-reek interior of the low-walled blackhouse as depicted in Tom Scott's *Caithness Interior*, 1913, could not be sharper (Fig. 28). The twenty-first-century visitor can experience the sensory shock of entering an eighteenth-century blackhouse – the half-light, smells, and low, narrowness of the interior space – at the recreated Highland village of Baile Gean at the Highland Folk Museum, Kingussie.[8] What is most striking are the slight interior furnishings of a culturally and geographically isolated subsistence society. It is a very different experience to entering the, relatively well-furnished, interiors of preserved late nineteenth-century croft houses now open to the public, such as the Arnol and Moirlanich longhouses. Whilst these interiors appear simple but comfortable, the interiors of the houses in the Baile Gean township are dark, earthy and more or less empty. The main

28. Tom Scott, *Caithness Interior,* 1913 (National Galleries of Scotland)

interior space is populated with only two or three items of self-made furniture, a stool, a settle and perhaps a kist or box bed. As described in eighteenth-century accounts, there are no chimney openings and the smoke drifts up through the half-light into the thatch from the central hearth. The mute brown expanse of the earth floor and walls also has a visual impact to eyes accustomed to plaster, paint and wallpaper. The largest of the recreated houses, the two-room Creel House, is intended as the larger dwelling of a tacksman (Fig. 29). The house has wattle walls, which increase the internal space, as described in the account of Inverie House in Glenelg. The Creel House has much larger interior spaces furnished with more furniture, including a dresser and box bed, and a greater number of manufactured goods such as the candlestick holder on the kist (Fig. 30).

The expression of good taste through the display of things was facilitated by

29. The Creel House, reconstructed early eighteenth-century tacksman's house, Highland Folk Museum, Kingussie (Highland Folk Museum)

30. Interior, Creel House, Highland Folk Museum, Kingussie (Highland Folk Museum)

'a shared material culture nourished by the flow of goods'.[9] The manufacture and transportation of goods, books and the ideas inside books throughout Britain created a common British culture based upon their consumption. A shared cultural identity emerged based upon shared consumer goods and underpinned by the accepted aesthetic standards displayed in the design of those goods. There was a rise in income and consumer spending in the eighteenth century, which particularly benefited those of middle wealth such as tradesmen, artisans, retailers and tenant farmers.[10] The tenant of a 70,000-acre sheep farm in the Highlands could afford to be a member of British consumer society.

The cultural historian Amanda Vickery suggests that 'a national society was created in eighteenth-century England by provincial elites who aped London taste and consequently failed to nurture distinctive regional tastes'.[11] A more complex relationship between goods and consumer tastes emerges in Scotland, in which Scottish buildings, developed within a European tradition, are furnished with English and Scottish goods in order to create a material world that is identifiably British. However, that is not to say that in building a new farmhouse the typical Highland tenant farmer wished to be considered English or British politically. The historian R. J. Finlay argues that ordinary Scots, who took advantage of the economic opportunities provided by the imitation of English practices, did not necessarily identify with the new political notion of Britishness. To the majority, the adoption of practices originating in England was because such practices represented the adoption of an attractive idea of modernity and economic improvement rather than a new, British, political identity.[12]

Social Rank and Decorum

At both the national and regional level, the standards of taste also defined people's positions within the social hierarchy. The appropriateness of the objects and goods a person owned in relation to their social standing was defined by the notion of decorum. Decorum was the key to the code of social manners. Decorum was inclusive and exclusive, connecting those within a group and pointedly excluding those not within that group. Decorum defined and maintained social hierarchies.[13] As such, when building or purchasing and furnishing a house, everything had to be socially appropriate. In architectural terms, decorum was the 'keeping of a due respect between the inhabitant and the habitation'.[14] The importance of decorum when making decisions about the home was also emphasised in the *Complete English Farmer,* a mid-eighteenth century practical farming, and what we would call 'lifestyle', manual for improving tenant farmers:

> I would never have my brother farmer live in a splendid house like his landlord, nor in a mean cottage like his day labourer; but in a comfortable, dry, dwelling-house, in which there should be neither profusion, nor want of convenience.[15]

The *Statistical Account* report for the parish of Archattan in northern Argyll shows that this was well understood in the Scottish Highlands:

> The farmers make a decent appearance; seem to enjoy the comforts and conveniences of life suitable to their station.[16]

The socially informed design rules of decorum are evident in the relationship between size and design in the typical improved farmhouse. A two-storey, three-bay plan and elevation is common to most tenant farmhouses. However, this formal uniformity incorporates considerable variations in the actual size of individual houses. Substantial gradations in size could be achieved by the addition of wings to the sides or to the rear (as a T or L-plan), but, the overall dimensions could also be increased with no alteration to plan or elevation design through the careful adjustment of the house's proportions. Substantial tacksmen-cum-tenant farmhouses such as Laudale House in Morvern can be equal in size to a five-bay pedimented country house (Fig. 22). The grandeur in scale alone of tacksmen's houses such as Laudale suggests a much greater wealth, at least, than the modest home of the typical Scottish tenant farmer. However, although finished to the highest craft standards, the largest farmhouse remains similar in form and ornament to the smallest farmhouse. Decorative features such as columned porticoes or pediments were associated with a higher social status than that of tenant farmer and their use would have been inappropriate irrespective of the farmer's actual wealth. Accordingly, an appropriately greater use of decorative ornament is evident in the columned entrance porches, projecting eaves, cornices and pediments featured in the new eighteenth-century houses of minor Highland landowners, as can be found in the countryside around Inverness. This area was characterised by a high number of wealthy but relatively small estates in contrast to the massive estates of the Central and Western Highlands (see Appendix 1, Table 2).

The Language of Taste

In eighteenth-century Britain taste and decorum were expressed visually through the language of classicism. The design principles of order and regularity and the emphasis of hierarchy upon which classicism is based correlated with the order and hierarchies of eighteenth-century British society. A tenant farmer was able to demonstrate good taste, and thereby consolidate his social position, by educating himself and his family to be receptive to classical design. Classicism is simply any form of art or design that is based upon classical antiquity. The revival and reinterpretation of the arts of classical antiquity, particularly that of Rome, had been the central theme of European art since the Renaissance began in fifteenth-century Italy. In the eighteenth century, European classicism in architecture was not a simple matter of bilateral symmetry and a sprinkling of classical decoration but required the strict observation of established design rules. Eighteenth-century classicism is characterised by the precise observation of codified rules of proportion that dictated the relationship between height and width in all elements of a building, from walls to windows, and the interrelationships between those elements. The eighteenth-century *Builder's Dictionary* explains this as the principle of *Eurithimia*: 'a term of architecture used by Vitruvius by which he intends only that agreeable harmony that ought to be between, the length, breadth, and height of each room in a fabric'.[17]

The quantitative analysis of eighteenth and nineteenth-century farmhouses in the Highlands shows that between 85 and 94 per cent are composed of symmetrical front elevations divided into three parts expressed by the 'regular' arrangement of a central doorway, flanking ground floor windows and three windows to the upper storey, aligned with the ground floor openings (Fig. 13). A further 64 to 86 per cent have rectangular symmetrical floor plans, with the three parts of the front elevation relating to the division of the plan into a central passageway, with a staircase to the rear flanked by symmetrical rooms, front and back. The remainder have a variety of rear extensions in addition to a core rectangular plan (see Appendix 1, Table 2). Some 17 per cent of houses surveyed have symmetrical single-storey flanking wings. These are not later lean-to additions but classical design features, which provide further harmony to the composition by articulating the relationship between the high, gable end walls and the site. As appropriate to the social rank of the tenant farmer, the use of classical ornament is very restrained across the farmhouses within the survey group. The most common features are plain raised margins to the windows and doors – a seventeenth-century construction feature adapted to articulate a regular elevation. Actual classical ornament is markedly absent. Features such as string courses, projecting cornices, window mouldings, pilasters or columns to entrance porches and central pediments do not feature in any great number in any Highland region, ranging from 0 to 5 per cent in most areas of the western and central Highlands to 30 to 40 per cent in areas with a high number of smaller country houses, such as Argyll, Eastern Inverness-shire and Easter Ross. Yet, these are classical buildings. In its proportions each plain, three-bay farmhouse is a carefully controlled, harmonic piece of classical design. A random sample of over a thousand farmhouses taken from across Scotland was analysed by Robert Naismith for the Countryside Commission of Scotland in 1989. Naismith's analysis of the relationship of the overall frontage of each building and its doors and windows showed that over 57 per cent were comprehensively controlled by a proportional principle based upon a geometric interrelationship of those elements. Naismith concluded that, 'the subjects surveyed leave no doubt that, for the most part, care in proportion is manifest in all parts of the designs'.[18]

The eighteenth century saw unprecedented uniformity in the design of ordinary domestic architecture across Britain and variations of the improved farmhouse can be found throughout Scotland, England, Wales and Ireland. However, the eighteenth century Highland, and also Scottish, farmhouse is not an imitation of English design. Like similar farmhouses in England, the eighteenth-century Scottish farmhouse evolved within the northern European classical tradition. But, there is no evidence to suggest that the everyday classicism of eighteenth-century rural domestic architecture in Scotland was a product of English influence rippling ever outwards from a notional focal point in south east England. As the architectural historian Elizabeth McKellar has observed, 'the reception and spread of classicism in the eighteenth century suggests not a top-down model but rather overlapping spheres of influence between the national and the provincial, the classical and the non-classical , the elite and the everyday'.[19]

Small Scottish houses were built by masons who were born, educated and employed in Scotland. The education of Scottish masons was informed by the traditions of Scottish Freemasonry. Freemasonry provided an extensive architectural education in the form of a seven-year apprenticeship for operative masons. Membership of a Lodge also provided a peer group and social forum for master masons within individual lodges and a professional network with lodges in other towns which maintained Scottish industry standards in design and construction. The rules of classicism were established as standard practice on Scottish building

sites through the Scottish Masonic system and through the distribution and sale
of books. Scotland had maintained a nationwide network of Masonic centres
since the seventeenth century. The Masonic system remained of great importance in the dissemination of architectural knowledge throughout the eighteenth
century. Under the supervision of the Scottish master masons, the broad classical
tenets of the Scottish Renaissance were modified to the codified rules of
eighteenth-century classicism on Scottish building sites. This can be seen in the
remodelling of the seventeenth-century laird's house type into the classical
proportions of the improved farmhouse.

The written theory and rules of classicism were also published in a number
of widely available books. The importance of publishing and the book trade in
the dissemination of ideas, cultural values, social standards and design rules in
eighteenth-century Britain cannot be underestimated. The 1710 Statute of
Queen Anne, 'An Act for the Encouragement of Learning by Vesting the Copies
of Printed Books . . . ', was the first British law to protect published authors'
rights or copyright, inaugurating the British mass-publishing industry. The
commercial publication and circulation of design books was enabled by the
Engraver's Copyright Act, 1735, which extended the protections of the 1710 Act
to printed designs. The book trade catered to an expanding consumer market for
design through the distribution of two-dimensional printed designs.
Architectural books were published in great variety and volume, 'disseminating
a common culture to anyone with access to them'.[20] In terms of volume,
London was the centre of the British publishing industry though there were
many provincial presses and a significant Scottish press was established in
Edinburgh, capable of catering for a more specifically Scottish market.

Under the broad heading of 'Architecture' three different types of book were
published, each serving a different purpose and aimed at a different market, viz.
architectural folios, pattern books and technical manuals. Architectural folios
were generally oversized, expensively produced volumes intended for a
gentleman's library, to be kept alongside other instructive and improving texts
such as *The Rudiments of Genteel Behaviour*, or, *The Complete Grazier: or, The
Gentlemen and Farmer's Directory.*[21] Popular architectural works included Andrea
Palladio's *The Four Books of Architecture*, first published in an English translation
in 1733, Colen Campbell's *Vitruvius Britannicus*, 1715, or William Adam's
Vitruvius Scoticus, published in Edinburgh posthumously in 1812.

Pattern books differed slightly in that they were, literally, books of patterns
or designs, offering details of ornament as well as complete designs. Their
primary purpose was to disseminate contemporary fashionable designs for archi-

tecture, furniture or textiles. Generally smaller volumes than folios, pattern books were intended for use by both patron and contractor, either by direct imitation of a design or, more often, as a source of general inspiration. In England, the standard arrangement of elevation and plan for 'small farm houses in the country' was established by Isaac Ware's *A Complete Body of Architecture,* 1756 (Fig. 31).[22] The English architect William Halfpenny's 1751, *Six new designs for convenient farm houses . . . adapted . . . to the northern counties in England and all Scotland,* was published in London but was also aimed at the Scottish market. However, the first Scottish pattern book of modest houses was George Jameson's *Thirty-three Designs with the Orders of Architecture,* first published in Edinburgh in 1765, based upon designs by William Adam.[23]

Most relevant to the production of everyday buildings, such as farmhouses, were builder's technical manuals. These were produced in great volume specifically for working masons and were used as a quick reference manual or as a study-aid by apprentices. These practical books did not generally include complete building designs but contained the mathematical and geometric information a mason required to understand the principles of classical design. The role of technical manuals in the dissemination of classical architecture as the universal architectural language of the eighteenth century has not been fully understood. However, their importance lies in the technical information and tables of proportion they provide, which allowed masons to design their own classical buildings. The most popular of these technical manuals in England was Batty Langley's *The Builder's Jewel,* first published in London, 1741, also published in Edinburgh in 1768.[24] *The Builder's Jewel* is a surprisingly small, pocket-sized volume, well suited to daily use in the workshop and building site. However, perhaps the most important architectural book in Scotland was *The Rudiments of Architecture,* first published in Edinburgh in 1772.

The Rudiments of Architecture is a combined technical manual and pattern book aimed exclusively at the Scottish market. As well as an explanation of the five classical orders as defined in the eighteenth century (Tuscan, Doric, Ionic, Corinthian and Composite), the book details the mathematical and technical drawing procedures a builder or house carpenter required to produce architectural elements and components which observed the rules of classical architecture. Plate XIV, for example, shows 'An Inspectional Plane-Scale for reducing Modules and Minutes to Feet and Inches' (Fig. 32). This table allowed the builder to calculate with great precision the dimensions of an architectural element according to the correct classical proportions (defined in modules and minutes). Plate XXVIII details the geometries of a staircase banister rail (Fig. 33).

Brewhouſe

Parlour
14 Sqᵉ

Kitchen

20 × 0

Dairy

Cellar

10.6

36 × 10

10.6

6.0

10   20   30   40   50   60 Feet

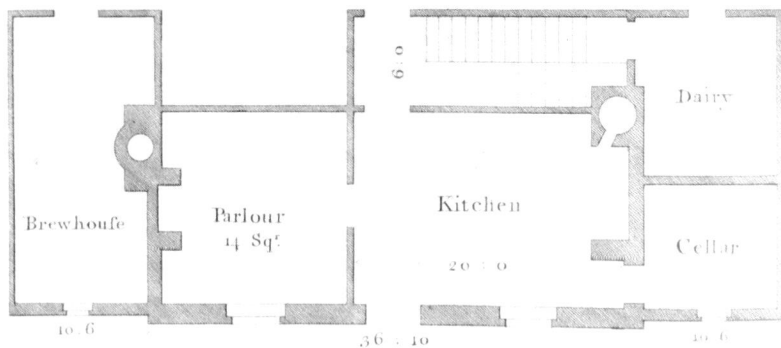

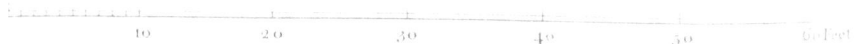

Small Farm near Biggleswade, at Calcot.

31. Isaac Ware, 'Small Farm near Biggleswade, at Calcot', A Complete Body of Architecture, 1767 reprint, plate 36 (Courtesy the Winterthur Library: Printed Book and Periodical Collection)

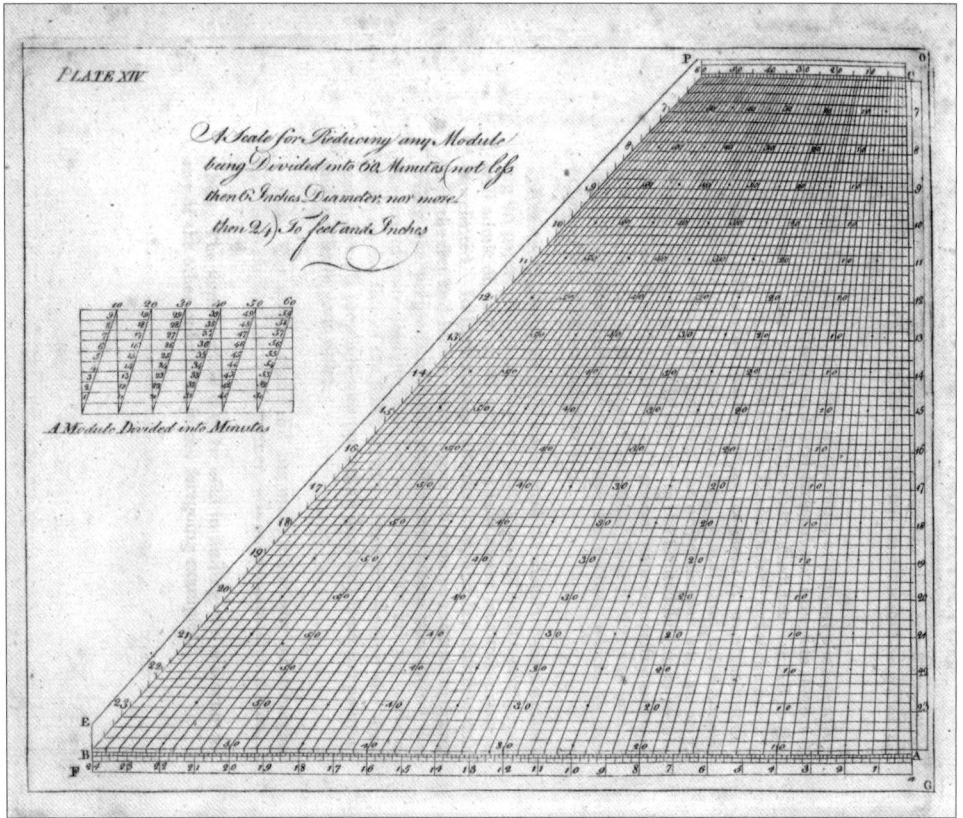

32. 'An Inspectional Plane-Scale for reducing Modules and Minutes to Feet and Inches',
Rudiments of Architecture, 2nd edn, 1778, plate XIV (National Library of Scotland)

In addition to chapters dealing with technical matters, the anonymous *Rudiments of Architecture* includes twenty-three designs for houses of various sizes, based upon George Jameson's *Thirty-three Designs*.[25] Accordingly, it is no surprise to find two variations of the improved farmhouse design illustrated (Fig. 34). *Design X* shows the archetypal two-storey, three-bay improved farmhouse (based upon plate nine in Jameson's *Thirty Three Designs*). *Design XI* is for a slightly larger, double-pile house with a basement floor and hipped roof of the sort built by the minor landowners of Eastern Inverness-shire and by the cadet branches of the Campbells in Argyll. The range of house types in the *Rudiments* demonstrates how the eighteenth-century operative mason designed and built suitable houses for clients across the social scale.[26]

The theoretical rules of classicism were disseminated through print and through the detailed knowledge of master masons. In his introduction to the

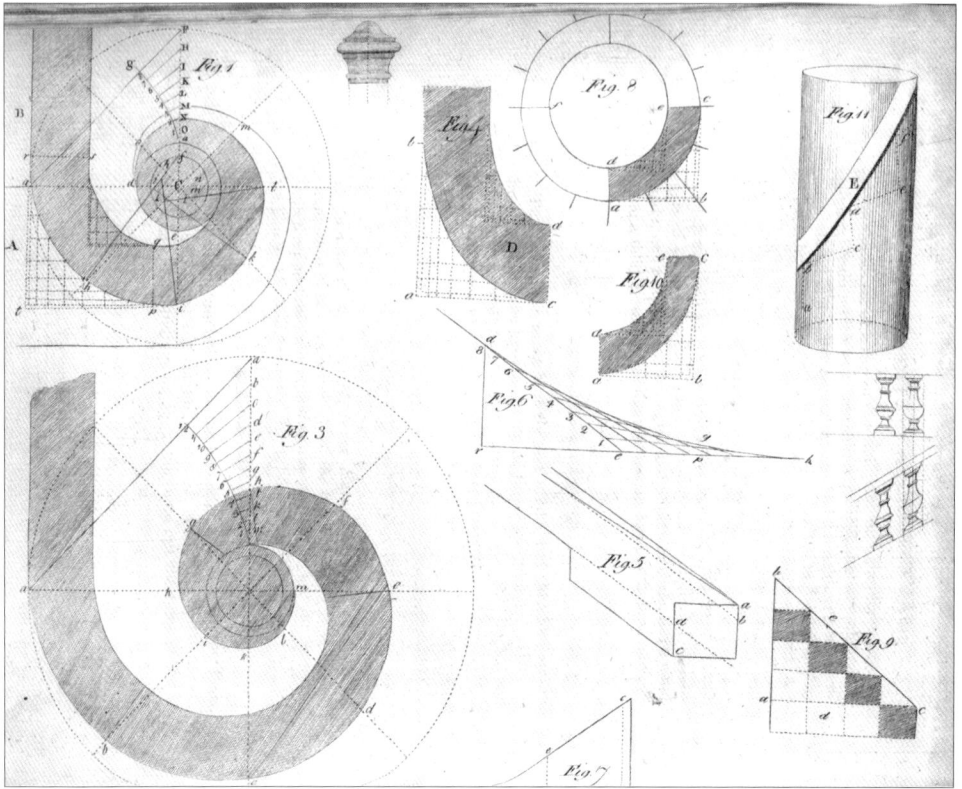

33. 'To form the Arch, or Mould, to the Hand Rail of a Pair of Stairs . . . ', *Rudiments of Architecture*, 2nd edn, 1778, plate XXVIII (National Library of Scotland)

1992 reprint of the *Rudiments of Architecture,* the architectural historian David Walker describes, 'the enormous influence the book had on the pattern of Scottish building in the boom period of 1770 to 1840 from which so much of our provincial housing stock still dates . . . the two-storey three-bay houses in Design X and XIX provided the standard pattern for farmhouse, manse and suburban villa . . . down to the mid-nineteenth century and even beyond . . . . The profound influence this little book had upon the character of the Scottish countryside has been an important but long forgotten aspect of Scottish history.' Walker continues, 'its five Scottish printings must have ensured that virtually everyone engaged in building or land management must have had a copy'.[27] However, the link between books and the physical evidence of the houses themselves must be inferred. There is no known written evidence such as letters, workbooks or journals that can prove that a Scottish mason used the *Rudiments of Architecture.*[28]

Design X.

Design XI.

Extends 54 Feet

Extends 60 Feet

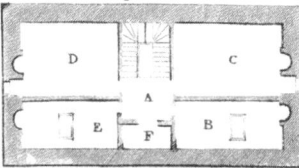

Fig. 3.

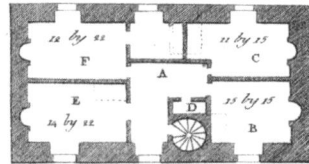

Fig. 3.

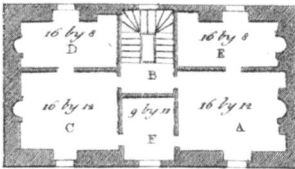

Fig. 2.

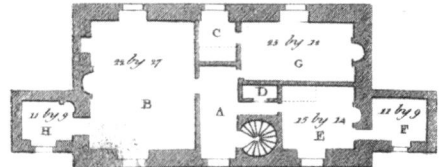

Fig. 2.

Fig. 1.

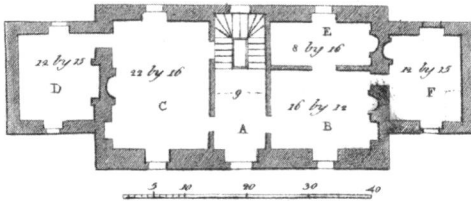

Fig. 1.

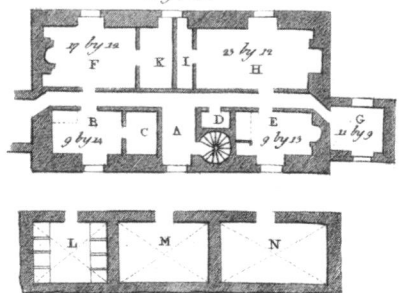

34. 'Design X', *Rudiments of Architecture*, 2nd edn, 1778 (National Library of Scotland)

The two-storey, three-bay design of the typical improved farmhouse was both a Scottish building and a product of the northern European classical tradition. It was a 'modern' building built by 'modern' people. To have in any way conceded to the region's environment by adopting any of the building techniques or features of the indigenous blackhouse was out of the question. The draughty discomfort gained from the very expensive importation of contemporary architectural tastes, skilled labour and building components is testament to the importance placed upon this form of cultural expression by improving tenant farmers, tacksmen and estate factors in the Highlands.[29]

CHAPTER 5

The New Highland Cottage

Cottages, single-storey, two-room dwellings, were built by improving landowners or tenant farmers to provide suitable housing wherever a permanent labour force was required as part of their wider programme of improvements. In the Lothians, wealthy tenant farmers built extensive complexes of farm buildings around the farmhouse, including terraces of single-storey cottages to house the farm's labourers. These were generally located in a straight line on an approach road to the farmhouse or in similar terraces some distance from the main farm to be closer to outlying fields. In the post-clearance Highland estates, a permanent labour force was required primarily in the new planned industrial villages that were to be the counterpoint to the new sheep ranches, but individual cottages were also needed to house shepherds and, in some areas, general farm labourers. The deliberate rejection of the indigenous blackhouse and its replacement with a 'modern' labourer's cottage was not the choice of the occupant, the ordinary landless Highlander, but an imposition by the landowner or tenant farmer. Like the 'modern' eighteenth-century farmhouse, the improved cottage was an architectural expression of the landlord or tenant farmer's identification with modernity and improvement. For the ordinary Highlander the unfamiliar design of the improved cottage imposed new living conditions and spatial experiences. In terms of construction and design, the typical cottage is similar to the improved farmhouse. In reference to their association with agricultural improvement, such cottages are commonly known as 'improved cottages'. As in the shorefront cottage on the Isle of Eigg depicted by William Daniell, the improved cottage is a harled stone-built gabled building with a slate roof and gable end chimneystacks on a two-room rectangular-plan; readily recognisable by its three-bay symmetrical front (Fig. 35).

The design of the improved cottage was established as a generic building type in the Scottish Highlands by the same social and cultural processes as the improved farmhouse: by architects, migrant masons, land surveyors and improving societies. Like the improved farmhouse, the improved cottage was a product of everyday eighteenth-century British classicism: plain, neat and

35. William Daniell, 'Scoor Eigg, on the Isle of Eig', *A Voyage Round the Coast of Scotland and the Adjacent Islands*, 1814–1822 (National Library of Scotland)

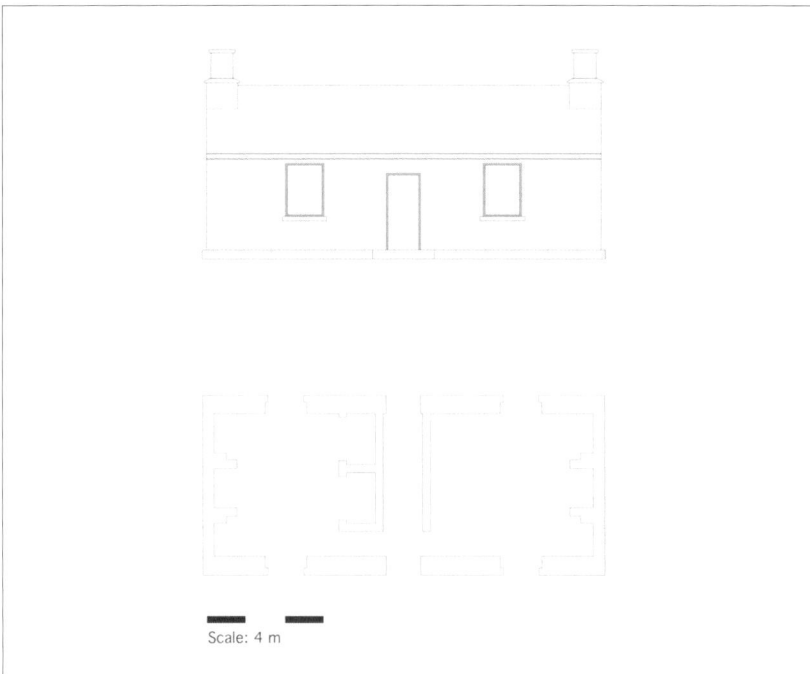

Scale: 4 m

36. Plan and elevation of a typical late-eighteenth century Scottish Highlands cottage (James Lingard)

regular. The building is regular in plan and elevation, each bay of the elevation relates directly to the internal plan and elements such as doors, windows and chimneys are positioned and proportioned to maintain an overall sense of architectural unity and balance (Fig. 36). However, in contrast to the tenant farmer's farmhouse, designed and built by master masons, improved labourers' cottages were frequently designed by professional architects as part of wider work on a client's estate, such as Robert Mylne's tenements at Inverarary for the fifth Duke of Argyll. Similar examples of estate cottages designed by eighteenth-century notable architects can be found throughout Britain. In contrast to the dissemination of improved farmhouse designs, architectural pattern books were of little influence in the development of the improved cottage since they were aimed at a middle class market and primarily contained designs for small country houses and large farmhouses. The exceptions were Nathaniel Kent's *Hints to Gentlemen of Landed Property*, London, 1799 and John Wood's Series of Plans for *Cottages or Habitations of the Labourer*, 1781, and it is unclear if either book had any direct, practical impact (Fig. 37).[1] It is relevant that both titles were aimed at the landowner as the expected provider of labourers' cottages. However, the three-bay symmetrical dwelling was an 'obvious' building type to most builders in eighteenth-century Britain and North America. It was a generic building type derived from the application of the most basic rules of architectural classicism: regularity, symmetry and proportion – as could be learned from any number of instructive manuals.

The improved cottage can be found throughout rural Scotland and in many other rural areas of Britain. Improved cottages in the Highlands are commonly of stone block construction generally laid in regular courses. Across Scotland, regional variations in building materials are evident according to local geological differences and the associated walling techniques. For example it is interesting to observe the use of traditional Highland random rubble, double-skin walling techniques in the side and rear walls of cottages in Ullapool, Wester Ross. Across Britain, the principle difference between eighteenth-century cottages in Scotland and England is the widespread use of brick and pan-tiles in England compared to the predominance of stone and slates in Scotland. It has also been observed that the Scottish cottage roof is often of steeper pitch than its English counterpart.[2] It is possible that this is a result of longstanding practices within the Scottish Masonic tradition; a steeply-pitched roof, often terminating in high crow-stepped gables, is a common feature of seventeenth-century Scottish burgh architecture. However, overall there are no significant variations between the form and dimensions of published English cottage designs, such as those by John

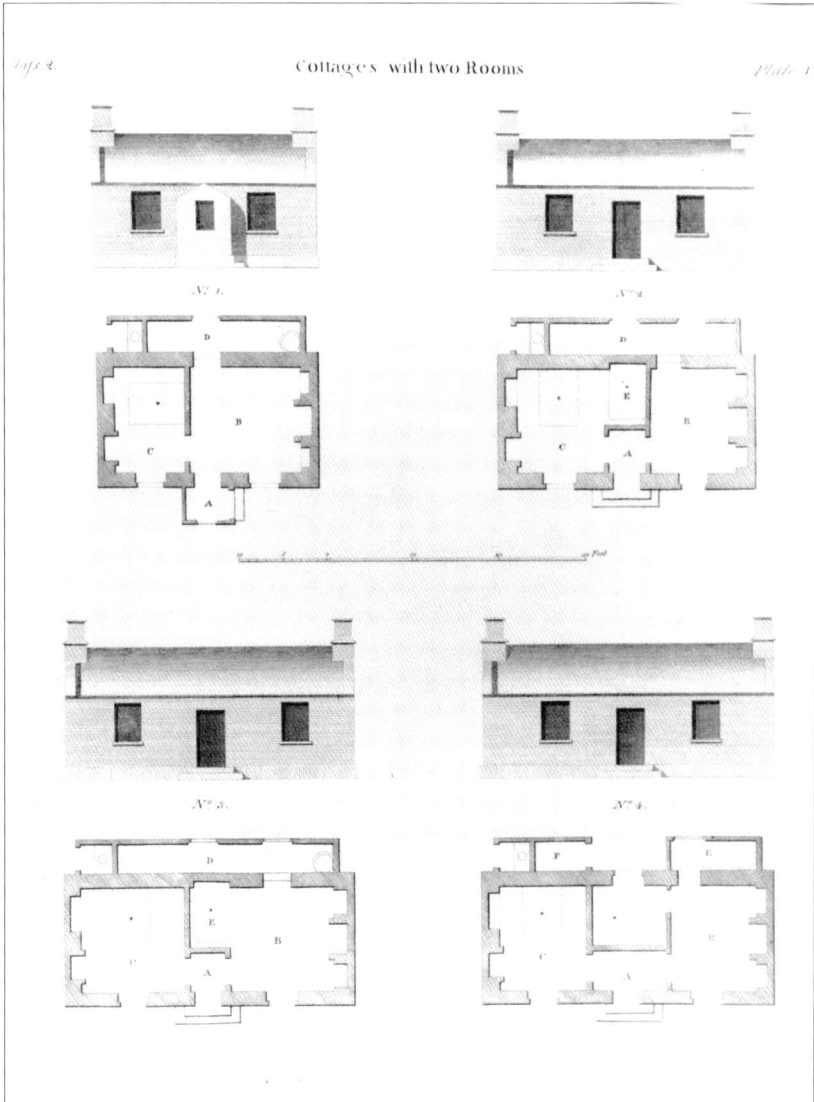

37. John Wood, 'Cottages with Two Rooms', *Series of Plans for Cottages or Habitations of the Labourer*, 1781, plate V (Courtesy – The Winterthur Library: Printed Book and Periodical Collection)

Wood, and those evident in extant cottages in the Scottish Highlands. Besides occasional architect-designed estate cottages, the majority of workers' cottages in the Scottish Highlands would have been designed by professional land surveyors. The employment of a skilled land surveyor was a vital aspect of any eighteenth-century improvement scheme. The mathematical and drawing skills

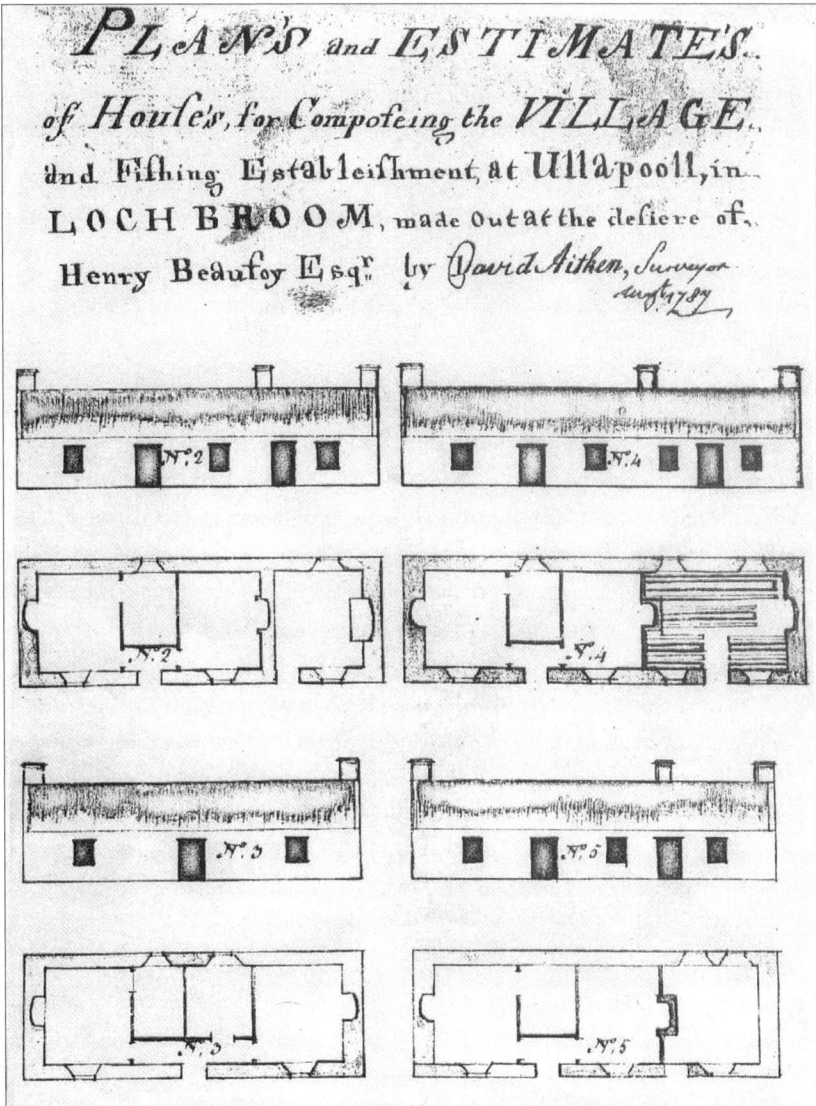

38. David Aitken, *Plans and Estimates of Houses for Composing the Fishing Establishment at Ullapool*, 1787 (National Archives of Scotland)

required for drawing estate maps and field enclosure schemes were readily translated into the design of simple classical cottages. For example, in 1787 the surveyor, David Aitken, was employed to survey the farm of Ullapool on Loch Broom, Wester Ross, and produced a series of cottage plans for an intended planned village (Fig. 38).

The Idea of the Cottage

The emphasis placed upon formal order and regularity in the design of the eighteenth-century cottage runs against our twenty-first century understanding of what a cottage should look like:

> Everything about it [a cottage] should be natural, and should appear as
> if the influences and forces which were in operation around it had been
> too strong to be resisted, and had rendered all efforts of art to check
> their power.[3]

This description of the ideal cottage by the nineteenth-century art critic John Ruskin remains familiar to us today. Ruskin's idea of the cottage developed from the eighteenth-century picturesque tradition which informed Romantic Highlandism in the nineteenth century that would in turn eventually lead to the popular *Brigadoon* view of the Highlands. In contrast to the deliberate order of eighteenth-century classicism, picturesque design idealised the irregularity, or happenstance, of the rustic cottage. This ideal is evident in the title of Robert Lugar's 1823 architectural pattern book: *Architectural sketches for cottages, rural dwellings and villas: . . . preceded by some observations on scenery and character proper for picturesque building.* Ruskin's idea of the cottage was an unplanned, anti-intellectual response to materials, climate and environment. Ruskin celebrated the 'natural' indigenous dwellings, such as the Highland blackhouses that had appalled eighteenth-century travel writers like Thomas Pennant who described them as 'molehills', and which the eighteenth-century improvers were so zealously keen to eradicate.

However, if the real dwellings of the rural poor appalled, the idea of the cottage held an honoured position within the classical tradition of eighteenth-century architectural criticism. In the preface to the first treatise on housing for rural workers, *A Series of Plans for Cottages or Habitations of the Labourer*, 1781, the English architect John Wood favourably compared the cottage with the great houses of the classical tradition:

> Considering the regular gradation between the plan of the most simple
> hut and that of the most superb palace; that a palace is nothing more
> than a cottage IMPROVED; and that the plan of the latter is the basis
> as it were of plans for the former.[4]

Wood's 'most simple hut' was a reference to the fashionable notion within eighteenth-century architectural criticism of the first cottage or simple hut. Building upon the Enlightenment philosophy of Jean-Jacques Rousseau, architectural theorists in France, notably Marc-Antoine Laugier, argued that classical architecture originated from a notional first cottage in which man dwelt when in an original State of Nature, adapting and perfecting Nature to create Architecture.[5] The argument was that, as classicism was the first architectural style, not only was it superior to all other styles such as Rococo and Gothick, it was an *a priori* universal truth. In Britain, Sir William Chambers took up the theory in *A Treatise on Civil Architecture*, 1759. Wood does not claim that a late eighteenth-century labourer's cottage was a representation of the 'first' cottage but simply that the theory supports the design of simple small-scale classical buildings. It is interesting that Wood does not equate the 'miserable hovels' he observed in the fallen nature of the eighteenth-century English West Country with Laugier's primitive hut (which could only be found in the original State of Nature). The gulf between the practical reality of an actual hut and the notional 'simple hut' was not lost on Dr Johnson. Dr Johnson dryly observed to James Boswell on leaving a 'simple hut' on the island of Coll during his *Journey to the Western Isles of Scotland*, that 'the philosophers, when they placed happiness in a cottage, supposed cleanliness and no smoke.'[6]

The Humanitarian Agenda

As discussed in the previous chapter, classicism was a powerful visual language in eighteenth-century British society. In the design of the improved farmhouse, classicism was used to indicate the tenant farmer's modernity and good taste. However, the humanitarian desire to improve the living conditions of the estate's population was also a motivation. The design of the improved cottage extended the tenant farmer or landlord's commitment to agricultural improvement to the welfare of their work force. The elimination of the turf and rubble and heather thatch of the blackhouse was partly undertaken for reasons of health and hygiene. To eighteenth-century Enlightenment thought, Improvement was the improvement of the 'quantity of happiness' of the whole population. The social historian, John E Crowley, has described the origins of this new social element in house design:

> In the middle of the eighteenth century . . . the word comfort was
> beginning to have the modern connotation of self-conscious satisfaction

between one's body and its immediate physical environment. Imaginative literature, political economy and humanitarian reform were giving new attention to concerns about lighting, heating, ventilation, privacy, ease, and hygiene in the design of the domestic environment.[7]

The improved cottage was part of a wider reform movement in which architectural cures for the social ills of eighteenth-century Britain extended beyond rural matters. The humanitarian reform movement of the later eighteenth century produced campaigns and vocal campaigners for many social causes. Most famously, Jeremy Bentham's campaign for prison reform produced his 1787 design for the *Panopticon*, or 'The Inspection-House for penitentiary houses, prisons, houses of industry, work-houses, poor-houses . . . hospitals, mad-houses and schools'. In urban housing, the reform of the rapidly growing industrial textile mills was the object of David Dale and Robert Owen's utopian workers' village and cotton mills complex of New Lanark, Lanarkshire, founded in 1786 and now a World Heritage Site. The humanitarian aspect of cottage design was also emphasised in Wood's *Cottages or Habitations of the Labourer . . . tending to the comfort of the poor . . . .* Unlike many architectural books of the period *Habitations of the Labourer* was not intended to encourage the newly affluent to build for themselves but to encourage landowners to build for others, urging them to improve the terrible state of the rural dwellings Wood had observed in the West Country, which he described as:

> shattered, dirty, inconvenient, miserable hovels scarcely affording shelter for beasts of the forest much less for the human species; nay it is impossible to describe the miserable condition of the poor cottager, of which I was too often the melancholy spectator.

The health problems Wood associates with living in an indigenous dwelling in Somerset had a direct parallel in the living conditions noted by observers of the eighteenth century Highland blackhouse. Thomas Pennant offered his opinion of a Highland blackhouse in *A Tour in Scotland*, 1776:

> The Houses of the common people in these parts are shocking to humanity, formed of loose stones and covered with clods, which they term devots, or with heath, broom, or branches of fir; they look, at a distance, like so many black molehills . . . The most wretched hovels that can be imagined.[8]

In contrast to the damp and dark thatch, low ceilings and earth floors found throughout rural eighteenth-century Britain, the standardised design of the improved cottage introduced large windows, gable end chimneys with flues, laid floors, slated or tiled roofs and stone walls, all of which were intended to bring in light and air and eliminate damp and smoke. To achieve these standards, as in the case of the new tenant farmhouse, skilled labour and materials had to be imported. For example six 'artisan's cottages' were built at the planned village of Ullapool by the fish merchant Robert Melvill. The labour and materials were shipped from Dunbar in East Lothian in June 1788:

> These certify that at the desire of Mr. Robert Melvill we have been on board the sloop Gilmerton of Dunbar, Robert Leslie Master, which vessel is loaded with and cleared at this Customs House for Ullapul in the port of Isle Martin, viz . . . thirty barrels of oatmeal, ten barrels of barley . . . we further certify that we mustered passengers on board the vessel above mentioned as follows; five builders, two joiners, a slater, a blacksmith, two labourers, *a* heckler, a netmaker, a fisherman, a cooper and a fishcurer. These persons being under engagements to Mr. Robert Melvill to work at Ullapul in their respective trades.[9]

Paying for a New Cottage

The improved cottage was a relatively expensive building that required imported building materials such as timber and slates and manufactured goods such as nails, hinges, glass and windows. For example, the Gilmerton's cargo also included:

> Eight thousand bricks and tiles, nineteen hundred and sixty seven pieces of fir timber . . . twenty cartloads of lime, six cartloads of household furniture, two pairs of cart wheels, one cart and a plough.[10]

Whilst keen to see blackhouses replaced with neat stone-built improved cottages, only exceptional landlords, such as the Duke of Sutherland at Tongue, were prepared to spend money on their tenants' re-housing (Fig. 39). A common practice amongst Highland landowners was for settlers to pay for and build their own cottages, but to do so according to strict building regulations in order to maintain architectural character and healthy living conditions within an estate's

New Stat. Account. Sutherland p 128.

THE MODERN HOUSE OF THE SMALL TENANTS OF THE REAY COUNTRY.

THE OLD HABITATION.

39. 'The Modern House of the Small Tenants of the Reay Country', *New Statistical Account of Scotland*, 1834–45 (National Library of Scotland)

housing stock. This was particularly associated with large scale re-housing schemes such as planned villages. The practice of settler self-build was recommended to the Highland Society of Edinburgh in 1787 by Sir James Grant of Grant, one of the earliest Highland improvers and founder of the planned village of Grantown-on-Spey:

> ... interfere as little as possible with building. It will inevitably bring a great deal of useless expense, any of the houses may remain uninhabited and those that are inhabited will not be taken near so much care for or so much enjoyed as those which they build for themselves.[11]

Typically, a secure long-term tenancy was offered with rights to quarry stone, lime, sand, and dig peat for fuel, at no charge. Each lot was big enough for a house and kail yard but not large enough to allow self-sufficiency. The landowner offered loans to the settler to offset the high cost of skilled labour and imported materials. Building regulations were drawn up to ensure that the same principles of regularity, symmetry and order that governed the layout of planned villages and tenant farmhouses would prevail in the houses of the ordinary labourer, but at no cost to the landowner. The British Fisheries Society's 1788 building regulations for the planned villages of Ullapool and Tobermory provide a good example:

> 1. Houses to be erected and completely built within three years.
> 2. Houses to be built of stone and lime or clay mortar and pointed with lime.
> 3. Houses to be built to the street line according to others in the street and according to the town plan in the agent's possession.
> 4. The ground floor to be six inches above the level of the middle of the street.
> 5. Houses to be built uniformly in terms of elevation and door and window dimensions.
> 6. No dormers or storm windows allowed.
> 7. Houses of two stories in any street must have side walls not less than seventeen feet high, doors six foot by three and windows five foot by three.
> 8. Houses of one storey in any street must have sidewalls not less than eight feet high, doors six foot by three and windows four foot by three.

9. If two houses share one lot the same uniformity of elevation must stand as if only one house with two doors placed near to and at equal distance from the centre.

10. All roofs must be slated.

11. All yards behind to be enclosed by walls.

12. Yards not to be used for any other purpose except dwelling houses including sheds.

13. A privy with roof, door and seat must be provided prior to inhabitation.

14. Before internally completed a flag pavement to be laid six foot wide with a curb stone two foot deep.

15. If the pavement is not laid by the feuar it will be done so by the Society's agent at the feuars expense.

16. Sewers and covered drains to be maintained by feuars.

17. No stones to be removed from a quarry after it is closed nor any new quarry opened without permission from the Society's agent.[12]

Building regulations proved to be an extremely effective method of ensuring architectural uniformity. The early cottages at Ullapool and Tobermory follow a consistent architectural pattern (Appendix 2). They are stone-built cottages predominantly rectangular in plan with regular symmetrical three-bay eleva-

40. The Ceilidh Place, West Argyle Street, Ullapool (Duncan Whitehead)

tions, small-pane sash and casement windows and gabled roofs covered with slates: the model of the late eighteenth-century 'improved cottage' (Fig. 40). The stipulation that houses were to be 'built uniformly in terms of elevation and door and window dimension' was followed to a remarkable degree. However, the side and rear walls are often of random rubble, constructed in the manner of field dykes, with a double skin of stones set in courses, the uneven edges facing the central cavity to create a smooth outer wall. This two-tier construction suggests that settlers employed masons to build the front elevation but constructed the other walls themselves, an obvious cost saving method.

The British Fisheries Society's building regulations produced a single, clearly defined building type without recourse to drawn plan and elevation. The high public profile of the British Fisheries Society ensured that the regulatory system was adopted as the standard building model in later planned villages throughout the Highlands. The plain, classically proportioned, improved cottage is now regarded as the generic building type of the Highlands. It is a building designed to sit within a rational improved agricultural landscape. The improved cottage was an architectural symbol of the spirit of improvement: commercial landlordism comfortably combined with humanitarian paternalism. In the Highlands, it was a radically new form of domestic architecture imposed by landowners and tenant farmers upon the landless labourer, the ordinary Gael.

CHAPTER 6

The Highland Planned Village Movement

At the peak period of the Highland house building boom in the late eighteenth century, ordinary Highlanders were faced with eviction from their homes and the possibility of destitution: 'an alarming time for the common people, a time of communal anxiety and insecurity'.[1] By the 1770s, the primary focus of agricultural improvement in the Highlands had shifted from the removal of the tacksmen to the forced removal and resettlement of entire communities and the eradication of indigenous settlements to make way for high rent-paying sheep farms.[2] The Highland planned village movement was conceived as the social and economic counterpoint to these measures. People were not to be abandoned, they were to be resettled in new villages located on cheap marginal land, often on the coast, where they would find employment in a new industry established by the landowner such as linen manufacturing or the fisheries. In this way, the establishment of a planned industrial village was viewed by Highland landowners as part of a new dual-estate economy, working profitably alongside the new sheep farms.

At the beginning of the eighteenth century, the farmlands of the glens and straths were widely peppered with hundreds of settlements, consisting of between ten and twenty dwellings, known as *clachan or bailtean*. There were no 'villages' in the Highlands. This was due in part to the Scottish system of burghs, chartered small towns, such as Tain, Dornoch and Wick in the northeast, which jealously guarded their exclusive civic rights, such as the right to hold markets. But the apparent lack of villages also relates to the English-influenced understanding of the term 'village' – that is: a small but permanent rural settlement with a village green, inn and parish church. The *bailtean* was a semi-permanent settlement that could be relocated to a completely new site within the lands of a particular clan chieftain following the periodic reorganisations of their holdings. The *bailtean* was vacated during the summer months when the residents moved to their summer lodgings, the shielings, in the high pastures. The settlement pattern of the *bailtean* was an irregular cluster of subtenants' dwellings around the home of the principal tenant or tacksman, the whole appearing very much like a herd of cattle huddled together against the elements; a natural evolved form within the landscape. The make-up of a typical bailtean farming community in Glenshiel in the 1790s was described in the *Statistical Account*:

> In the parish are 17 farms, each of which is occupied by a number of
> tenants so that each forms a village. The tenants graze their cattle
> promiscuously, each restricting himself to a number of heads; and the
> arable ground they occupy in like manner.[3]

This pattern is evident in a mid-eighteenth-century survey map of the farm of Ullapool, Lochbroom, Wester Ross (Fig. 41). The surveyor has laid out the lines of the intended planned village but has also shown the *bailtean* of Blairdu, Kannchrine and two others, both called Ullapool; all are sited on what is noted as 'Good Pasture'.[4] Another contemporary account described the negative effects of enclosures upon these indigenous settlements and their communities in Wester Ross:

> The oppression of the landowners is a general complaint in the
> Highlands, and the consequence is, that great numbers of the people
> are forced to emigrate to America, while others go to service in the low
> countries and manufacturing towns. And thus the population of these
> corners is not near so great as might be expected in such an extent of
> territory. Another circumstance, which is unfriendly to population, is
> the engrossing of farms for sheep walks. This mode of farming has been
> introduced lately into some parts of this parish and proved the occasion
> of reducing to hardships several honest families, who lived tolerably
> happy on the fruits of their industry and frugality. Whoever would wish
> to see the population of this country flourishing should do all in their
> power to put a stop to the sheep traffic . . . Whole districts have already
> been depopulated by the introduction of sheep; so that where formerly
> hundreds of people could be seen, no human faces are now to be met
> with, except a shepherd and his dog.[5]

A similar process of depopulation had followed enclosures in the Lowlands forty years earlier. In Haddington, East Lothian, it was reported that 'the whole district is in a state of high cultivation, and all inclosed except a few fields in the neighbourhood of the burgh . . . The increase of the number of poor in this place, is in great degree owing to the prevailing customs of the heritors and farmers in the country preserving no cottagers, unless such as are absolutely necessary for persons employed in cultivation.'[6] Similarly in Morham, East Lothian, 'we find that the population . . . has diminished through the frequent union of farms'.[7]

41. *A Survey and Plan for a Village at Ullapooll*, Annexed Estates Commission, 1757 (National Archives of Scotland)

The Highland Planned Village

In the nineteenth century, the brutality of forced Highland Clearances brought infamy to the process of enclosure and resettlement. However, in the later eighteenth century the Highland landlord did not generally seek to remove people entirely, only to have them resettled on less productive and less profitable land, and many deplored the depopulating effect of the 'evil of emigration'. The late eighteenth century is described by Eric Richards as the 'Classical Age' of the Highland Clearances, when an attempt was made to save and develop the Highlands and its population in a new modern model prior to the admission of failure and total capitulation to sheep in the nineteenth century.[8] Such was the resistance to depopulation and emigration that Scottish landowners lobbied Henry Dundas, Secretary of State for Scotland, to introduce a ban on emigration from Scottish ports in 1775, though the legislation had little practical effect.[9] Many people resettled in the crofting townships. These were areas of poor marginal land, often on the coast, to which people were relocated and provided with small, often unproductive, consecutive strips of land to farm individually. This created the single-strip settlement pattern typical of crofting communities. However, the principal agent of resettlement was the establishment of new planned villages. Planned villages were to be the centres of new non-agricultural industries, such as the herring fishery, part of a new type of dual-economy estate, functioning profitably alongside large-scale sheep ranching.[10] In spatial terms, the contrast between the settlement pattern of the irregularly-clustered dwellings of the indigenous Highland *bailtean* and the ordered geometry of the grid-plan village could not be greater: the former very much of its place, the latter designed, ordered and imposed.

'The entire history of the modern Highlands is pockmarked with broken schemes for development, with dreams of economic growth, fishing, manufacturing, mining, villages and new rural enterprises, mainly dashed by the problems inherent in the region's geographical disadvantages.'[11] In the eighteenth century, however, unlike the ill-favoured, last resort that was the crofting system, the planned village was viewed as the 'focus par excellence' of the dual-economy estate: sheep farming in the glens and fishing on the coast.[12] This was a view common to the majority of eighteenth-century landowners, not only in Scotland but also in many regions of England under intensive agricultural improvement, notably in East Anglia and the Home Counties. The geographer David Turnock has observed that, 'like the model of agricultural improvement the planned village formula offered security and advantage to all . . . with careful promotion some of the projects were enormously successful and developed into true urban communities but there were others which failed to gain any momentum and did not grow beyond the level of a small rural settlement'.[13] In Scotland, following seventeenth-century urban schemes such as Edzell, Campbeltown, Stornoway, Langholm and Galashiels, the eighteenth-century planned village movement began with agricultural villages in the Lothians where early precedents were set with villages such as Yester (now Gifford) founded by the Marquis of Tweeddale in 1708 and Ormiston founded by John Cockburn in 1714.[14] Across eighteenth-century Scotland as a whole, the historian T. C. Smout identified four principal types of planned village in his pioneering article of 1970, *The Landowner and the Planned Village*, namely agricultural villages, fishing villages, villages with small rural industries, and the factory village. The last was comparable with similar factory-based village developments in the emerging industrial centres of northern England, such as Josiah Wedgwood's Etruria, Staffordshire, founded on the Trent and Mersey Canal in 1769 to house the workers at Wedgwood's new pottery. Overall in Scotland, geographer Douglas Lockhart has estimated that over five hundred planned villages were founded during the 'long eighteenth century'.[15] In a separate study Lockhart has further estimated that at least 91 of those villages were established in the Highland region.[16] This figure does not include a further 130 in the north east region, which contains considerable areas of the Highlands' eastern border country. The planned village movement in the Highlands was part of the wider phenomenon of the Highland building boom. A remarkable rate of urban growth for a region with only a handful of permanent towns and villages at the beginning of the eighteenth century, with the majority of planned villages founded in the brief period from *c*.1780 to 1850.

Early planned villages in the Highlands followed three distinct examples; the model estate village, the industrial estate village for all types of industry and manufacture, and the government scheme village. The first Highland planned villages of the Age of Improvement emerged in the mid-eighteenth century. These were typical of the eighteenth-century model agricultural villages established throughout Britain as part of wider estate enclosure and improvement schemes such as the Duke of Perth's grid-plan settlement at Crieff, 1731. However, the most celebrated is Inveraray, Argyll, the seat of the Dukes of Argyll. Inveraray has been described as 'without equal among small British towns'.[17] The old village of Inveraray was transplanted to the shore of Loch Fyne in 1751 from its former location adjacent to Inveraray Castle. Inveraray was a model estate village built to express the cultured tastes of the Dukes of Argyll. The 1751 cruciform plan was drawn up by John Adam, son of William and eldest brother

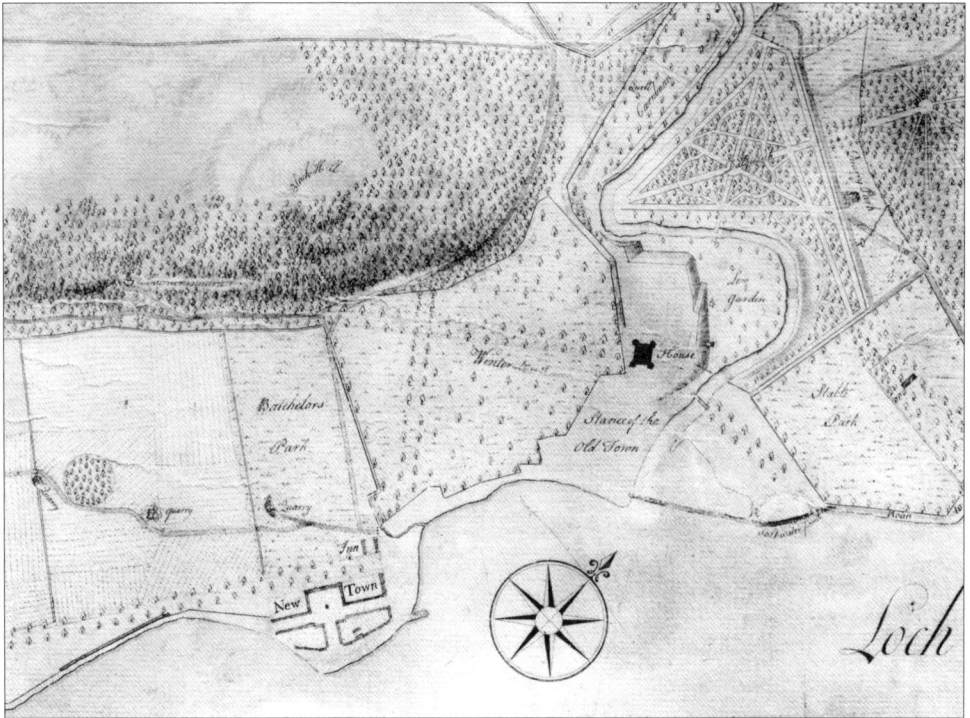

42. *Inveraray Castle Estate plan* (Reproduced courtesy of RCAHMS)

of Robert, but was not fully laid out until 1771 by the Scottish Neoclassical architect, Robert Mylne for John, fifth Duke of Argyll (Fig. 42).[18] The axial main street is terminated by Mylne's elegant dual-denomination church (Fig. 43).

Daniel Campbell of Shawfield's planned village of Bowmore, Islay, is worth mentioning in this context as a direct, if small-scale, imitation of the planned grandeur of Inveraray by a cadet branch of the House of Argyll. Like Inveraray, Bowmore was established following the removal of a village, in this case, Kilarow adjacent to Islay House, in 1768 (Fig. 44). The village is also dominated by an axial main street leading to the shore which terminates in an elegant circular-plan neoclassical church.[19] The refined architecture and planning of Inveraray was intended for the visual pleasure of the Dukes and their noble guests. In this respect, Inveraray was typical of the British eighteenth-century estate model village and can be compared to other aesthetically driven planned villages, such as Lord Dorchester's Milton Abbas, Dorset, 1773, designed by William Chambers (1723–96) to replace the old village which disrupted the sweeping vistas of Dorchester's new Arcadian landscape laid out by Lancelot 'Capability'

43. Inveraray, Main Street (Crown Copyright: RCAHMS)

Brown (1716–83). Inveraray and Milton Abbas form part of an exclusive architectural group of prestigious estate villages of the mid-eighteenth century, which
also includes the Earl of Harcourt's Nuneham Courtney, Oxfordshire, and
Harewood, Yorkshire, by John Carr (1723–1807), both laid out in the 1760s.[20]
    Through the 1750s and 1760s, the grand architectural statement of Inveraray
was countered by a parallel development on the eastern margins of the
Highlands where a different village type emerged: new industrial centres
intended to be the catalysts for economic growth and the development of
regional market economies.[21] In the north-eastern counties of Banff, Moray and
Inverness-shire, a circle of improving landowners, such as Sir Archibald Grant of
Monymusk and Sir James Grant of Grant, established villages not as personal
architectural statements but as nascent centres for an anticipated regional textile
industry. The geographer Ian Adams identifies this north-eastern group of
landowners and their shared pool of land surveyors as the influential North East
School of surveying and planning.[22] In contrast to the aesthetically-conscious
urban design programme underway at Inveraray, these villages were plain and
practical: simple grid-plans laid out on unimproved marginal land.[23] It was the
fervent belief of the outward-looking, improving, commercial Highland
landlord that models of improvement could be imported directly into the region
and that in time the Highlands would develop a market economy similar to that
of the Lowlands.[24] The earliest north-east planned village was New Keith,

44. Bowmore, Islay (Crown Copyright: RCAHMS)

founded by the Earl of Seafield, *c.* 1750, as a grid-plan linen manufacturing centre.[25] This was followed by other grid-plan villages such as Sir James Grant of Grant's Grantown-on-Spey, Inverness-shire, laid out on a grid-plan by the north-eastern surveyor Alexander Taylor in 1767, which won a prize at the Highland Society of Edinburgh.[26] There were also numerous smaller, less well-known villages: such as Joseph Cumine of Auchry's Cuminestown, Aberdeenshire, 1765; Urquhart, Morayshire; Longmanhill, Banffshire; Fetterangus, Longside; and New Deer, St Fergus and Mintlaw, Aberdeenshire.[27]

Sir John Sinclair wrote in 1825, 'a village cannot be expected to prosper unless it is advantageously situated and erected according to a judicious plan'.[28] The north-east planned village was a particularly utilitarian form of town planning, which the architectural historian Spiro Kostof has described as the 'practical model . . . factual, functional, cool, not in the least magical . . . the concept that motivates colonial towns and company towns'.[29] In terms of both function and appearance, it was these early industrial villages of the north-east, not the aesthetics of neoclassical Inveraray, which were the prototypes for the subsequent

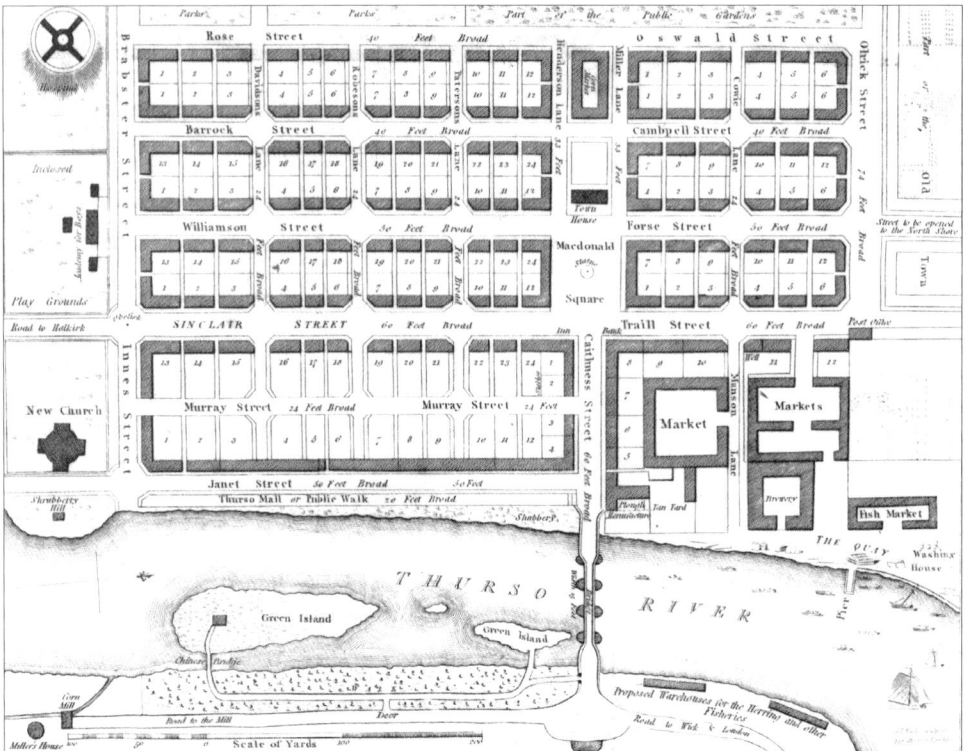

45. 'Plan of Thurso', *A General View of the Agriculture of Caithness*, 1812 (Crown Copyright: RCAHMS)

planned village movement in the central and western Highlands. In the early nineteenth century, Thurso New Town was a particularly grand scheme under-taken by Sir John Sinclair to provide an urban centre for wider agricultural improvements on his Caithness estates (Fig. 45).

Easdale Island near Oban, in the West Highlands, is an example of a mid-to-late eighteenth-century planned village that was established not to exploit the sea but the island's slate geology. Slate quarrying on the island was first recorded in the mid-seventeenth century when Easdale slate was used to roof Caisteal-an-Stalcaire, Appin in 1631.[30] The Marble and Rock Company of Netherlorn, later the Easdale Slate Company, was formed by a partnership in 1745 between the landowner, the Earl of Breadalbane, also deputy chairman of the British Fisheries Society, and three other Campbells: Colin Campbell of Carwhin, Charles Campbell of Lochaline and John Campbell, cashier to the Royal Bank of Scotland. In its first year the company produced over one million slates, rising to a peak of seven million per year in the 1840s. By the 1840s there were over

4,000 residents in the parish of Kilbrandon and Kilchattan, and 500 on Easdale Island, all of whom were directly or indirectly dependent on the slate industry. The company exported slates throughout Britain and to the United States and throughout the British Empire: Canada, the West Indies, Australia and New Zealand. The slate quarriers' village on Easdale was laid out in an irregular U-shape around the long and narrow harbour, totalling 114 single-storey improved cottages, with a central 'town' square flanked with neat terraces of cottages on three sides (Fig. 46).[31] Easdale, like Tobermory just across the Sound of Mull, is a venture closely linked to the improving Campbells and underlines the fact that in the plans of the landowner, both public and private, the dual purpose of the Highland planned village was to turn a profit through the industrial exploitation of natural resources and to provide employment, thereby preventing emigration. The specific focus of that industry, whether herring, slate or linen, was a matter of opportunism. The Highland planned village was to be a place of work dedicated not to beauty, the ornament of the landowner's estate, but to the efficient pursuit of a profitable industry.

However, the imposed order of the grid-plan need not only define a place of industrial efficiency but could also be employed to represent different urban concepts. For example, in contrast to the emphasis upon economic rationality

46. Easdale from the Hill, 1930s

embodied in the grid-plan of the industrial planned village, James Craig's (1744–95) grid-plan for the first Edinburgh New Town, 1766, is a political allegory representing the union of Scotland and England and the modernity and prosperity of a new Britain. Outside Edinburgh, the idea of political order was expressed in the gridded Highland villages of the Annexed Estates Commission. At a national British level, the establishment of villages in the Highlands emerged as a matter of government policy in the 1750s. In the decades after Culloden it was not only accelerated commercial landlordism at work in the Highlands but also a shift in government policy, in which 'state sponsored terrorism gave way to state sponsored improvement' in partnership with Highland landowners.[32] The government's interest in the Highlands was born of broader political concerns than simply regional economic development. Of these, military recruitment and the growing need for new natural resources – whether slate, kelp, wool, hemp or fish – were perhaps the primary motivations. The loyalty and bravery of the new Highland regiments in the Seven Years War, 1756–63, against the French in Canada had brought the Highland clansmen to the attention of the British Army as a vast resource of excellent but expendable troops. The Highlands were also promoted by Whig polemicists, such as John Knox (1720–90), as an untapped economic resource, which could supply the raw industrial materials and food produce required to maintain the factories and towns of the nascent industrial revolution in England and Lowland Scotland. It was a situation heightened by the British government's economic and political pain induced by the loss of the American colonies in 1786.[33] The government was therefore keen to support any private or public improvements in the Highlands that prevented emigration and increased economic productivity.

An early outcome of this policy was the establishment of the Annexed and Forfeited Estates Commission in 1752. The Commissioners of Annexed and Forfeited Estates, mostly Scottish Whig non-Highland landowners, were tasked by the government with the social and economic improvement of thirteen of the largest Highland estates forfeited to the state by rebel Jacobite clan chiefs after the '45.[34] They were to have a 'particular attention . . . to the enlargement, or new erection of towns and villages'.[35] The Commissioners called these settlements *coloniae,* based upon the Roman Empire's veteran settlements established to pacify conquered territory, in this instance, Britain's own veterans of the Seven Years War.[36] However, for the most part, the villages established by the Commission were not a great success. This was principally because the sites were chosen for their strategic location, at key loch-heads and glen passes such as Kinloch Rannoch sited on the eastern loch-head of Loch Rannoch, and

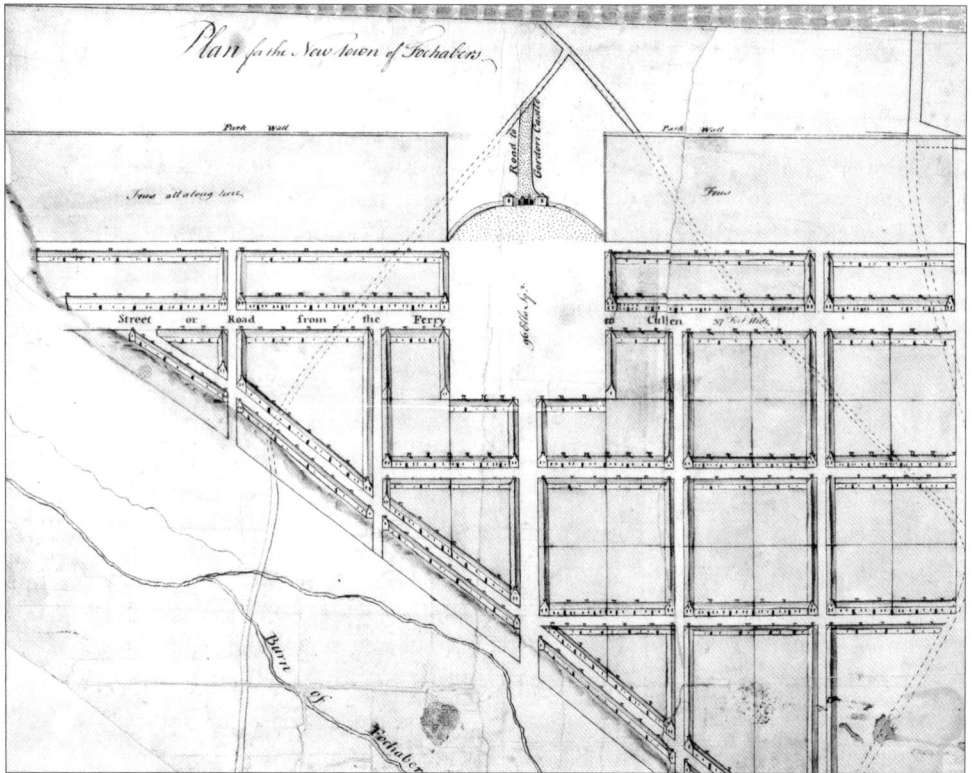

47. John Baxter, *Plan of Fochabers*, 1764 (National Archives of Scotland)

Callendar in the Trossachs north of Stirling, rather than for their agricultural or industrial advantage.

Despite its decommissioning in 1784 and its limited success on the ground, it has been argued that the Annexed Estates Commission still had a 'formative role in shaping the agenda for Highland improvement' through its influence amongst Highland landowners.[37] Fochabers, Moray, for example, was initially planned by the Commission in 1764 but was developed by the fourth Duke of Gordon from 1775–90 (Fig. 47). The village was laid out on a standard grid-plan with a central U-shaped square by the fourth Duke's architect-surveyor, John Baxter (d. 1798) in conjunction with the remodelling of Gordon Castle. Fochabers is unusual in this respect: what was first conceived as an Annexed Estates village was developed as an estate village similar to Inveraray but was eventually established as a typical north-east industrial village.[38] Despite the Commission's provision of housing, settlers did not always settle; at Strelitz, Coupar Angus, for example, 69 houses were built but only nine settlers remained after 1764.[39] The money wasted on house building was a lasting lesson for those involved in the Highland planned village movement. Annette Smith neatly summarises the Annexed Estates Commission planned village programme as follows: 'in its conception, the plan of providing for disbanded soldiers and sailors, increasing the population of the Highlands and Islands, importing necessary trades, and building houses of a higher standard than was usual, all in one step, was a splendid one. In its implementation, little can be said in its favour.'[40] Nonetheless, the Commission played a 'formative role in shaping the agenda for Highland improvement'.[41]

Following the decommissioning of the Annexed Estates Commission in 1784, the establishment of the British Fisheries Society was the next attempt at the development of the Scottish Highlands on a national level. Again, the focus of the initiative was to be the foundation of planned villages. The British Fisheries Society was a quasi-governmental improvement society founded in the late eighteenth century in order to establish fishing villages in the Highlands. The planned villages of the British Fisheries Society, considered fully in the next chapter, are important in the context of the transformation of the Highlands as they became the planning model for the wave of later Highland planned villages established from the late eighteenth to mid-nineteenth century.

The new villages of the improving landowner and those resulting from government initiatives were born of the same eighteenth-century commitment to the dual Scottish Enlightenment principles of economic and social improvement through the practical application of reason. However, they were also closely linked in practice through the frequent appearance of the same landowners, surveyors and architects, at all levels of activity – from small-scale private to national public projects. This intimate relationship is best explained through, what historian Andrew Mackillop has termed, the 'patriotic partnership'.[42] This was an ideological and practical partnership between improving Highland landowners and the Hanoverian government.[43] One practical outcome of this partnership in the 1760s was loans made by the Trustees for Manufacturers and Fisheries to manufacturers willing to settle in private planned villages. For the Highland landowner it was, therefore, a matter of patriotic duty as well as personal finance to improve an estate's productivity and to prevent emigration. It was also a patriotic duty to support and serve on government-sponsored bodies committed to Highland improvement.[44] Like most landowners in Britain, the typical Highland landowner was, if not directly a member of the government through a cabinet position, usually the Member of Parliament for their constituency. They sat on government commissions relating to the Highlands, though not the Annexed Estates Commission, and were involved in improving societies such as the Highland Society of London, founded in 1778 and chaired by John, fifth Duke of Argyll (1723–1806).[45]

The activities of the Dukes of Argyll are a good example of the patriotic partnership and the blurring of the line between public and private initiative. The House of Argyll was central to the 'improvement' of the Scottish Highlands throughout the eighteenth century. The Dukes set the standard for improvement in the Highlands with a programme of wide-ranging and innovative developments to their Inveraray estates. The improving influence of the Dukes of Argyll amongst the cadet branches of the Campbells and their tenant farms in Argyll has been discussed previously. But the Dukes of Argyll also exerted wider political influence through their favoured position with successive Whig governments. It is therefore not surprising that amongst his various improving activities John, fifth Duke of Argyll, was also the first chairman of the British Fisheries Society.

Landowners, improving societies and government alike viewed the planned village as a panacea to the social disruptions brought about by agricultural improvement in the Scottish Highlands. The pioneering planned villages of the north-eastern Highlands were intended to house the indigenous population of estates who had been displaced by enclosures and the establishment of large single-tenant farms. Unlike the model estate village, such as Inveraray, these villages were to be primarily a place of industry where the people of an estate would be profitably employed for the benefit of themselves and the landowner. Theoretically, a successful industrial centre provided an estate with a dual economy of sheep ranches on the pasturelands and industrial settlement on otherwise unprofitable marginal land. The planning and architecture of these pioneering Highland planned villages reflected their utilitarian character with an emphasis upon the grid-plan and the plain, uniform, classical architecture of terraced improved cottages. Whilst the majority of early Highland planned villages were established by private landowners, those established by government-backed bodies, the British Fisheries Society in particular, were of great importance due to their influence on the subsequent schemes of private landlords throughout the Highlands.

CHAPTER 7

The British Fisheries Society

The British Fisheries Society was a national improvement scheme backed by major Highland landowners that, through the establishment of planned fishing villages, aimed to provide permanent work and housing for the rural poor displaced by agricultural improvements in the Highlands.[1] The Society established a utilitarian planning model which fundamentally influenced the subsequent Highland planned village movement. The British Fisheries Society also made a significant contribution to urban history in the Highlands with Thomas Telford's innovative plan for its last development of Pulteneytown. Pulteneytown remains the most complete example of Telford's work as a town planner.

The British Society for Extending the Fisheries and Improving the Sea Coasts of the Kingdom of Great Britain, to give it its full name, was a quasi-governmental body incorporated as a joint-stock company by Act of Parliament in July 1786. The Act followed a period of quick lobbying by the Highland Society of London in response to the 1785 Fisheries Act which, through changes to the bounty regulations, permitted large offshore fishing 'busses', which dominated the herring fishery, to buy directly from small boats. Throughout the early modern period a succession of parliamentary Acts were passed by Scottish, English, and post–1707 British, governments determined to encourage the expansion and promotion of the fisheries to increase the national wealth. It was the British government's ambition to mount a large scale, offshore herring fishery capable of rivalling the Dutch.[2] The geographer James R. Coull writes that 'from the late seventeenth to the early nineteenth centuries the promotion of the fishery was seen as a proper field for government financial incentives, policy was for long dominated by the objective of increasing exports: this was done by giving export bounties and by exempting from the heavy salt duties salt which was to be used for curing herring for export.'[3]

However, despite its name, the British Fisheries Society was much more closely concerned with agricultural improvement and the management of the subsequent social and economic change within the Scottish Highlands than the national fisheries. The significance of the 1785 Fisheries Act for the group of

Highland landowners who founded the British Fisheries Society was that, by letting inshore boats sell directly to offshore busses, it provided a legislative opportunity for economic development in the Highlands as an inshore fleet of small boats made planned coastal villages a real possibility.[4] New fishing settlements were seen as a means of regional development in the Highlands and the aims and activities of the British Fisheries Society was therefore part of the much longer process of transformation in the Scottish rural economy.[5]

Following the demise of the Annexed Estates Commission in 1784, the establishment of the British Fisheries Society, 1786, was the next attempt on a national level to create a network of planned villages throughout the Highlands. By 1786 the Society's mandate for establishing planned fishing villages was to increase economic productivity in the Highlands and to thereby prevent emigration. The composition of the Society's first Board of Directors reflects the change in national attitude towards the Highlands from one of suspicion to one of inclusion. The Board of Directors of the British Fisheries Society is a superlative example of the 'patriotic partnership' between landowners and the government at work.[6] The society's founding Board of Directors comprised the inner circle of the Scottish Whig political and landowning establishment; besides boasting the great improver, John, fifth Duke of Argyll (1723–1806) as Chairman, the Earl of Breadalbane was Deputy Chairman and other board members included the Marquis of Graham, the Earl of Moray, the Earl of Abercorn and the Earl Gower. To this august group can be added several Members of Parliament and figures associated with Highland landownership and the Scottish Enlightenment, familiar names such as Sir John Sinclair, Sir Adam Fergusson, Sir James Grant of Grant, Sir Henry Beaufoy, Sir William Pulteney and Sir George Dempster.

The Planned Villages of the British Fisheries Society

The British Fisheries Society established four villages along the coastline of the Scottish Highlands (Fig. 48). Ullapool, Lochbroom, Wester Ross, and Tobermory, Isle of Mull, were founded in 1788, Lochbay, Isle of Skye, 1790 and Pulteneytown, Wick, Caithness, 1808. Tobermory and Lochbroom both had established reputations amongst the Scottish fishing fleet for good harbours with safe anchorage.[7] Lochbroom was also famed for the size of its herring shoals and the Annexed Estates Commission had previously considered establishing a village there. The contracts for the purchase of both sites were exchanged on 28

48. Ullapool, Loch Broom, 1930s (Crown Copyright: RCAHMS)

February 1788.[8] Following the start of works at Tobermory and Ullapool, one thousand acres at Lochbay, Isle of Skye, were purchased in December 1790.[9] Lochbay was considered 'one of the first situations for a seaport town in Europe' but despite grand designs the settlement was the Society's great failure.[10] The Society's final and most successful venture was the development of the New Town and harbour of Pulteneytown, from 1808, adjacent to the historic burgh of Wick, Caithness.[11] Pulteneytown, first suggested by Thomas Telford, was a change in strategy for the Society, from the establishment of entirely new settlements to the strategic development of an existing fishing town.[12]

From a central office in London the British Fisheries Society established and maintained a standard building programme at all its settlements. Once the purchase of land was agreed at each settlement a town plan was commissioned and then laid out by a surveyor and the Society's agent on site. The Society then built three key public works: a harbour, an inn, and a storehouse. Building contracts were advertised in the Scottish press, with all contracts and works approved and reviewed by the Board of Directors (for a full catalogue of the Society's civil engineering and building works see Appendix 3).[13] Besides the public works, the Society adopted a standard policy for all its settlements regarding the domestic architecture of the settlers. The Society stipulated that all settlers were to build houses at their own expense but according to strict building regulations. In return settlers were offered long leases on favourable terms.[14]

Several studies have considered the buildings of the British Fisheries Society's settlements within their different regional contexts, notably the work of Elizabeth Beaton, Jean Munro, Geoffrey Stell and the inventory volumes produced by the Royal Commission on Ancient and Historic Monuments of Scotland.[15] However, the architectural works and town planning of the British Fisheries Society are not generally considered collectively as a distinct historic and architectural group. The Society's villages were planned, designed and managed centrally by a Board of Directors in London, including the appointment of architects, surveyors and building contractors. The Board's centralised control enabled a consistent and architecturally coherent programme of works to be implemented across all the settlements irrespective of their regional geographic locations. The imposition of a standardised settlement pattern and uniform architectural character across the region by the British Fisheries Society was a significant developmental factor in the emerging urban form of planned villages throughout the Highlands through the late eighteenth and early nineteenth centuries.

Taken as a group the Society's town planning and architectural works can be divided into two chronological periods each with their own architectural character. This dual character directly relates to changes on the Board of Directors and individual Director's preferred architects and surveyors. The first design period, 1786–90, encompassed the establishment of the first two settlements of Tobermory and Ullapool and was dominated by John, fifth Duke of Argyll.[16] The Duke was the principal patron of the architect Robert Mylne (1733–1811) and Mylne's austere neo-classical style is very much in evidence in the design of the Society's inns and storehouses. During the same period Mylne was responsible for improvements at the Inveraray estate and designed numerous estate buildings, such as the circular-plan Maam Steading, Glenshira, 1787–9.[17] Another important figure in this first period was James Maxwell (1757–1829), the fifth Duke of Argyll's Chamberlain on Mull and the British Fisheries Society's first agent at Tobermory. Educated at Glasgow University and previously employed by the Commissioner of Argyll Estates in Edinburgh, Maxwell was the sort of modern professional preferred by the Dukes of Argyll.[18] It was Maxwell who, with no training as a surveyor or architect, was eventually responsible for the design of the town plan and several of the public buildings at Tobermory. The employment of the North-East School surveyor and former Annexed Estates Commission employee, David Aitken, for the survey and town plan of Ullapool, reflects the Society's close links with the wider Scottish landowning establishment. Overall, the first period of the Society's activities can be inter-

preted as a model of the patriotic partnership at work. Influenced by the architectural style of Mylne and the planning model of the early industrial villages of
the North-East, the urban design of this period is characterised by a plain, often
austere, classicism well-suited to the rational and efficient pursuit of industry.

The second architectural period of the Society's activities, 1790–1817, encompassed the establishment of the latter two settlements of Lochbay and
Pulteneytown and was dominated by Sir William Pulteney (1729–1805).
Pulteney was appointed a director of the Society in 1790 and Chairman in 1800,
when he succeeded the fifth Duke of Argyll and assumed control of the Society's
architectural patronage. Pulteney was the principal patron of the architect and
civil engineer Thomas Telford (1757–1834) whose contemporary style and
engineering skill characterise Lochbay and Pulteneytown. Pulteney was the
Whig Member of Parliament for Shrewsbury, 1768–1805, and husband to Lady
Bath, heiress of the fourth Earl of Bath, which made Sir William one of the
richest commoners in Britain. Like his protégé, Pulteney was born in the
Scottish Borders and had close links with the Scottish Enlightenment (he was
one of Adam Smith's pall-bearers).[19] Through Pulteney's influence Telford came
to dominate all aspects of the design process at Lochbay and Pulteneytown.

Town Planning

The British Fisheries Society's first two settlements, Tobermory and Ullapool,
were laid out on grid-plans, the archetypal planning model of the eighteenth-
century estate village or company town.[20] However, the Society's immediate
design source was Sir James Grant of Grant who suggested that: 'it may be
proper at the first establishment to line out the intended town on a regular plan
according to the characteristic situation of the ground that the streets may be
regular and convenient'.[21] The town plan of Tobermory was drawn up by James
Maxwell following the Duke of Argyll's rejection of a rather confused radial-plan
submitted by a Campbeltown surveyor, George Langlands.[22] Maxwell's decep-
tively simple plan of 1790, placed the town's core public buildings on the harbour
front along the town wharf below the site's steep bank (Fig. 49). This
arrangement included the storehouse and customs house, which were located on
the edge of the Society's land and together formed a small U-shaped yard open
to the seaward side. Above the bank Maxwell laid out a hierarchical, grid plan of
rectangular blocks aligned in two columns three blocks deep. This formed a
street system of three streets and a central cross-street. The front two blocks on

Argyle Terrace were further subdivided into five settlers' plots, three facing the sea and six plots facing inland onto Breadalbane Street. A parallel service lane separated the garden plots of the two streets. Another two blocks enclosed Breadalbane Street on the landward side, this time divided into seven plots. Therefore, moving inland from the harbour, each block consisted of one more

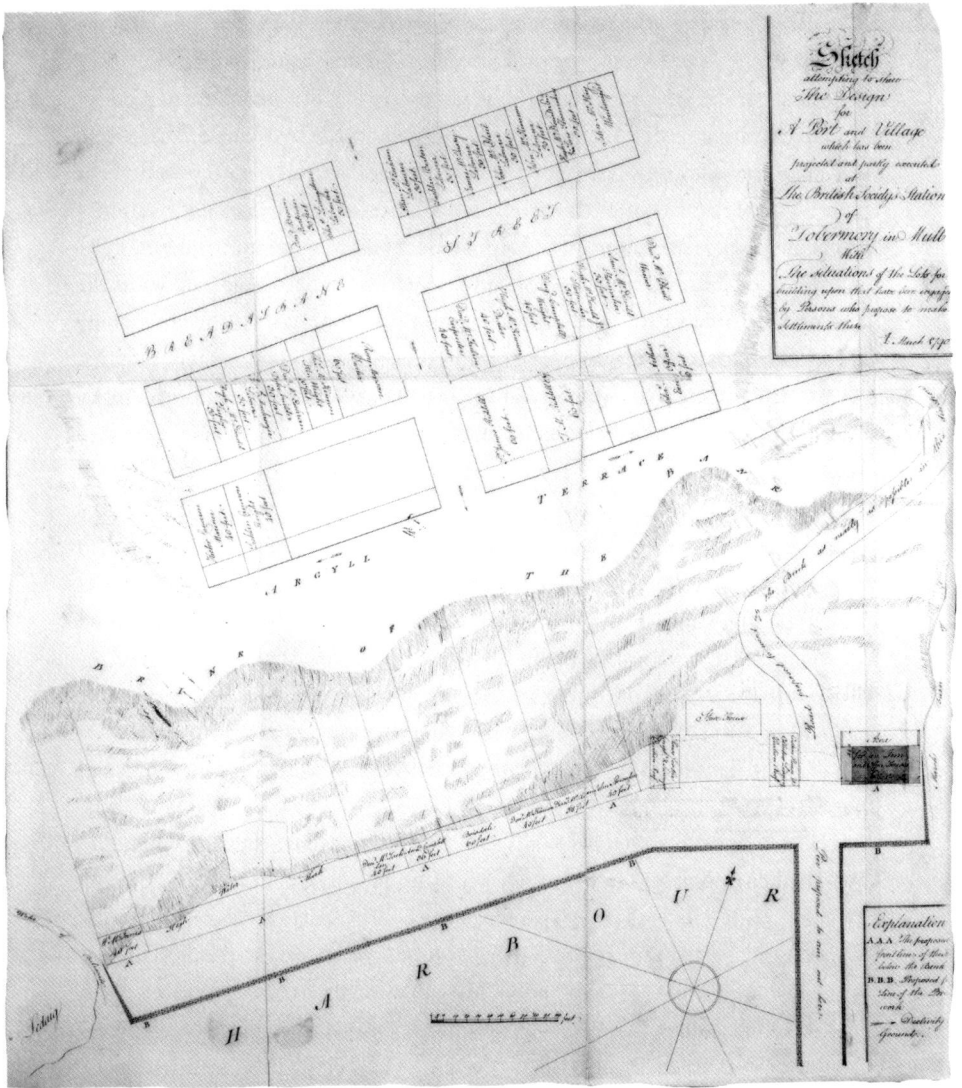

49. James Maxwell, *Sketch attempting to show The Design for A Port and Village which has been projected and partially executed at the British Society's Station of Tobermory in Mull*, 1790 (Crown Copyright: RCAHMS).

plot than the one before it. As the landward plots decreased in size their rental value decreased correspondingly.[23]

Ullapool was laid out to a simpler grid plan by the surveyor David Aitken in 1789. David Aitken (active 1763–1804) had previously worked for the Annexed Estates Commission, as well as numerous private landowners in Ross and Cromarty and Inverness-shire. Aitken had trained under the north east surveyor Alexander Sangster, who trained under John Forbes with the best known surveyor of the North East School, Peter May.[24] These associations put Aitken at the heart of the North East School of surveyors. David Aitken's town plan for Ullapool has been lost but a sketch of the plan was made by Donald Macleod of Geanies, Sheriff of Ross-shire, who inspected the village in 1789 on behalf of the Society.[25] Macleod of Geanies's sketch shows that the plan was intended to be a regular grid, as at Tobermory, with a similar adaptation to the practicalities of the site (Fig. 50). The main street, Shore Street, marked 'C.C.', runs parallel to the shore and features a terrace of housing and public buildings. As the bank along the foreshore was smaller than at Tobermory, the rising ground was incorporated into the rear gardens, or kail yards, of the building plots on Shore Street. Argyle Street, immediately above the bank, marked 'D.D.', runs parallel. These two parallel streets are intersected at the mid-point by a central cross-street named Quay Street, marked 'E.E.', which runs down to the town pier. Potential expansion of the grid was restricted to the west by the mouth of the Ullapool River but to the east the grid could be, and later was, expanded by a further block and cross-street, Ladysmith Street. As the sketch shows, Shore Street was laid out parallel to the shore, not parallel with Argyle Street as intended by Aitken, upsetting the uniformity of the grid plan blocks. This was the lasting result of an error by one of the early building contractors at Ullapool, Robert Melvill, who ignored the town plan when building the stores and herring-houses.[26]

The Society's links with the north east through Sir James Grant of Grant and David Aitken are evident in the utilitarian planning and architecture of Ullapool and Tobermory. The high public profile of the Society subsequently ensured that Ullapool and Tobermory became the design template for the proliferation of planned villages founded in the Highlands through to the mid-nineteenth century. Of the thirty-five eighteenth- and early-nineteenth-century Highland planned villages listed in Nic Allen's Gazetteer of Highland Planned Villages, only three, Grantown-on-Spey, 1769, Portree, 1763, and Lochboisdale, 1786, pre-date Ullapool and Tobermory.[27] All of those that post-date Ullapool and Tobermory were laid out on the standard British Fisheries Society grid-plan. In

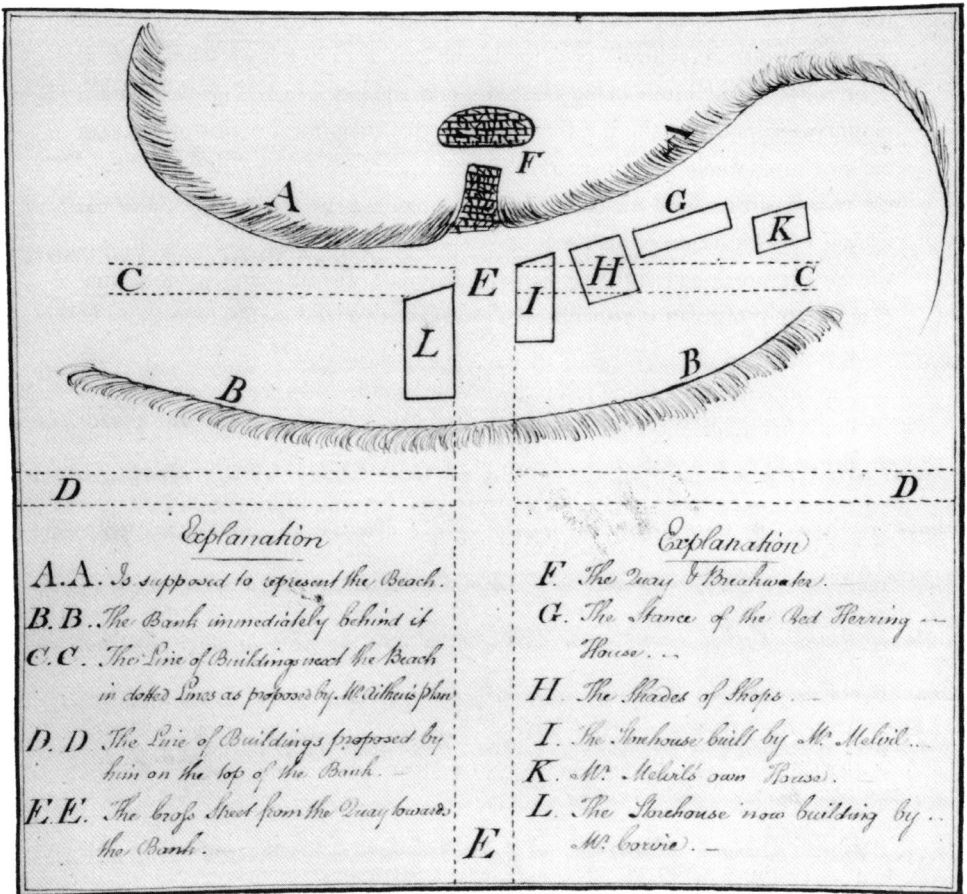

50. Donald Macleod of Geanies, *Sketch of David Aitken's plan of Ullapool*, 1789. Depicting the builders' divergence from the laid out street line (National Archives of Scotland)

terms of function, twenty-one were established as fishing villages, whilst the remaining twelve were intended as centres for textile manufacturing.[28] To the twenty-first-century visitor to the Scottish Highlands the straight terraces of the typical planned village appear bleak and contrast unfavourably with the perceived romance of the Highlands. This has much to do with our romantic image of the Highlands inherited from the nineteenth century, which ignored the true, predominantly eighteenth-century, industrial character of the built environment in the Highlands.

Thomas Telford's, largely unexecuted, 1790, plan for the Society's third settlement at Lochbay, Isle of Skye, marked a radical departure from the industrial grid-plan villages of the Society's first phase of activity. In contrast, to the imposed grid-plan, Telford's plan for Lochbay is a sophisticated scheme based upon a system of interlocking crescents and squares which engage with the natural topography of the site (Fig. 51). The two main focal points of the plan are the church square and the market square. In contrast to the early settlements, the two squares offer a focus for civic life inland, away from the sea and the fishery. In justification of his rejection of a standard grid-plan drawn up for the site by the north-east surveyor, James Chapman, Telford gave the following description of his plan for Lochbay:

> The bottom of the rising ground with the middle street for a centre the market is made of a semi circle shape with street of the same surrounding it; this form is chosen in order to render the market place warmer, to help the ascent of the streets that communicate with the

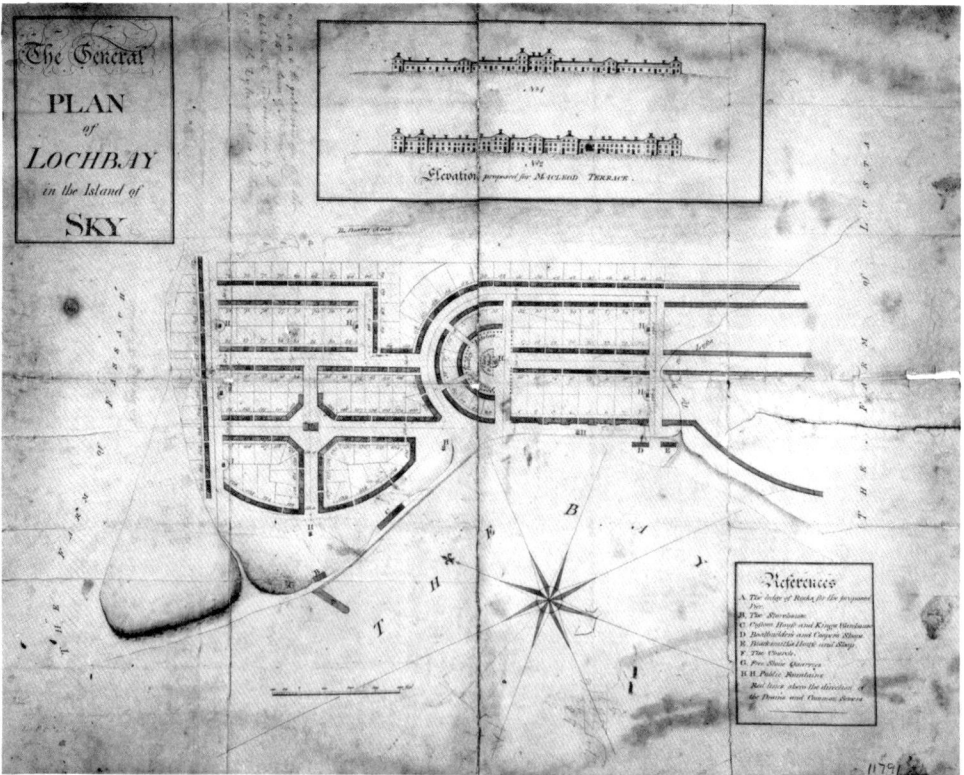

51. Thomas Telford, *The General Plan of Lochbay in the Island of Sky*, 1790 (National Archives of Scotland)

higher ground and to prevent a current of air from the streets above. The streets of the higher ground are laid out on the same principles of gaining easy ascent and preventing cross drafts of air for which purpose there is a row of houses which defend the ends of each of the streets. The large reversed crescent is made to suit the form of the ground, and to get the easiest possible ascent from the lower to the higher ground. On the top of the rising ground in the centre of a lozenge is the church.[29]

Telford describes the scheme solely in practical terms of climate and geography with no reference to the contemporary, fashionable nature of the design and its novelty in the context of the industrial Highland planned village.[30] Of course, by the late eighteenth century, crescents and squares were no longer considered a radical invention, even on the small-scale of the model estate village but the British Fisheries Society villages were remote industrial settlements not model estate villages built to be admired. It is frustrating that Telford makes no reference to his design influences, only his intent, in either his correspondence or later biographical writings. It can be inferred from Telford's diverse national work schedule during this period that he took his inspiration from markedly similar street forms he encountered on his travels elsewhere in Britain. For example, the crescent terraces and unified elevations with terminating pavilion wings in the proposal for Lochbay are reminiscent of Robert Adam's Lowther Village, 1766, which Telford visited when working in Cumbria in 1789.[31] As an avid follower of contemporary architecture, it is also likely that Telford had a second hand familiarity with John Wood the Younger's widely-celebrated Royal Crescent, Bath, completed in 1775, though he did not personally go to Bath until 1792 when he worked as a surveyor at Sir William Pulteney's Bathwick estate.[32] A familiarity with the plans and elevations of Georgian Bath would explain the strong similarities between Lochbay's proposed lozenge-shaped church square and Thomas Baldwin's Laura Place, 1788–92, and its semicircular colonnaded market square with Baldwin's Cross Bath, 1786.[33] However, Telford's deployment of the crescent as an enclosed street with its void filled by the semicircular central marketplace was an innovation. The crescent in this period was still only employed as an open form and Telford's proposal for the 'crescent-street' had no British precedent.[34]

Following the high costs which mounted up at Ullapool, the Directors of the Society were unwilling to invest money in Lochbay and Telford's plan remained largely undeveloped. Pulteneytown, therefore, was Telford's greatest contribution to the British Fisheries Society and to urban planning in Scotland. Pulteneytown was the Society's final venture and differed from the previous settlements as it is a New Town adjunct to the historic burgh of Wick not a pioneer settlement. Telford drew up a preliminary town plan in 1807, which featured a large shallow crescent facing away from the sea, similar to Peter Nicholson's 1806 plan for the ferry port of Ardrossan, Ayrshire, which Telford had visited (Fig. 52). However, Telford substantially remodelled the plan for the final version of 1810.[35] The town plan of Pulteneytown is essentially a simple cross-plan running roughly east-west with a central open square, Argyll Square. Telford enhanced the scheme by designing the central square as a chamfered rectangle (Fig. 53). Argyll Square is bisected lengthwise by the east-west axis of Grant Street and Dempster Street. The square is also flanked by enclosed angular, or canted, crescents, Breadalbane Terrace and Brown Street. All the residential streets were named after directors of the Society.

As with Lochbay, Telford explained his fashionable departure from the industrial grid-plan established by the Society purely in terms of geography and climate, 'one great objective in forming the new plan was to exclude the north wind. At present the wind blows right across the flat evenly but it will hit the wall of the crescent and be forced down a side street'.[36] Telford's presentation of a fashionable and aesthetically-considered plan to the practical and money-minded Directors of the British Fisheries Society in language which extols only its practical benefits is a fascinating example of the civil engineer's self presentation and understanding of his clients.

As with Telford's proposed scheme for Lochbay there are strong formal similarities between the urban spaces of Pulteneytown and Thomas Baldwin's scheme for the Bathwick estate, Bath. The chamfered rectangle of Telford's Argyll Square is very close to the chamfered rectangle of Thomas Baldwin's Sydney Gardens, Bath, 1788–92.[37] In contrast to the Lochbay scheme, the probability of Bath having had a direct influence upon Telford is high as he had worked as a surveyor at Bathwick since 1792 and had overseen the completion of the scheme following Baldwin's dismissal as City Surveyor.[38] And, Telford was impressed with what he had seen at Bath:

> Modern Bath has been created by a Mr. Wood, an Architect, a man of very superior talents to whom, if I will, I hope do justice . . . I know of no instance in Ancient or Modern History of the conjunction of so many favourable circumstances . . . far excell'd the Bath of Diocletian or any of the Roman Works.[39]

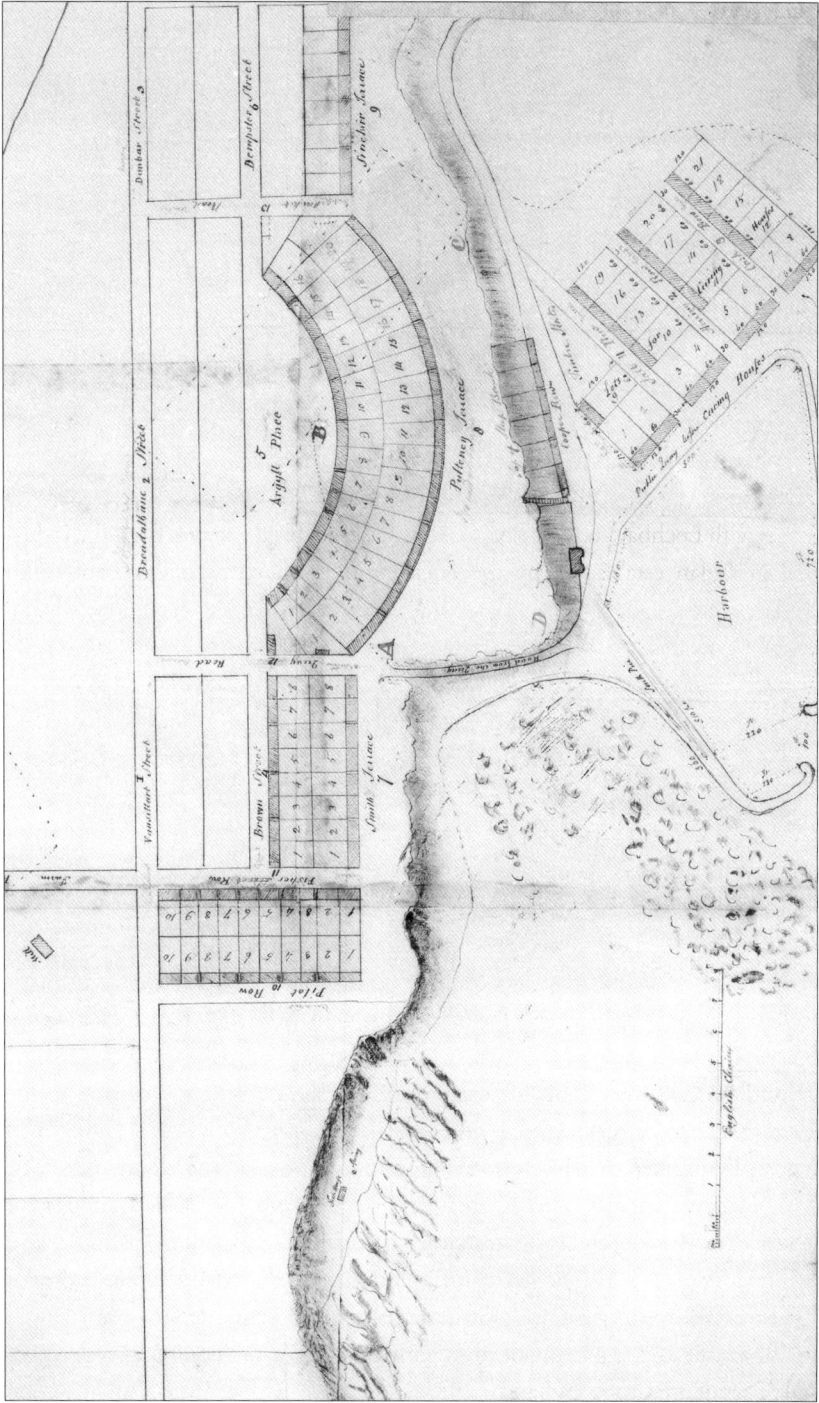

52. Thomas Telford, initial scheme for Pulteneytown, 1807 (National Archives of Scotland)

53. Pulteneytown, Wick, Caithness (Crown Copyright: RCAHMS)

Telford's use of the fashionable urban forms of the crescent and square in the context of a planned industrial settlement in the Highlands – and selling it to practically-minded clients – was a unique contribution to Scottish urban history. It also demonstrates that, in his work for the British Fisheries Society, though his designs may have been largely imitative, their social application was innovative by providing enclosed civic spaces for industrial workers away from the centre of industry. Perhaps of greatest significance in terms of urban design, was Telford's use of zoning to separate work from leisure: the clear division of Pulteneytown into a residential zone and an industrial zone each with a distinct architectural character. The genteel urbanity of the residential zone's crescents and squares juxtaposes with a strict geometric grid-plan in the separate industrial zone. Telford's architectural zoning has no eighteenth-century British precedent and should be more widely recognised. The industrial zone, known as Lower Pulteneytown, was laid out on ground close to the harbour and planned as a grid of nineteen plots grouped into four rectangular blocks, each block comprising two plots facing the harbour and four plots facing those of the next parallel block. The grid, and the correspondingly austere warehouses and depots were built according to strict building regulations, which emphasised the functional and industrial nature of the zone. The industrial aesthetic was further empha-sised by the original street names: Salt Row, Herring Row and Cask Row.[40] The repetitive geometry of Lower Pulteneytown was a forerunner of Telford's unrealised London Docks scheme for a monumental warehouse and embankment complex on the Thames, 1800, and pre-empted his later schemes for Gloucester Docks, 1826 and St Katherine's Docks, 1827–8, built 'to rival the London Dock Company and the West India Docks'.[41] Pulteneytown is the most innovative example of eighteenth-century town planning in northern Scotland and the most complete example of Telford's work as a town planner. The historic significance of Pulteneytown was recognised by Historic Scotland when desig-nated 'Group Category A' in 2002.

Harbours

The Society's harbour developments are matters of civil engineering not archi-tectural history, however, the capital investment in harbour works was consid-erably greater than any amount invested in architecture or planning (Telford's creative town planning at Lochbay and Pulteneytown were only accepted by the Board of Directors as they cost no more to design or lay-out than a basic grid). For example, Robert Mylne's elegant neo-classical inn at Tobermory cost £792 whereas the harbours works cost £8,000, while the harbour works at Pulteneytown cost over £10,000 against no financial investment in buildings. More than any architectural work, the completion of the harbour was the primary factor in the eventual success or failure of a settlement. The 700ft breastwork at Tobermory, quickly well-built by Stevenson's of Oban, 1791, allowed the settlement to develop its fishery and its status as a trading port immediately.[42] In contrast, the harbour works at Ullapool were poorly constructed by the contractors, Melvill and Miller, and required expensive

ongoing alterations immediately after completion. By the early 1800s Ullapool
had declined into poverty as larger vessels could not use the harbour which cut
off the village from the offshore herring busses upon which an inshore fleet
depended.[43] Despite a harbour scheme drawn up by Sir John Rennie and
Thomas Telford in the early 1790s, the harbour at Lochbay was not actually
completed until 1802.[44] The large numbers that were initially willing to settle at
Lochbay eventually emigrated to North America, citing the Society's unwill-
ingness to commence works at Lochbay that led to their decision to emigrate.[45]
In contrast, Telford's massive double-harbour complex at Pulteneytown, 1807–
13, was the principal cause of the settlement's success, providing the infrastructure for an existing town and fishery to expand. Telford's first biographer,
Samuel Smiles, wrote in the mid-nineteenth century:

> Wick is now, we believe, the greatest fishing station in the world. The
> place has increased from a little poverty-stricken village to a large and
> thriving town . . . The bay is at times frequented by upwards of a
> thousand fishing-boats and the take of herring in some years amounts
> to more than a hundred thousand barrels.[46]

Pulteneytown harbour was funded by the British Fisheries Society and the
Commission for Highland Roads and Bridges. This joint enterprise was born
out of Telford's highly influential *Survey and Report on the Coasts and Central
Highlands of Scotland*, produced for the Treasury in 1802, in which he recommended the construction of harbours along the northern coastline of Scotland.
Pulteneytown harbour was the British Fisheries Society's last project and the first
harbour project by the Highland Roads and Bridges Commission, marking the
transition to the next phase of the patriotic partnership in the Highlands, in
which the emphasis shifted to government infrastructure schemes for canals,
roads, bridges and harbours not planned villages, which were left to private
landowners. From 1806 to 1821, the Highland Road and Bridges Commission
was prolific in the construction of harbours and piers in northern Scotland.[47]

The Society's Inns

In 1789 the fifth Duke of Argyll wrote to his factor, James Maxwell, regarding
the works at Tobermory. He stressed that the inn was '. . . a building that ought
to be very particularly studied and attended to . . . strangers will of course set the

edge of their criticism upon the Inn in the first place'.[48] This was a deliberate design strategy previously employed by the Dukes of Argyll at Inveraray. The inn was intended as a place for the accommodation of travelling gentlemen, not the use of the village residents. Accordingly, the inn was the only building in which the Board of Directors expressed an interest in appearance beyond the uniform late eighteenth-century commercial classicism implied by the phrase much-used in the period: 'neat and regular'. Robert Mylne's work for the Society was almost entirely focused upon the design of inns. Robert Mylne was a contemporary of Robert Adam and a fellow Scottish émigré resident in London. Mylne is known for his innovative, early-career design for Blackfriars Bridge, London, and a handful of country house commissions, such as Pitlour House, Fife, 1787, executed in a severely-restrained neo-classical style reminiscent of Ledoux.[49] Much of Mylne's practice was devoted to infrastructure improvement schemes (canals, river navigations, roads, bridges) notably for the fifth Duke of Argyll at Inveraray.

The Tobermory Inn, 1790–1, was Mylne's first and principal design for the Society. Illustrated in Mylne's plan and elevation, the inn was an archetypal post-Palladian, Improvement-era small-scale house: a plain but well-proportioned, two-storey, three-bay classical building flanked by single-storey pavilion wings clearly visible in William Daniell's watercolour of the village (Fig. 54). The pavilions were ornamented with blind arched-niches and ball-finials. An inn of identical design was planned for Ullapool (Fig. 17). An initial plan drawn up by the contractor, Roderick Morrison, outlined a two-storey, three-bay building, 'built of stone and lime, roofed with slate . . . and two wings one for the kitchens and servants the other as a byre and hay loft'.[50] Morrison's plans were sent to Mylne who produced 'a new elevation and section of the Inn . . . only enlarging the Inn by addition of a sunk storey and drawing its wings closer up to the body'.[51] Completed before the inn at Tobermory in 1790, this inn, which was heavily altered in the early twentieth century, was considered by Macleod of Geanies to be, 'an excellent one, but the Reporter fears will come to a much greater expense than the situation can afford any equal return from it'.[52] Telford surveyed the building in 1790 and concurred that, 'there seems to be an excellent inn and offices at Ullapool, too good perhaps for the probable resort to that place'.[53]

At Lochbay, only a temporary inn was built during the Society's period of ownership; the present building dates from the 1840s. The lack of a landmark British Fisheries Society inn at Lochbay is symptomatic of the general lack of development at the site. The Pulteneytown Inn, designed by Thomas Telford,

54. William Daniell, 'Tobermory on the Isle of Mull', *A Voyage Round the Coast of Scotland and the Adjacent Islands*, 1814–1822 (National Library of Scotland)

stands on a prominent position overlooking the main harbour. The Round House, as it is known locally, was built by a local contractor, George Burn, in 1808.[54] The intended Pulteneytown Inn demonstrates that, as with the town plan, Telford liked to experiment with contemporary trends in architecture. The fashionable Picturesque-style of the early nineteenth century, disseminated by a new generation of architectural books, such as Robert Lugar's *The Country Gentleman's Architect*, 1807, is evident in features such as the hipped roof with over-sailing eaves, central roof-ridge chimneystacks and advanced, bowed window bays. Telford considered the completed building, 'an example of neatness'.[55] However, on completion Burn decided to make the landmark building his own house thus depriving Pulteneytown of a quality inn, although many small private whisky-shops and cook-houses sprang up around the harbour to meet demand.

The Society's Storehouses

A storehouse for the storage of equipment and materials relating to the fishery, such as nets, salt and barrels, was the third of the British Fisheries Society's three core public works. Essentially, the warehouses erected by the Society were plain functional buildings typical of eighteenth-century commercial classicism and similar to the bonded warehouses of Scottish ports such as Leith, Edinburgh, and the Port of Glasgow: well-ordered, two to three-storey, stone-built and slate-roofed, buildings of regular elevation and rectangular-plan.[56] The *Rudiments of Architecture* includes a design for this ordinary, functional building type (*Design XX*). Similar examples can also be found at many of the smaller Caithness fishing stations that sprang up in response to the success of Pulteneytown, such as Lybster, Staxigo and Clyth.

The size and quantity of storehouses built by the British Fisheries Society varied considerably from one settlement to the next. The first storehouse to go up was the three-storey King's Warehouse at Tobermory in 1789.[57] This building was designed and built by contractors Richards and Rodgers of Perth following alterations by Robert Mylne, who considered the original plans for a four-storey building, 'much too lofty for that climate'.[58] James Maxwell's 1791 sketch of the harbour shows a regular, gabled, three-storey building with a segmental-arched door to centre similar to that illustrated in the *Rudiments of Architecture* (Fig. 49).[59] The sketch also shows the Tobermory Customs House and Lodgings, 1789–91, flanking the storehouse to form a U-shape complex facing the wharf. The symmetrical two-storey buildings with hipped roofs were a revised version by Maxwell of an elegant but costly design by Mylne.[60] The U-plan arrangement created a small public space for official and commercial transactions.

In contrast to the regular scheme at Tobermory, the presence of two competing contractors at Ullapool resulted in a straggling street-line of mismatched stores and curing houses along the shore. The principal building along the shore remains the three-storey Great Storehouse with a first-storey forestair, built by William Cowie of Tain, 1789–90, marked L on Geanies' sketch map (Fig. 55). A smaller storehouse for salt and casks had been previously completed in 1788 by Melvill and Miller of Dunbar and roofed with pan-tiles shipped from Aberdeen. Geanies' sketch shows how Melvill's poor alignment of the storehouse, marked I, with Aitken's street plan forced Cowie to build the Great Storehouse with an asymmetrical floor plan.[61] These buildings were supplemented with a further three-storey curing-house and a large workshop with a pyramidal roof, both by Melvill and Miller.

A small, single-storey storehouse, designed by Thomas Telford, was built at Lochbay in 1795 but it soon fell into disrepair. In contrast, the industrial archae-ologist John Hume has commented that 'the finest group of curing depots [in the Highlands and Islands] is at Pulteneytown' (Fig. 56).[62] The store and curing houses of Pulteneytown's industrial zone were built by private investors. The uniformity of materials, construction and design was controlled by building

55. The Great Storehouse, Ullapool, Lochbroom (Crown copyright: RCAHMS)

regulations stipulated by Telford. Plots were initially sold at roup auction in 1808 with eleven taken; by 1817 all twenty plots were taken. Ever fashionable, the repeated blocks of storehouses built under these regulations relate Telford's Lower Pulteneytown to the contemporary architectural trend for 'relentless repetition and obsessive geometry . . . of heroic geometry' in large building complexes such as docks, prisons, barracks or asylums.[63]

Settlers' Houses

As previously discussed, the design and construction of settlers' houses at Tobermory and Ullapool were controlled by building regulations intended to ensure uniformity of materials and design. The Society's strict building regulations ensured that the same design principles of regularity and order that governed the town plan and public buildings of each settlement would prevail in the settlers' houses, but at no cost to the Society.[64] Both villages still predominantly comprise uniform straight terraces of stone-built, slate-roofed, single or two-storey, three-bay symmetrical cottages. Telford initiated a change of strategy

56. Converted storehouse,
Wick Heritage Centre, Lower
Pulteneytown, Wick, Caithness
(author)

at Lochbay, providing two elevations for the proposed Macleod Terrace, which was to have been built along the main shorefront. Both designs were for unified Palladian façades as pioneered by John Wood in Bath, Queen's Square, 1736, and Grand Circus, 1754 (Fig. 51).[65] As initiated by John Wood in Bath the continuous façade was intended to allow the individual property owner or builder, who bore the cost of building, to design the internal plan as they saw fit whilst maintaining the overall architectural unity of the row. 'Elevation No. 1' was for a three-storey central block flanked by pedimented pavilions linked by plain single-storey terracing. 'Elevation No. 2' was designed on the same principle but arranged for two-storey terraces.[66] Again, the similarity of these elevations with Robert Adam's Lowther Village, Cumbria, 1766, is notable.[67] The flaw in Telford's scheme was that the intended occupants were neither the wealthy seasonal residents of Bath nor the recipients of a landowner's largesse as in the case of a model estate village such as Lowther. Later at Pulteneytown, Telford achieved a workable synthesis of the continuous façade and the Society's self-build regulation by removing the hierarchical Palladian element and prescribing the same plain and symmetrical, two-storey, three-bay elevation for all houses.[68]

The early planned villages of the British Fisheries Society had an impact upon the urban development of the Scottish Highlands far out of proportion to their small number, demonstrating the ability of a national body to remotely impose a consistent and, more or less, uniform 'modern' planning and design model upon distant and unconnected areas irrespective of regional building and settlement traditions. The adoption of Robert Mylne's restrained neo-classical architectural style by a high profile and influential national body, and the industrial planned village model developed in the north east of Scotland, set both the aesthetic and operative agendas of the subsequent Highland planned village boom in the late-eighteenth to mid-nineteenth centuries. The planned villages of the British Fisheries Society and its successors had little success in establishing a long-term sustainable economy in the Scottish Highlands but, in terms of the built environment, the Highland planned village totally superseded the indigenous *bailtean* as the common settlement pattern in the Highlands and continues to define the character of the Highland built environment today. In contrast, Thomas Telford's later innovative planning for the British Fisheries Society at Lochbay and Pulteneytown was of little wider influence. However, Pulteneytown was the Society's singular success, becoming the greatest fishing port in Britain in the nineteenth century and Telford's town plan is today recognised as the most original and architecturally significant example of Georgian town planning in the north of Scotland.

CHAPTER 8

From Northern Scotland to North America

Through the eighteenth and early nineteenth century, new modern British farmhouses were built for a new Highland population of improving tenant farmers. The establishment of vast sheep ranches entailed the eviction of thousands of indigenous small tenant farmers, and planned villages were established for their resettlement. Many also rebuilt their homes on marginal crofting land in an attempt to continue their traditional way of life. Others migrated to the growing industrial towns of the Lowlands. Many, however, chose to emigrate from Scotland to North America and, later in the nineteenth century, to Australia, New Zealand and South Africa. The history of agricultural improvement in the Highlands is also the history of emigration. During the peak period of the Highland building boom, c.1775–1815, emigration to North America meant Canada. From the late eighteenth century thousands of Scots emigrated to Nova Scotia, Canada, settling there principally in Pictou and Antigonish Counties on the province's north coast. What type of house did those immigrant Highlanders in Canada inhabit on the edge of the British Empire?

This final chapter considers the domestic architecture of Scottish Gaelic immigrants in Canada from the blackhouse to the timber-framed colonial house; the Highland house transformed once more. In contrast to the transferable building traditions of Lowland Scottish mason settlers, virtually no element of the Scottish Highland vernacular building tradition was established in Nova Scotia and Scottish Highland emigrants adopted a new architecture with near total uniformity. A new environment introduced new building materials, namely timber, and construction techniques, however, in terms of form and style this was the same understated classicism adopted by the new tenant farmers in the Highlands of Scotland. Scottish Gaelic immigrants in Nova Scotia went to great lengths to retain their Gaelic traditions in language and literature, music and dance, but quickly and completely rejected their indigenous building traditions. They abandoned the low, earth and field-cleared stone walls and turf or thatch roofed dwellings of the blackhouse; instead they opted to inhabit the classically ornamented and proportioned houses typical of colonists throughout the north-eastern seaboard of North America from the mid eighteenth century. Breaking with their self-build tradition, they employed carpenters who were trained craftsmen, probably using architectural pattern books, who built houses designed and ornamented according to the principles of eighteenth-century British, or British American, classicism. By contrast, the highly skilled masonic building traditions of Lowland Scottish emigrant masons asserted its influence in Nova Scotia, albeit in a specific and localised way: on the townhouses of Pictou Town.

Lowland masons showed their capacity for economic migration beyond the outer edges of Scotland to North America. The Highland emigrants' rapid switch from an evolved vernacular to colonial classicism, whilst fiercely guarding other aspects of Gaelic culture, was not just a practical shift, due to the ready availability of building materials in one location against those in another, from stone and earth to wood; rather, it was a more fundamental change: from evolved vernacular to conscious design. This change suggests a distinction of values between the material and non-material that allowed the Gaels, like many other immigrant ethnic minority groups in North America, to adapt successfully to life within the broader cultural structure of the early modern Atlantic world.

Highland Emigration to North America

Highland emigration was a consequence of a rapidly rising population, a fragile economy and the changes in land use and tenure introduced by agricultural improvement.[1] Throughout the eighteenth century, pockets of Highland settlement had been established in Georgia, North Carolina and the Mohawk and Hudson valleys of New York.[2] Emigration to North America increased rapidly in the late eighteenth century, despite efforts to discourage emigration through the establishment of planned industrial villages.[3] Following the American War of Independence (1776–83), British emigration to North America meant Canada and the former French colony of Quebec, the isolated fishing communities of Newfoundland and, for Scottish Gaels, Nova Scotia. Nova Scotia was the last British North American colony to be opened up for settlement, following the expulsion of the French Acadians in the 1750s.[4] Scottish Gaelic emigration to Nova Scotia reached a peak in the 1830s and then another in the 1850s, following the forced evictions of the nineteenth-century Clearances.[5] The Scottish Gaels who disembarked in Nova Scotia established themselves in close-knit farming communities in the Pictou and Antigonish regions of northern Nova Scotia, often led by tacksmen (Fig. 57).[6]

The first small party of two hundred Scottish Gaels to land in Nova Scotia departed from Lochbroom aboard the *Hector*, landing at Pictou Harbour on 15 September 1773, fourteen years before the establishment of Ullapool by the British Fisheries Society. At the present-day Pictou Heritage Centre, the arrival of the *Hector* is described as analogous to the arrival of the Puritans' *Mayflower* in seventeenth-century New England, marking the foundation of Scottish Highland culture in Canada.[7] In reality, however, the Scottish Gaels were but one of many distinct ethnic groups – also including Irish, English and Germans – who established their own ethnic, regional centres within the province in the late eighteenth century, and it was not until the nineteenth century that Scottish Gaels emerged as the dominant ethnic group in north-eastern Nova Scotia. In 1763 (prior to the arrival of the *Hector*) the total population of the province already stood at 13,374, of which over half – in other words, the largest cultural group – had come from New England, principally Connecticut.[8] The provincial capital, Halifax, was founded in 1749 as a British naval port and town, with a population of 2,576 settlers. In contrast to the small number aboard the *Hector*, in the brief period of 1772–4 alone, a thousand settlers emigrated from Yorkshire to Cumberland County, close to Pictou County.

The two hundred Gaels aboard the *Hector* arrived to find the land immedi-

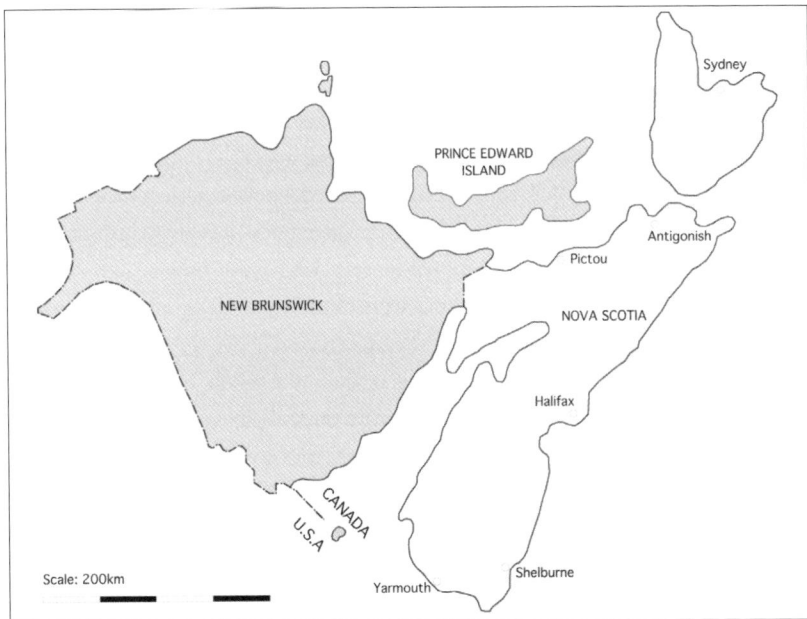

57. Map of Nova Scotia, New Brunswick and Prince Edward Island (James Lingard)

ately around the town of Pictou already settled by earlier continental migrants, principally those from New England, and took grants further inland and further along the coast. By 1769 the town already had a population of sixty-seven. The region to the east of Pictou, present day Antigonish County, was settled in the 1770s, shortly after the arrival of the *Hector*, by community groups of Roman Catholic Gaels, particularly from the Western Isles, who had often been encouraged to leave and organised into emigrant parties by Catholic priests. The general population of the province was further swelled by the Loyalist exodus from New England in 1783, following American Independence. Between 1783 and 1785, fifteen thousand Loyalists landed at Halifax alone. New port towns such as Digby, Shelburne and Sydney, Cape Breton, were established by Loyalists with the support of the British government, and the populations here rapidly grew to several thousand strong. From these initial ports of arrival, settlers dispersed within a few years to locations throughout Nova Scotia: to small towns and farms in the Annapolis Valley, to the Bay of Fundy and to north-eastern counties including Pictou and Antigonish. The population of Shelburne, for example, peaked at ten thousand in 1785 but had dwindled to three hundred by 1818. By 1815, the total population of Nova Scotia had risen to 75,000. Within this multi-ethnic migration, the late eighteenth-century trickle of Scottish settlers in Pictou and Antigonish Counties grew exponentially during the early nineteenth century, reaching a peak in the 1830s, following the first of many post-Clearance waves of emigration from the Scottish Highlands. Between 1815 and 1838, 39,243 settlers disembarked at the ports of Halifax, Sydney and Pictou; of this total, the majority – 21,833 – had embarked in Scotland.[9]

The prospect of legal freehold was the principal appeal of emigration to Nova Scotia where colonial settlement patterns presented a new experience for Scottish Gaels. The process of surveying and laying out regular lots in British colonial settlements was not an anarchic wilderness land-grab but a well-ordered government-monitored process.[10] Lots were distributed along the coast, along the course of rivers and around the shores of lakes. This was not so much a matter of drinking water but of access, as initially the whole region was densely forested and travelling to new grants was only possible by watercraft. Settlers in the mid-nineteenth century were often able to buy plots of land already developed to some degree, from pioneer settlers. Through continuous habitation, often by the same families, this early pattern of settlement is still much in evidence today and can be read in the names of townships, such as Lower South River, River John, Caribou River, Sutherland River, Scotsburn, South Side Harbour, Cape Jack and Loch Broom.

Settlement in Nova Scotia brought new challenges and a radically-different type of house. In the early nineteenth century, Nova Scotia was still mostly covered by ancient forest, providing an abundance of house-building material. The early establishment of sawmills capable of producing timber boards meant that relatively sophisticated timber-framed houses, clad with clapboards or shingles, could be built. The first sawmill in Pictou County was opened by James Patterson in 1786.[11] The evidence of the surviving colonial building stock in Nova Scotia suggests that the construction of 'colonial farmhouses' with classical proportions rose steadily from 1800 (see Appendix 4, Table 1).[12] Only three houses survive from before 1800, with survivals reaching a peak towards the end of the 1840s (281 extant houses), and then a decline from the 1850s (only fifty colonial-style houses built) with the advent of the North American, high-gabled 'Gothic Vernacular' style, which would continue throughout the nineteenth century. Of the 529 surviving houses, 369 were probably built for the Scottish families who registered the land freehold; the vast majority of these were of Highland or Scottish Gaelic origin, compared with thirty-nine English, twenty-four American, seventeen Irish and eighty French Acadian families who returned to the Province in the early nineteenth century.[13]

Settlement in Pictou and Antigonish counties in the early-to-mid nineteenth century was dominated by people of Scottish Highland origin or descent. The early ownership of the majority of farmhouses can also be related to names of Scottish Highland origin. By the 1840s, a single, uniform house type had been adopted by Scottish Gaelic settlers and their immediate descendants in Nova Scotia, and the longstanding vernacular building traditions of the Highlands had by then been completely rejected. There is an overwhelming uniformity in the architectural form, plan and elevation, architectural ornament, building materials and construction methods amongst the pre-1850 farmhouses extant throughout both Pictou and Antigonish counties. A similar sameness of building construction and architectural form to that observed in the new farmhouses and cottages of the Scottish Highlands built in the same period (Fig. 58).

The Highlander's House in Nova Scotia

The typical house was one-and-a-half storeys in height, rectangular in plan and symmetrical in elevation, and either three or five bays wide with a regular arrangement of rectangular windows, door and chimney (see Appendix 4, Table 2). The rectangular plans of these houses are generally of a length to width ratio

58. A typical early nineteenth-century colonial farmhouse, McDonnell House, St Andrews, Antigonish County, Nova Scotia (author)

of 3:2. Beside the widespread use of plain mouldings to doors, windows and wall margins, wooden classical features such as cornices, pilasters and complex mouldings have been applied to the doors and windows (Fig. 59).

The typical floor plan is of a rectangle divided into three internal spaces that broadly correspond with the tripartite main elevation.[14] The internal partition walls then further break up these three internal spaces: either into a four-room arrangement, of two rectangular rooms to each outer space – one to the front and one to the back – flanking the central space, which contains the staircase, central chimney stack and entrance hall; or into a three-room arrangement, with a large kitchen occupying the entire rear of the house (Fig. 60). The stairs are accessed either directly from the lobby to the front, or from a back kitchen whenever the staircase is located to the rear of the chimneystack. Typically, the upper attic storey is lit by gable-end windows, sometimes with additional gabled dormers. Centrally-placed, twin brick stacks are also evident in houses built towards the middle of the nineteenth century, an arrangement that allowed for the expansion of the central hall area and staircase. Many examples also feature a small, single-storey extension to the side or rear, known as an 'ell', which was used as a summer kitchen in order to spare the main accommodation from the

59. Classical ornamentation: MacGillivary House, Upper South River, Antigonish County (author)

flies and heat. The ground floor rooms follow the eighteenth-century 'polite' formal arrangement: of parlours and kitchen, with livestock removed to a barn or field enclosure. Internal lathe and plaster was commonly employed, even in rural regions of Nova Scotia, from the late eighteenth century onwards. In addition to this interior finish classical mouldings were applied to internal doors, window frames, fire surrounds, skirting and dado rails, thereby accentuating the air of order and formality. The formal subdivision and ornamentation of rooms contrasts starkly with the flexible internal space of traditional Highland black-houses, which were often only partially subdivided by box beds.

The typical farmhouse is a timber-framed building clad in a sacrificial layer of clapboards (see Appendix 4, Table 5). Early timber-frame construction in Nova Scotia used posts and beams, and in some techniques diagonal braces, connected by means of a variety of joint profiles and wooden pegs, with nails being employed from the mid-nineteenth century onwards. The original outer cladding of shingles or clapboards covered a thick board sheathing attached to the frame, the board also serving to augment lateral strength. The use today of modern vinyl siding demonstrates the living character of this vernacular tradition, of continuously replacing the outer sacrificial layer of cladding. The

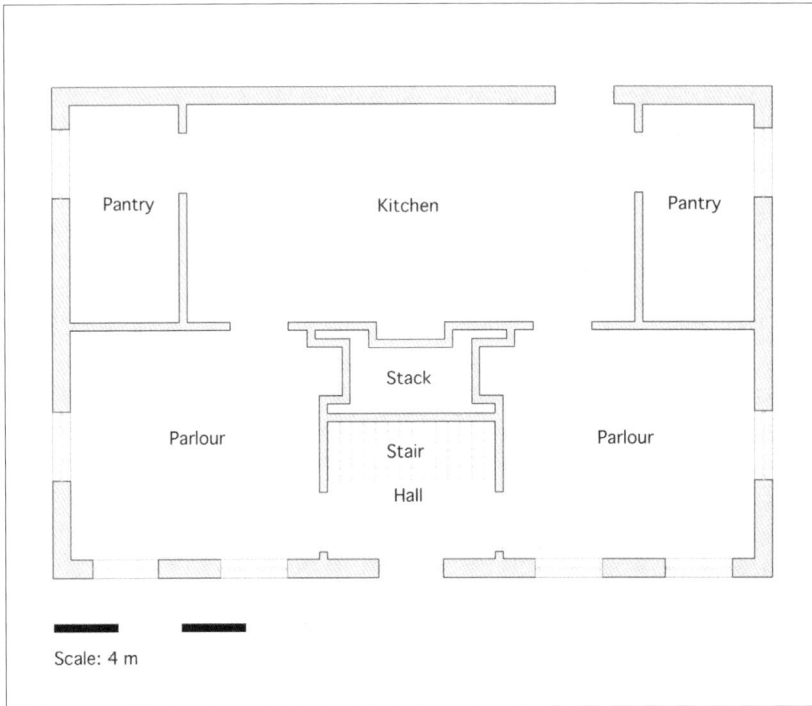

60. Sketch plan of a typical early nineteenth-century Nova Scotia farmhouse
(James Lingard)

majority of roofs surveyed are gabled and were originally covered with wooden
shingles, although they are now usually covered with asphalt tiles.

Each of the houses surveyed stands upon a raised foundation, itself often
incorporating a small cellar or crawl space, which provides a degree of damp and
frost proofing. The majority still stand upon their original stone foundations
with a minority standing upon replacement concrete or brick foundations (or,
in a very few cases, none at all). The chimneystack and foundation were the first
parts of the house to be built and provided the formal central axis and architectural plinth for the structure. The original central chimneystacks and hearths
were also made of stone, but very few remain, most having been replaced in the
later nineteenth century in brick or with stove pipes. For example, the house
built at 116 Water Street, Pictou (*c.* 1845), by William Brownrigg, a Scottish
emigrant, is a symmetrical one-and-a-half storey, three-bay timber-framed
building, which has retained its large, stone-built, central chimneystack.[15]

A surprisingly high number of original doors and windows have also
survived. The panelled timber door, which now predominates, was probably

made by the local house carpenter, whereas the twelve- or four-pane sash-window frames, together with their glass panes, were often imported as prefabricated units. These features can be seen in the McDonnell House, located in the settlement of St Andrews, a district in the centre of rural Antigonish County. This house was built (circa 1830) for Donald McDonnell, who emigrated from Glengarry in 1790. The McDonnell family worked as blacksmiths, farmers and storekeepers in St Andrews until the early twentieth century.[16] In the roof, dormer windows of various types, dates and combinations are also common. Windows placed in the apex of the end of the gable are the most common type of upper storey window, but traditional gabled dormers are also widespread. The relatively high number of roof dormers reflects the need to gain as much headroom and light as possible within the confined space of an upper attic storey.

The five-bay Fraser House, at Lower South River, Antigonish County, is one of the earliest houses extant in the county, dating from 1803 (Fig. 61). The original owner, Archibald Fraser, emigrated from Strathglass in the heart of the Scottish Highlands in the late eighteenth century. The original 150-acre grant remains in the possession of the Fraser family, but the farmhouse itself is in an

61. Roof shingles exposed: Fraser House, Lower South River, Antigonish County (author)

advanced state of dereliction.[17] The house remains largely unaltered, being in its early nineteenth-century form and displaying original features such as clapboarding, interior panelling, panelled doors, and classical mouldings to the interior and exterior openings. The original split-wood roof shingles can also been seen, under a corroded tin roof. A handful of early farms also feature a timber-framed barn. These are simple, rectangular-plan, gabled buildings, which were erected adjacent to farmhouses. The primary purpose of such barns was to house the farmer's livestock, especially in winter, including chickens, pigs, horses and cattle. Barns of this type were commonplace, developed to support the self-sufficient small-scale holding of mixed livestock typical of a self-sufficient, colonial farm. Very few of these early barns remain, although mounds of derelict timber boards frequently point to their former existence, since subsistence farming has all but disappeared.

Lowland Masons in Nova Scotia

Pictou, the county town of Pictou County, is an exception to the architectural character of small Nova Scotian towns in general. Uniquely, amongst the Province's many small historic towns, Pictou has a large number of stone-built houses. These stone houses in Pictou come in various sizes, including single-storey cottages, two-storey houses and tenements or apartment blocks, but all were executed according to the design rules of eighteenth-century classicism. In Pictou a direct connection exists between emigration from Scotland and architectural practices in Nova Scotia, but this connection stems from the masonic traditions of Lowland Scotland, not from the Highland Gaels. Lowland masons contrasted with these Scottish Gaels – small-scale farmers settling in rural areas – in being highly skilled economic migrants, attracted to 'Pictou Town' as its wealth increased in the early nineteenth century.

Two small houses, or rather cottages, in Pictou Town that immediately suggest a Scottish ancestry are the Pictou Men's Club, in Shore Street, and 10 Coleraine Street. The single-storey, five-bay Pictou Men's Club closely resembles a Scottish improved cottage, despite its extra bays and raised foundation, not commonly found in Scotland. Pictou Men's Club was built (*c.* 1827) as the Pictou Town residence of Henry Blackadder, the County's member for the Nova Scotia House of Assembly (Fig. 62). Besides its overall classical proportions, the building also displays construction features commonly found in Scotland, particularly in the Lothian region around Edinburgh, such as stone 'skews': an additional stone course to the gable-ends, which raises the walls slightly above the roofline.[18]

Number 10 Coleraine Street is a small but architecturally significant building, reputedly dating from 1796 (Fig. 63). In this region steeped in Scottish Highland myth and memory, 10 Coleraine Street acquired the name of 'Long House', due to its elongated, rectangular plan, seemingly reminiscent of traditional blackhouses. This name, however, was inappropriate, as the unusual length of the building is simply due to a later timber-framed addition to one end. The first official record of the building's ownership dates from 1827, when the house was owned by a Scottish emigrant blacksmith, John McKay. The building has an unusual combination of stonewalling and a central hearth, a feature typically associated with timber-framed houses in Nova Scotia. It is also unique within the context of the stone buildings of Pictou Town, in that its stone walls are of a double-skin construction, separated by a central airspace of roughly thirty centimetres: a walling technique generally associated with the Scottish Highland blackhouse. In this respect, the building includes the only known example of traditional Highland building methods in Nova Scotia.[19] It is, however, probably not unique in Atlantic Canada, since recent archaeological excavations in Newfoundland have also found evidence of blackhouse construction.[20]

Perhaps the most readily identifiable Scottish construction feature in Pictou

62. Pictou Men's Club, Shore Street, Pictou Town (author)

63. 10 Coleraine Street, Pictou Town (author)

Town is the five-sided, canted dormer window (Fig. 64). This type of window construction is the only architectural element transferred directly from Scotland to have had any influence beyond the stone houses of Pictou Town, and to have transferred to timber-frame house construction in Nova Scotia. The Lowland masons working in Pictou Town were able to pursue their trade due to the high quality of the building stone along the nearby Northumberland Shore, a brown sandstone that was exported in the nineteenth century to Boston, New York (Brownstones), Philadelphia and throughout the American mid-west.[21]

The 1838 Census of Pictou County lists over twenty stonemasons and thirty-three house carpenters resident and working in early nineteenth-century Pictou Town. These builders were predominantly migrant Lowland Scots. The list of masons' names in the 1838 census for Pictou Town shows a predominance of names of Lowland origin, such as Burnett, Walker, Logan and Munro.[22] For instance, 46 Church Street is a two-and-a-half storey, stone-built house, similar to a contemporary Scottish inn in both form and function, built by the Lowland mason, John Lorrain (Fig. 65). The building was constructed in 1820 on a site purchased from a John Marshall for fifty pounds, and operated as 'Lorrain's Inn' in the early nineteenth century.[23] Lorrain's inn was advertised for sale in the *Colonial Patriot*, 18 June 1831:

> Tavern in Church Street known by the sign of John Lorrain's Inn . . . ,
> which has been fitted up in the neatest and best style. It can therefore
> warrant the most genteel and comfortable accommodation with the
> best attendance both to Travellers and private parties.[24]

The large number of stone houses and stonemasons active in Pictou Town was
an anomaly in early nineteenth-century Nova Scotia, where masons were
generally only required to lay foundations and build chimneystacks. The
relatively high number of stone buildings in Pictou reflects the port's high status
and its wealth in the early to mid nineteenth century – a United States Consulate
was established and numerous merchant shipping companies and boat building
yards flourished – a situation that attracted the Lowland masons. Pictou rapidly
grew to become the second busiest port in the province after Halifax, where the
labour force, also well-represented by Lowland Scots masons, was raising terraces
of stone-built town houses, warehouses and government buildings. Pictou
Town's 22 masons and 33 carpenters can be compared with the 10 stonemasons
and 35 carpenters working in the same period in Shelburne, or three masons and

64. Canted dormer windows: 70–72 Water Street, Pictou Town (author)

65. 'Lorrain's Inn', 46 Church Street, Pictou Town (author)

66 carpenters in Yarmouth, both county towns of similar size to Pictou Town on the South Shore, an area dominated in the late eighteenth and early nineteenth centuries by Loyalist settlers from New England.[25]

Classicism in Colonial Canada

The high degree of formal and stylistic uniformity, or 'architectural sameness', of the farmhouses of Pictou and Antigonish counties is clear. This is because like the improved tenant farmhouse in the Scottish Highlands they are classical buildings. As in the case of the improved farmhouse, the use of a classical system of proportion is evident in the consistent use of the ratio of 3:2 in the rectangular form of the elevation, floor plan and windows of houses across the survey group. The extensive use of classical ornament is also evident in both the exteriors and interiors of the houses, principally in the form of simple mouldings to openings, such as windows and doors; but this can extend to delicate Robert Adam-influenced demi-lune fanlights, as is the case in the Fraser House. Other houses feature combinations of pilasters capped with simple capitals applied to the outside edges of the main elevation or projecting dentil-moulded cornices. The MacGillivary House, Upper South River, Antigonish County (built *c.* 1830) features an ornate classical cornice, corner pilasters and classical mouldings to the doors and windows. Likewise, the interior of the McCulloch House, Pictou (*c.* 1820) features classical mouldings to the doorframes and skirting (Fig. 66).

As in Scotland, the successful execution of a classical building required the work of skilled craftsmen familiar with the principles of classical proportion and adept at modelling classical ornament. Pioneer colonial farmers lacking any architectural training could not build to such an exact specification. The Scottish Gaels brought neither the traditions of classical architectural composition nor of timber-frame construction with them from Scotland. Not only was no formal architectural training available in the Highlands but also there was no timber. The classical farmhouses of Antigonish and Pictou counties must therefore have been designed and built by craft-trained house carpenters, not by Gaelic farmer-landowners. Carpentry was a highly-trained craft tradition well-established in eighteenth-century colonial North America with guild organisations and traditions similar to the Scottish Freemasons. The 1838 census of Nova Scotia, the first

66. The parlour, McCulloch House, Pictou, Pictou County (author)

to include occupations, shows that at this date the number of house carpenters resident in Pictou and Antigonish Counties equalled that in southern counties such as Shelburne and Yarmouth. What is surprising is that the names of the house carpenters cited in the census for Pictou and Antigonish are predominantly of Scottish Highland origin, such as Macleod, MacKay, MacDonald and Fraser. This suggests that, although Highland emigrants in the late eighteenth century would initially have had to employ house carpenters already established in Nova Scotia, by the main phase of house construction in the 1830s and 1840s they had acquired the relevant trade skills and architectural knowledge to undertake such work themselves. There is no known documentary evidence relating to the organisation and training of house builders in Pictou and Antigonish counties, but, given the total lack of training in classical architectural in the Scottish Highlands, it is probable that those Scottish Gaelic names listed in the 1838 census refer to second generation immigrants, trained as apprentices in Nova Scotia, as the demand for houses – and therefore for house building skills – increased exponentially.

The architectural uniformity in those areas settled by Scottish Gaelic communities is consistent with early farmhouse architecture throughout Nova Scotia. There is no evidence of any formal properties or construction features that distinguish Scottish Gaelic homes from those found elsewhere in the province. For example, Ross Farm, New Ross, Lunenburg County, in central Nova Scotia to the south of Halifax, is a model example of the Nova Scotia farmhouse (Fig. 67). Ross Farm was built in 1817 by Nova Scotia-born Captain William Ross, who was one of 172 soldiers disbanded from the Nova Scotia Fencible Infantry at the end of the Napoleonic War, in 1816.[26] This building expresses through architectural form how Gaeldom was quickly assimilated into a wider British colonial culture, which extended throughout and beyond Nova Scotia.

The formal origins of the early farmhouses of Nova Scotia can be traced back to New England. The architectural link between Nova Scotia and New England was first noted in a 1962 article by pioneering historian Alan Gowan, in which he simply noted that, 'if you come to houses . . . from Nova Scotia, they will remind you of something you have seen in Maine or Massachusetts'.[27] More recently, in *Homeplace: the Making of the Canadian Dwelling*, Peter Ennals and Deryck Holdsworth have also concluded that 'housing solutions conveyed to the region by early colonists or planters and Loyalists offered a powerful model which was quickly absorbed by later arrivals from Britain'.[28]

The continental migration of New Englanders to Nova Scotia in the second

67. Ross Farm, New Ross, Lunenburg County, Nova Scotia, 1817 (author)

half of the eighteenth century was on a scale vastly greater to that of emigrants from any other sub-national or ethnic group, or geographic area. Following American Independence, many Loyalist refugee-settlers were able to build New England-style houses upon arrival in Nova Scotia, due to the British government's provision of tools and building materials, a helping hand that was not extended to Highland settlers in Pictou and Antigonish. Timber-framed houses were also imported in 'flat-pack' kit-form directly from New England. For example, T'her End, a typical five bay farmhouse at Chester, Lunenburg County (*c.* 1780), was imported from New England and then erected on the Chester waterfront by sea captain David Evans, who later served in the Royal Navy during the Napoleonic Wars.[29]

The classicism evident in Nova Scotia's farmhouses was initially imported from New England in the mid-to-late eighteenth century. In New England, the mid-to-late eighteenth century farmhouse had developed from an English timber-frame and clapboard house type introduced there by seventeenth-century emigrants from southern England. Through the eighteenth century, in parallel with architectural developments in Britain, including Scotland, not only bilateral symmetry of plan and elevation but also a classical system of proportion and ornament became commonplace in New England farmhouse design.[30]

The Architecture of the British Atlantic World

The dissemination of classicism in eighteenth-century New England followed the routes of migrant labour and imported architectural manuals between Britain and North America.[31] Research by Abbott Lowell Cummings has established that the earliest architectural text known to have been employed in New England was Joseph Moxon's eminently practical *Mechanick Exercises*, published in London in 1678.[32] Cummings has also demonstrated that the most popular titles available in eighteenth-century New England were William Salmon's *Palladio Londinensis* (London, 1737), Francis Price's *The British Carpenter* (London, 1753), and Batty Langley's *The Builder's Jewel* (London, 1741). Cummings has found evidence that at least 170 different architectural titles, all printed in London, were available in eighteenth-century New England. Amongst these titles, eighty-four surviving books have been linked with known buildings or house carpenters active in New England.[33]

In eighteenth-century Nova Scotia, British – or British American – architectural standards were introduced and established by the craftsmen who were amongst the early Planters and, later, Loyalist refugees from New England after American Independence. They were also imported in print directly from Britain by Halifax merchants, as can be traced through the pages of the *Halifax Gazette* (1752–67) and the *Nova Scotia Gazette* (1767–89). Trade advertisements show that the same imported texts used in the house construction industry in New England were also being imported into Halifax, for example:

> Just imported via Boston and to be sold by Robert Fletcher;
> Hoppus' Admeasurement of Timber; Ryland's Mechaniks;
> ree Mason's Pocket Companion.
> (*Nova Scotia Gazette*, 14 July 1772).[34]

Advertisements placed by Halifax merchants also provide evidence that the physical tools and architectural components of the building construction industry were also being imported:

> To be sold for ready money, by Joseph Scott at his store near
> Mr. Fairbanks wharf . . . The best assortment of Carpenters,
> Joyners, Masons, Bricklayers, Painterers and Shoe Makers tools:
> steel cross-cut saws, locks, hinges, nails and spikes of all size.
> (*Halifax Gazette*, Saturday 9 June 1753)[35]

> Just imported at Mr. Samuel Shipton's near the north gate . . . sashes
> painted and glaz'd 8 × 10, glass 8 × 10, 7 × 9 . . . bricks, lumber, and
> House frames of two-storeys, 36 × 18.
> (*Halifax, Gazette*, Saturday 18 April 1752).[36]

Although the connection between surviving houses, documented house carpenters and printed works in New England has thus been established, it has not yet been possible to make such definite connections for Nova Scotia and caution is therefore advisable; for while there is documentary evidence of the sale of imported architectural books, tools and components in Halifax, it is not possible to establish their actual use by known house carpenters in the province. All that can be inferred is that the continued sale of architecture-related texts and materials in Nova Scotia suggests that they were being used to produce the extant classically-designed farmhouses found throughout the province.

The economic mechanism behind this cultural transfer was, of course, the trade cycle between North American ports, such as Philadelphia, Boston and Halifax, and British ports such as Southampton, Plymouth, Bristol and Glasgow: the traffic in 'goods, persons, books and ideas'.[37] In this context, Scotland had a significant influence through the migration of Lowland masons as is evident in Pictou Town and Halifax. But in terms of print, London had an overwhelming influence as not only was it the centre of British book production but also the centre of transatlantic book distribution. London-printed books pervaded the stocks of booksellers throughout Britain and North America, 'disseminating a common culture to anyone with access to them'.[38]

In recent years historians of early modern Britain and North America, such as Bernard Bailyn, Nicholas Canny and Jack P. Greene, have explored the possibility of a 'British Atlantic World' that emerged in the seventeenth century and became established through the eighteenth century.[39] It is suggested that the principal movement within this British Atlantic world was an outwards ripple from London and the English Home Counties – the centre of eighteenth-century British politics, economics and culture – to a federation of sub-national groups spread throughout Britain and the British Atlantic.[40] Nova Scotia's position within the British Atlantic World was reflected in newspapers such as the *Halifax Gazette* and the *Colonial Patriot*, which regularly covered stories from locations such as London, Edinburgh, Glasgow, Dublin, Boston, New York, Philadelphia, Williamsburg, Charleston, Bermuda and the Caribbean. At a smaller scale, the geographer James T. Lemon's description of the position of the average English colonial farmer within eighteenth-century British North

America applies equally to the situation found in Scottish Gaelic settlements in Nova Scotia:

> [North] America was still a part of England and of Europe; in fact, from one perspective it was England and Europe on the move. Americans of European origin and descent organised themselves into households, local communities, and regional structures. At the household level, most lived much of their lives within nuclear families on dispersed farms largely held in freehold tenure . . . farmers were linked through political, religious, and economic institutions and social and cultural ties to England and to the larger Atlantic world.[41]

The Colonial Farmhouse and Gaelic Identity

Ennals and Holdsworth state that 'it is clear that the Scottish . . . folk dwelling did make its way to Atlantic Canada . . . quite simply stone and thatch were abandoned in favor of wood'.[42] While this may be true for materials and related construction, the presence of a broadly rectangular floor plan and a tendency towards bilateral symmetry in the Highland vernacular 'blackhouse' does not translate into the careful classical proportions and architectural mouldings of the early Nova Scotia farmhouse adopted by Highland immigrants. The history of the Highland house in North America is one of radical transformation, not of continuity. The timber-framed farmhouse, widespread in Nova Scotia before the arrival of the first Scottish Gaels, was universally imitated by them over both the traditional Highland vernacular and the pioneer log cabin. The deliberate transition from the stone-and-turf vernacular tradition to an unfamiliar, timber-framed, classical classically styled house type represents a total break with tradition and a desire to embrace the new and modern. Even if the choice of timber over stone might have been a practical choice, fields still had to be cleared of stones, and the elegant but poorly insulated New England timber-framed house was certainly not as straightforward a response to a new environment as would have been a log cabin, which would have been better insulated and easier to build. Indeed, there is evidence from Cape Breton that the desire to adopt the New England style even extended to the superficial cladding of log cabins with clapboard veneers to form a symmetrical, three-bay facade.[43]

The extant building stock in either Pictou County or Antigonish County offers no evidence to support the notion that Highland emigrants transferred the traditional architecture of the Highlands to North America, apart from a single and notable exception, that of the wall construction of 10 Coleraine Street, Pictou Town. The Highland Settler Project (under the direction of James Symonds, at Sheffield University) has carried out archaeological excavations of sites settled by pioneer emigrant Highland Gaels in Pictou County and Mabou, Inverness County, Cape Breton. These digs have also found no evidence of traditional Highland building forms or techniques. Instead, excavations have discovered stone foundations consistent with the standard Nova Scotia farmhouse.[44]

The Nova Scotia farmhouse was light and airy, in stark contrast with the windowless, smoke-filled Highland blackhouse. It was a new house for a new life: as a colonial farmer and landowner. The change in social status from that of tenant, or more often subtenant, in Scotland, with no legal security of tenure, to that of independent landowner was a massive cultural and economic shift for the typical Scottish Gaelic settler and the principal attraction of emigration to Nova Scotia. Nevertheless, certain elements of the Nova Scotia farmhouse could have exerted an appeal to the Highland settler's nostalgia. The Highland blackhouse and the Nova Scotia farmhouse are both symmetrical buildings with a rectangular plan and central fireplace. In the midst of the smooth plastered walls and classical architectural mouldings of its doors and windows, the central chimneystack of the Nova Scotian farmhouse would have evoked the central hearth of the blackhouse.[45] As James Symonds has observed, 'the hearth enclosed in a stone chimney-stack still stood at the centre of the house, a kind of fulcrum around which Gaelic society revolved. The long standing symbolism of the central hearth was retained in the new wooden houses, no doubt affording some spiritual comfort.'[46]

The rejection of a redundant, and incommodious, vernacular architectural tradition did not represent a loss of the Gaelic settlers' shared cultural identity. Indeed, settlers and their descendents maintained their Scottish Gaelic culture through their language, literature, music and dance. Instead it expressed a modern and improving attitude within a culturally vibrant Gaelic society when given the freedom of choice brought by relative prosperity and landownership.

As in Britain, and perhaps even more so in present day Nova Scotia, a romanticised nostalgia for the pre-improvement Highlands persists (Fig. 68). For instance, the 'Lone Shieling' was built in northern Cape Breton (in 1947), from field-cleared stones and with a thatched roof. It is a roughly three-quarter scale replica of a traditional Highland blackhouse. Yet the 'Lone Shieling' is not actually a Highland house but a monument to Nova Scotia's constructed

Highland memory. For, as James Symonds observes, 'the thought of assembling the necessary stones in order to construct a remembrance of home could only have occurred to later generations with sufficient leisure to indulge such sentimental inclinations.'[47]

It is possible that the adoption of the colonial house was intended as a display of political – British – allegiance. The building type was introduced in the 1760s by 'New England Planters', mainly from Connecticut, who settled in present-day Kings, Yarmouth, Annapolis, Shelburne and Queens counties. These early settlers were joined two decades later by Loyalist refugees from the newly-formed United States of America. The Scottish Gaels who adopted this house type were likewise famously loyal to the British government and monarchist.[48] From 1783 onwards, Nova Scotia became a focal point for British military and political activity, as can be seen from the name of Pictou's newspaper: *The Colonial Patriot*. Nevertheless, whilst Nova Scotia's colonial society was highly politically aware, such a consciousness did not translate to domestic architecture, as the same house type also continued to flourish in the independent United States, and to do so well into the nineteenth century.[49]

It is most likely that, as in the case of the tenant farmer in the Highlands,

68. Contemporary mural celebrating the arrival of the first Scottish Gaels on the *Hector*, Pictou Town (author)

building uniform houses expressed the Highlanders' new social standing, social conformity and sense of community'. The universal adoption of the classical colonial house form, over and above any pragmatic change in building materials – from sod and stone to timber – and in related construction techniques was a collective expression by the Scottish Gaelic community in Nova Scotia of their newly acquired status as landowners: simultaneously proud to be Gaelic and proud to be modern colonial farmers. Accordingly, as with the improved farmhouses of the Scottish Highlands the design of the colonial farmhouse places the social display of good taste above practical matters such as insulation and warmth. In this context, the high level of uniformity among the houses studied confirms a high level of social conformity within British colonial society in Nova Scotia. It also demonstrates a high level of social equality amongst settlers of all ethnic origins.

The social indicators of eighteenth-century British society are also evident in the typical farmhouse in Pictou or Antigonish County, Nova Scotia: a place similarly designed and maintained for the practice of the social theatre of eighteenth-century manners and etiquette. The regular, well-ordered front elevation, or façade of the colonial farmhouse, like the improved Highland farmhouse, acted as a highly visible statement of the occupants' good taste and membership of genteel British, or British Atlantic, society. In Pictou and Antigonish Counties, however, while considerable variation exists in the subdivision of interiors, there is almost none in the arrangement of the façade. The application of symmetrical clapboard façades to log cabins shows the importance for settlers of outward appearance, despite its seeming superficiality for us today.

The average Nova Scotian farmhouse inhabited by Scottish Gaelic settlers was not furnished with homemade Highland vernacular furniture but with local, artisan-made versions of fashionable, early-nineteenth-century furniture and imported ornaments, tableware, prints and books.[50] The social centre of the colonial farmhouse was the same decorated interior domestic space of the parlour, furnished with the same imported objects of British material culture, as that of the improved farmhouse in the Scottish Highlands. Both houses stood geographically at the edge of British society but both sought to recreate the same domestic spaces, filled with the same goods, as could be found in Edinburgh or London.

The trans-Atlantic migration of Scottish Gaels from the Scottish Highlands to Nova Scotia resulted in the transformation of their domestic architecture from the indigenous blackhouse tradition to timber-framed structures displaying a taste for contemporary architectural design. The almost total uniformity of

Scottish Gaelic settlers' houses in Pictou and Antigonish Counties demonstrates a conformity with contemporary British and British American architectural taste for the formal rules and ornament of classicism. Given freehold property and relative prosperity, the Scottish Gaels in North America chose to adopt the same architectural designs and social practices as the new modernising tenant farmers who had taken over their traditional farmlands in the Scottish Highlands. Yet, the same Scottish Gaelic colonial communities fiercely retained and upheld their traditional language, literature, music and dance. The evidence from Canada suggests that the Scottish Highland blackhouse held no particular cultural significance for the Scottish Gaels; it represented nothing more than effective shelter and was abandoned as soon as circumstance permitted. By contrast, for farmers and landowners throughout the British Atlantic world, including tenant farmers in the Highlands and colonial Gaelic farmers in Canada, a taste for the new classical architecture indicated wealth, status, education and modernity.[51]

Tables to Show House Building Patterns in the Scottish Highlands, 1700–1850

Table 1. Chronological periods of construction for listed rural domestic architecture across the Scottish Highlands, 1600–1850

Period of Construction	Caithness	Western Isles	NW Sutherland	SE Sutherland	Easter Ross and Cromarty	Wester Ross	Eastern Inverness-shire	Western Inverness-shire	Northern Argyll	Southern Argyll and Bute	Period Total
Early 17th										1	1
Mid 17th		1									1
Later 17th	1				1		1	1		2	6
Early 18th	1				2			1	1	1	6
Early–Mid 18th	1	1			3	1	2	1	4	3	16
Mid 18th	3	1	3		1	2	2	2	1	3	17
Mid–Late 18th	3	1	2	1	3	2	3	3	9	2	29
Later 18th	7	2	2	2	18	4	13	8	12	11	79
Late 18th–Early 19th	3	3	5	3	13	3	6	5	11	8	60
Early 19th	4	3	5	5	23	6	12	9	7	23	97
Early–Mid 19th	4	5	4	6	12	6	9	2	6	10	64
Mid 19th	5	1	1	1	8	2	8	2	1	2	31
Region Total	32	17	22	18	84	26	56	34	52	66	407
Re-modelled											
1750–1800	1	2		1	2		5		1	3	15
1800–1850	10	13	1	2	8		14	9	12	5	74
1850–1900	3	5	2		17	4	11	8			50

Chart 1.

Chronology of rural houses built in the Scottish Highlands, 1600–1850
(information taken from Scottish Statutory List, chronological periods as
recorded by Historic Scotland)

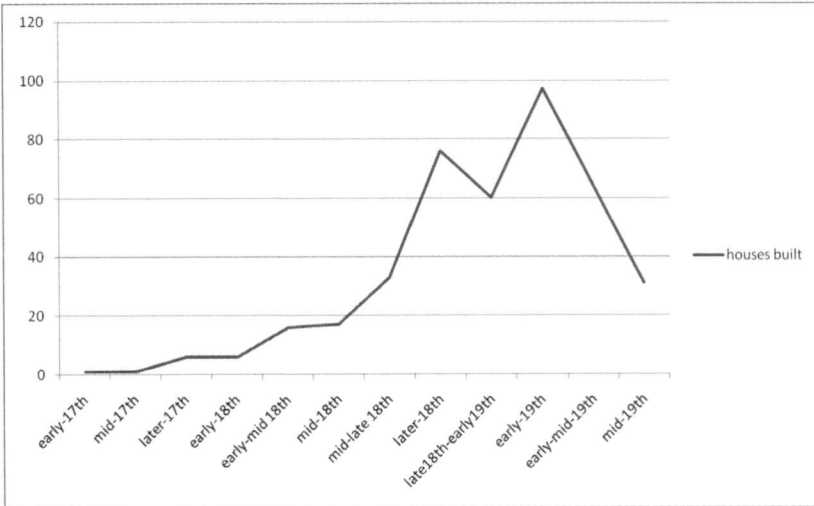

Table 2. Building materials, architectural form and ornament of listed rural domestic architecture across the Scottish Highlands, 1600–1850

Building Element	Caithness	Western Isles	NW Sutherland	SE Sutherland	Easter Ross and Cromarty	Wester Ross	Eastern Inverness	Western Inverness Skye & Isles	Northern Argyll	Southern Argyll & Bute	Highland Total
total number of houses	32	17	22	18	84	26	56	34	52	66	407
number greater than three bays	22	11	18	17	65	17	43	28	43	50	314
greater than three bays	11	6	4	1	19	9	13	6	9	16	94
walling technique											
render	29	15	18	17	54	24	34	23	38	48	300
render sides and rear	1	1	0	1	10	2	10	6	4	6	41
random or squared rubble	33	17	20	17	77	26	48	30	50	65	383
rubble with ashlar margins	25	4	16	14	53	19	45	19	6	24	225
ashlar	0	0	2	1	7	0	8	4	2	1	25
roof shape											
gabled	30	15	22	18	64	21	32	29	37	51	319

Building Element	Caithness	Western Isles	NW Sutherland	SE Sutherland	Easter Ross and Cromarty	Wester Ross	Eastern Inverness	Western Inverness Skye & Isles	Northern Argyll	Southern Argyll & Bute	Highland Total
crow-stepped gables	0	0	5	3	20	3	4	1	3	2	41
nepus gable	5	1	1	1	0	2	3	1	0	1	15
gabled with stone skews	7	7	2	2	15	4	5	2	8	11	63
hipped	3	2	0	0	20	5	24	5	15	15	89
roofing materials											
slates	33	17	22	18	84	26	56	34	52	66	408
pan-tiles	0	0	0	0	0	0	0	0	0	0	0
other	0	0	0	0	0	0	0	0	0	1	0
window shape											
principally tall rectangular	33	17	22	18	84	26	56	34	52	66	408
dormer windows	2	9	7	5	23	9	22	12	16	21	126
other	3	2	1	4	0	9	14	15	9	6	63
window frames											
multi-pane vertically sliding	33	14	22	18	84	26	54	34	52	65	402
sash and casement other	0	3	0	0	0	0	2	0	3	1	9

Table 2 continued

Building Element	Caithness	Western Isles	NW Sutherland	SE Sutherland	Easter Ross and Cromarty	Wester Ross	Eastern Inverness	Western Inverness Skye & Isles	Northern Argyll	Southern Argyll & Bute	Highland Total
doorway shape											
square head	33	17	22	18	84	0	52	31	51	64	400
other	0	0	0	0	0	0	2	3	1	2	8
storeys											
two storey	21	9	17	18	52	18	27	20	31	44	257
two storey with attic	6	8	3	0	14	8	12	13	13	10	87
two storey with attic and basement	0	0	0	0	13	1	7	1	13	2	37
two storey with basement	0	0	0	0	0	0	6	0	1	7	14
three storey +	5	0	2	0	5	1	4	0	7	3	27
elevation											
asymmetrical	5	1	4	2	5	1	2	3	2	1	26
symmetrical	28	16	18	16	79	25	54	31	50	65	382

Building Element	Caithness	Western Isles	NW Sutherland	SE Sutherland	Easter Ross and Cromarty	Wester Ross	Eastern Inverness	Western Inverness Skye & Isles	Northern Argyll	Southern Argyll & Bute	Highland Total
plan											
rectangular	21	11	15	14	69	21	31	23	42	57	304
M-gable	3	0	1	0	1	2	2	1	2	1	13
L-plan	5	4	5	4	4	2	5	3	5	3	40
T-plan	1	1	0	0	4	0	7	5	2	2	22
U-plan	3	1	1	0	4	1	8	2	1	2	23
H-plan	0	0	0	0	2	0	3	0	0	0	5
number of bays											
three	23	16	18	15	65	17	43	28	43	50	318
four	2	0	2	1	0	1	1	0	0	3	10
five	7	1	2	2	15	6	8	3	8	9	61
six +	1	0	0	0	4	2	4	3	1	4	19
additions											
single storey wings to sides	10	1	3	4	11	4	8	7	7	11	66
two storey wings to sides	2	0	0	1	5	1	1	0	2	3	15
single storey wing to one side	1	3	1	4	8	5	3	3	7	9	44
two storey wing to one side	1	0	4	4	6	3	2	4	0	0	24

Table 2 continued

Building Element	Caithness	Western Isles	NW Sutherland	SE Sutherland	Easter Ross and Cromarty	Wester Ross	Eastern Inverness	Western Inverness Skye & Isles	Northern Argyll	Southern Argyll & Bute	Highland Total
additions (continued)											
bowed/canted bays	0	0	0	0	13	4	18	2	1	8	46
addition to rear	9	7	8	11	34	7	38	17	18	21	170
stair tower	4	0	1	2	2	1	5	4	2	2	23
porch	5	7	6	10	16	6	19	12	15	6	102
Classical ornament											
portico with columns	1	0	0	0	13	1	7	3	3	7	35
portico with pilasters	1	0	1	1	7	0	5	0	4	12	31
entrance stair	2	0	2	0	12	3	10	3	0	9	41
wallhead cornice	10	0	2	2	16	2	15	6	5	14	72
window/door mouldings	12	0	5	2	34	3	22	5	13	23	119
central pediment	2	0	1	1	3	2	6	2	3	10	30
string or band course	4	0	0	6	22	0	15	2	1	21	71
Historic Revival ornament	5	0	2	2	9	1	3	0	3	5	30
Listed steadings	8	4	8	5	16	12	13	10	11	19	106

APPENDIX 2

Table to show Building Patterns at the Planned Villages of Ullapool and Tobermory, 1786–1820

Details of properties		Ullapool	Tobermory
Walling material	sandstone	26	27
Walling technique	random rubble	22	25
	square-cut blocks	4	2
Roof shape	gabled	26	27
	stone copings	12	0
Roofing materials	thick slates	26	27
Window shape	square	3	2
	rectangular	23	25
	gabled dormer windows	16	11
Window frames	vertically sliding sash	26	27
Doorway shape	square head	26	27
Number of storeys	single storey	5	2
	one-and-a-half storey	15	11
	two storey	5	12
	two-and-a-half storey	1	2
Plan	asymmetrical rectangular	3	5
	symmetrical rectangular	23	22
Links	individual house	8	4
	semi-detached	8	1
	part of a row	10	22

APPENDIX 3

British Fisheries Society Catalogue of Works

Tobermory

Town Plan: James Maxwell, 1790. Hierarchical grid-plan focused upon waterfront industrial buildings.[1]

Harbour: breastwork: contractor, Stevensons of Oban, 1789–91. 700ft. £600. Pier: civil engineer; Thomas Telford, contractor; Stevensons of Oban, 1814; £8,000. 300ft. Stone rubble.[2]

Inn: architect, Robert Mylne; contractor, Stevensons of Oban, 1790; minor alts. Thomas Telford, 1791; £792. Symmetrical two-storey, three-bay, rectangular-plan gabled building with single storey wings. Harled random rubble, slate roof.[3]

Storehouse: design by James Maxwell; contractor, Rodgers and Richardson of Stanley, Perthshire, 1789; alts. 1792 to form King's Warehouse. £693. Symmetrical three-storey, rectangular-plan gabled building (60ft x 18 ft x 24ft). Harled random rubble, slate roof (demolished).[4]

Customs House and Officers' Lodgings: designed by James Maxwell; contractor, Stevenson of Oban, 1789–91. £484. Two symmetrical two-storey, rectangular-plan buildings with hipped roofs 'arranged at right angles to the storehouse to form a courtyard'. Harled, random rubble, slate roofs (demolished).[5]

Bridge, Water of Baliscate: architect, Thomas Telford; contractor, Stevenson of Oban, 1792–3. Single span, stone bridge with raised parapets.[6]

Smithy: contractor, Rodgers and Richardson, 1790. £110. Single-storey, rectangular-plan, gabled structure (demolished).[7]

Boat Builder's Shed: architect, Thomas Telford; contractor, Rodgers and Richardson, completed by tenant David Urquhart, 1789–92. Single-storey, three-bay, rectangular-plan building with hipped roof. Harled random rubble, slate roof (demolished).[8]

Ullapool

Town Plan: David Aitken, 1789. Simple grid-plan focused upon waterfront industrial buildings. Regularity of grid compromised by early building contractors Meville and Miller.[9]

Harbour: military engineer, Sir John Call; contractor, Melville and Miller of Edinburgh, 1789–90. £4,629 7s 9d. 136ft pier and breakwater. Infilled random rubble (marked F on Geanies' plan).[10]

Inn: architect, Robert Mylne; contractor, Roderick Morrison of Tanera, Lochbroom, 1788–90. £450. Symmetrical two-storey, three-bay, rectangular-plan, gabled building with single storey wings. Harled random rubble, slate roof (not marked on Geanies' plan. Located to right of building K).[11]

Great Storehouse: contractor, William Cowie of Tain, Inverness-shire, 1789–90. Symmetrical three-storey, rectangular-plan building with hipped roof high, external forestair. Harled random rubble, slate roof (marked L on Geanies' plan).[12]

Storehouse: contractor, Miller and Melville, 1788. £350. Asymmetrical two-storey, trapezoid-plan building with hipped roof (46 ft x 14 ft x 12.5 ft) Random rubble lined with brick, pantiled roof, tiles imported from Aberdeen (demolished) (marked I on Geanies' plan).[13]

Red Herring House: contractor, Melville and Miller, 1788–9. £268. Symmetrical two-storey, rectangular-plan, gabled building (18 ft x 110 ft long x 22 ft). Random rubble originally with pantiled roof. Internally subdivided into six smoking rooms containing wooden hanging frames (marked G on Geanies' plan).[14]

The Shades: Artisans workshops. Contractor, Melville and Miller, 1788. £186. Symmetrical single-storey, square-plan building (36ft x 36ft). Open sided, stone pillars supporting pantiled, hipped roof (demolished) (marked H on Geanies' plan).[15]

Church and Schoolmaster's House: contractor, Melville and Miller, 1789–90. £197. Single-storey, rectangular-plan, gabled building with timber-galleried interior. Random rubble with pantiled roof (demolished). Minister housed in adjacent cottage of similar dimensions as artisans' cottages (demolished). Replaced by Parliamentary Highland Church and Manse (street DD on Geanies' plan).[16]

Artisans' Houses: 'Red Row', West Argyll Street. Contractor, Melville and Miller, 1788–9. £156. Terrace of six plain single-storey, gabled cottages (22ft x 13ft x 7ft). Random rubble originally with pantiled roofs rehung with slates (street DD on Geanies' plan).[17]

Lochbay

Town Plan: Thomas Telford, 1790–1. Planned as series of crescents linking two town squares; one semicircular, one lozenge-shaped (unexecuted).[18]

Harbour: civil engineers, Sir John Rennie and Thomas Telford; contractor, John Forsyth of Avoch, 1796–1800. Completed by Abercrombie of Glasgow, 1800–2. £1,246. Pier, 100ft. Breastwork 60ft. Infilled random rubble.[19]

Inn: architect, Thomas Telford; contractor, Angus Shaw of Dunvegan, 1790. Estimated at £30, settled for £299 in 1801. Single-storey, rectangular-plan, gabled building intended as a temporary structure (90ft x 15ft x 9ft). Random rubble with thatched roof (demolished). Present Stein Inn probably built early 1800s by landlord Donald Maclean.[20]

Storehouse: architect, Thomas Telford; contract, John Forsyth of Avoch, 1795. £116. Single-storey, rectangular-plan gabled building (60ft x 20ft x 18ft). Random rubble, brick floor, slate roof, external forestair (demolished).[21]

Church and Schoolhouse: architect, Thomas Telford; contractor, John Forsyth of Avoch, 1793–6. £170. Single-storey, rectangular-plan, gabled building. Random rubble with thatched roof (demolished). Elegant neoclassical design by Telford rejected due to high expense (estimated at £882). Superseded by Waternish Parish Church and Manse (Parliamentary Highland Church).[22]

Smithy: architect, Thomas Telford; contractor, John Forsyth of Avoch, 1798–9. £88. Plain single-storey, three-bay, rectangular-plan gabled building. Random rubble with slate roof (ruinous).[23]

Fishermen's Cottages: contractor, James Cummings, Dunvegan, Skye, 1795. £343. Terrace of four single-storey, gabled cottages. Random rubble with thatched roof. Built at suggestion of Society's agent, Dr Porter, to attract settlers (ruinous by 1823).[24]

The British Fisheries Society's lands at Lochbay were sold to Macdonald of Skeabost for £2,800 in 1837.[25]

Pulteneytown

Town Plan: Thomas Telford, draft plan 1807, final plan 1810. Town plan divided into residential zone and industrial zone. Residential zone laid out in crescents around a central square. Industrial zone laid out in strict grid-pan.[26]

Harbour: civil engineer, Thomas Telford; contractor, George Burn of Wick, 1807–13. Estimated cost £10,000 (£7,500 provided by Highlands Harbours, Roads and Bridges Commission). Final cost £12,669. Large harbour basin abutting warehouse wharves, enclosed by two piers and breakwater: south pier, 600ft; breakwater, 560ft; breastwork, 280ft; north pier, 280ft. Second harbour: engineer, Joseph Mitchell; contractor, George Burn, 1820. £2,828, paid with revenue form harbour dues. Smaller rectangular basin (230ft x 560ft).[27]

Inn: 'The Round House'. Architect, Thomas Telford; contractor, George Burn, 1808. Cost unknown. Symmetrical two-storey, three-bay, rectangular-plan building with bowed advanced bays, oversailing eaves to hipped roof. Harled Caithness slabstone with slate roof. Burn took the building as his own house on completion.[28]

Warehouses: building regulations by Thomas Telford, tenants self-build. 1807–17. Symmetrical three-storey, rectangular-plan gabled buildings with arched-pend to centre (60ft x 22ft x 18ft). Squared Caithness slab-stone with slate roofs (mostly semi-ruinous).[29]

Water Mill: architect, Thomas Telford; contractor, George Burn; timber mill machinery by John Sinclair of Watten, Caithness, 1808–9. £649. Three-storey, rectangular-plan gabled building. Squared Caithness slab-stone with slate roof (demolished).[30]

Wick Bridge: architect, Thomas Telford; contractor, George Burn, 1805–7. £2,000 (£1,000 funded by Highlands Harbours, Roads and Bridges Commission. £517 funded by the Corporation of Wick). Three-span bridge, elliptical arches, raised parapets (156ft x 30ft). Squared Caithness slab-stones (demolished 1875).[31]

Roads: Bridge of Wick to Harbour Road: Civil engineer, Thomas Telford; contractor, George Ross, 1808. £70. Metalled surface (18ft x 600ft). Harbour to New Town Road: contractor, George Burn, 1807–9. £22. Metalled surface (18ft x 150ft). 'The Black Steps': broad flight of stone steps from Harbour to New Town; engineer Joseph Mitchell; contract, George Burn, 1820.[32]

Watercourse: civil engineer, Thomas Telford; contractor, George Ross of Tain, Inverness-shire, 1807–8. £4,475. Stone-faced culvert from Loch of Hempriggs to Pulteneytown (3ft x 12ft x 2 miles with 112ft underground). Work included six stone-built single-span bridges (5ft x 17ft) (mostly demolished).[33]

Table to show House Building Patterns in Nova Scotia, 1780–1850

Table 1.
Survey of houses in Pictou and Antigonish counties, 1780–1850

	Antigonish Sub-total	Pictou Sub-total	Total
Date of original construction			
1780s	0	2	2
1790s	1	0	1
1800s	10	6	16
1810s	3	6	9
1820s	17	28	45
1830s	35	91	126
1840s	139	142	281
1850s	0	50	50
House types			
Farmhouse	200	269	469
Town house	4	45	49
Tenement and shop	1	7	8
Inn	0	1	1
Mansion	0	2	2
Number of settlements	58	99	157
Number of houses	205	324	529
Origin of builder (farm owner)			
Acadian (France)	62	18	80
Ireland	11	6	17
USA	8	19	27
Scotland	123	246	369
England	4	32	36

Table 2.

Form and ornamentation of houses in Pictou and Antigonish counties,
1780–1850

	Antigonish sub-total	Pictou sub-total	Total
Plan			
Rectangular	194	272	466
Square	2	4	6
Temple	5	38	43
L-Plan	4	8	12
Cross-Plan	0	1	1
Elevation Symmetrical			
Yes	177	245	422
No	28	79	107
Number of bays			
2	10	55	65
3	121	198	319
4	9	16	25
5	65	52	117
6	0	3	3
Number of storeys			
1	2	7	9
1½	195	270	465
2	7	22	29
2½	1	23	24
3	0	2	2
3½	0	0	0
Main windows: type			
Rectangular	200	318	518
Square	1	2	3
Other	4	4	8
Chimney			
Central	144	198	342

Table 3.
Materials and construction of houses in Pictou and Antigonish counties,
1780–1850

	Antigonish sub-total	Pictou sub-total	Total
Wall			
Wood			
Log	0	1	1
Boards	118	216	334
Shingles	49	46	95
Vinyl	38	45	83
Brick	0	2	2
Stone			
Mason Squared	0	11	11
Rubble	0	3	3
Basement			
Stone	199	294	493
Brick	0	6	6
Concrete	6	11	17
None	0	3	3
Roof			
Gable	198	308	506
Flat gable	2	4	6
Salt box	12	2	14
Hipped	3	10	13
Dormer windows			
Shed dormer	14	31	45
Wallhead Gabled	19	23	42
Wallhead Canted	0	1	1
Roof gabled	42	50	92
Roof canted	2	13	15
Gable end	128	217	345
2-Symmetrical	7	34	41
1-Symmetrical to centre	43	40	83
3-Symmetrical	0	1	1
Gothic	11	16	27

	Antigonish sub-total	Pictou sub-total	Total
Chimney			
Stone	18	48	66
Brick	139	238	377
Stovepipe	36	16	52
None	12	23	35
Door			
Wood	171	240	411
Other	34	84	118
Margins			
Timber	165	221	386
Other	0	17	17
None	40	87	127
Windows			
Modern	56	77	133
Sash and case			
2-Pane	8	72	80
4-Pane	53	86	139
8-Pane	27	12	39
12-Pane	61	77	138
Roof			
Wooden			
Shingles	21	6	27
Other	0	0	0
Tin			
Modern	7	16	23
Old	14	23	37
Asphalt tiles	163	278	441
Slates	0	1	1
Construction			
Frame built	205	310	515
Other	0	14	14
Off Centre	30	28	58
Gable	10	31	41
Multiple Centre	12	36	48
Multiple Gable	2	10	12

	Antigonish sub-total	Pictou sub-total	Total
Door			
Central	173	241	414
Off Centre	28	75	103
Left	3	4	7
Right	1	4	5
Ornament			
Door pediments	31	38	69
Door pilasters	31	32	63
Door fanlight	28	43	71
Moulded door frame	54	98	152
Moulded window frames	62	105	167
Cornice (wallhead)	35	60	95
Pilasters to corner – plain	30	64	94
Pilasters to corner – ornate	18	12	30
Additions			
Single storey			
Left	48	40	88
Right	30	45	75
Rear	29	47	76
Two-storey			
Left	2	3	5
Right	4	4	8
Rear	5	2	7
Porch	31	76	107
Pedimented advanced porch	0	5	5

Table 4.
Skilled timber and stone workers resident in four Nova Scotia counties, 1838*

	Pictou Town	*Pictou*	*Antigonish*	*Shelburne*	*Yarmouth*
Masons	22	12	3	10	3
Carpenters	33	27	15	35	60
Shipwrights	8	–	–	–	–
Joiners	4	–	–	3	4
Cabinetmakers	5	–	–	1	1

* K. E. Mackay, 1838 Census of Pictou County, Genealogical Association of Nova Scotia, Halifax, 1995, transcribed from original manuscripts: RG1/vol. 449/166a–166f; 1838 Census of Antigonish County, Genealogical Association of Nova Scotia, Halifax, 1999. Transcribed from original manuscripts: RG1/vol. 449/176–9; 1838 Census of Shelburne and Yarmouth Counties, Genealogical Association of Nova Scotia, Halifax, 2002, transcribed from original manuscripts: RG1/vol. 449/170–183.

Notes

Introduction

1. A particular debt is owed to historians Robert Clyde, Tom Devine, Robert Dodgshon, Allan Macinnes, Andrew Mackillop, Eric Richards and Christopher Whatley who have in recent years changed our understanding of the social and economic history of the Highlands in the eighteenth century and advanced the debate surrounding the question of Highland, Scottish and British identity in the eighteenth and nineteenth centuries.

2. The Highland line runs from the Kintyre peninsula in the southwest through Perthshire in central Scotland, and through Highland Aberdeenshire to the northeast coast. The southwest Highlands comprise Argyll and the Isle of Bute. The Central Highlands are the Grampian Mountains and the coastal plain of the Laigh of Moray. The Northern Highlands include the flat boggy country of Caithness and Sutherland, Ross and Cromarty and the Black Isle and the area around the Beauly Firth, Inverness-shire. The Inner Hebrides are made up of numerous small islands lying close to the mainland including the principal isles of Skye, Mull, Jura and Islay. The Outer Hebrides, or Western Isles, are dominated by the Long Isle of Lewis, the Uists and include the small remote island of St Kilda.

3. Elizabeth McKellar and Barbara Arciszewska (eds), *Articulating British Classicism: New Approaches to Eighteenth-Century Classicism* (Aldershot, 2004). Another recent exception is Peter Guillery, *The Small House in Eighteenth-Century London: a social and architectural history* (London, 2004). The framework of material culture is a well-established approach in North American architectural history; see, for example, Bernard L. Herman and Gabrielle M. Lanier, *Everyday Architecture of the Mid-Atlantic: Looking at Buildings and Landscapes* (Baltimore, 1997).

4. Alfred L. Kroeber, *Style and Civilisations* (Cornell, 1957); S. J. Shennan (ed.), *Archaeological Approaches to Cultural Identity* (London, 1989).

5. See Amanda Vickery and John Styles (eds), *Gender, Taste and Material Culture in Britain and North America, 1700–1830* (New Haven, 2006), pp. 23–5. Also Guillery, *The Small House in Eighteenth-Century London.*

6. Shennan, *Archaeological Approaches to Cultural Identity*, p. 2.

7. Marjory Harper and Michael E. Vance (eds), *Myth, Migration and the Making of Memory: Scotia and Nova Scotia c.1700–1900* (Halifax, 1999).

8. John S. Martell, *Immigration* (Halifax, 1942).

9. John D. Kornwolf, *Architecture and Town Planning in Colonial North America* (Baltimore, 2002); Peter Ennals and Deryck Holdsworth, *Homeplace: the making of the Canadian dwelling over three centuries* (Toronto, 1998).

10. See Robert Olwell and Alan Tully (eds), *Cultures and Identities in Colonial British America* (Baltimore, 2006); Elizabeth Mancke and Carole Shammas (eds), *The Creation of the British Atlantic World* (Baltimore, 2005); David Armitage and Michael Braddick (eds), *The British Atlantic World, 1500–1800,* (New York, 2002).

Chapter 1

1. T. C. Smout, *A History of the Scottish People 1560–1830* (London, 1969), pp. 270–80.
2. Roger A. Dodgshon, *From Chiefs to Landlords; social and economic change in the Western Highlands, c. 1493–1820* (Edinburgh, 1998), p. 50.
3. Tom M. Devine, *Clanship to Crofters' War: the social transformation of the Scottish Highlands* (Manchester, 1994), pp. 6–13.
4. Thomas Garnett, *Observations on a tour through the Highlands and part of the Western Isles of Scotland (*London, 1800).
5. Ingval Maxwell. *Building Materials of the Scottish Farmstead* (Edinburgh, 1996), p. 1. The folk-culture approach to Highland material culture, embodied by I.F. Grant's *Highland Folk Ways*, that typified early enquiries into the Highland blackhouse tradition is today complimented by the scientific methodologies of university-based researchers and professional archaeology teams, and the research and publication programmes of the Scottish Vernacular Building Working Group, Royal Commission on the Historic and Ancient Monuments of Scotland and Historic Scotland's Technical Conservation Research and Education Unit.
6. In 'Traditional Dwellings of the Uists', *Highland Vernacular Building*, SVBWG (Edinburgh, 1989), pp. 51–70, Bruce Walker has argued that, notwithstanding the numerous regional variations in walling and roofing materials and construction, the differences between the western Highlands and the Central Highlands have been exaggerated and that longhouses were also common in central and eastern Scotland in the early eighteenth century. Excavations of four settlement mounds on the *machair* at Bornais, Uist, led by Niall Sharples, have traced the origin of the Western Isles longhouse to Norse settlements of the ninth century. See N. Sharples (ed.), *A Norse Farmstead in the Outer Hebrides: Excavations at Mound 3, Bornais, South Uist* (Oxbow, 2005).
7. Bruce Walker, 'Earth Building in Scotland', *Terra Britannica*, ICOMOS UK (London, 2000), pp. 22–3.
8. SAS/ vol. 14, p. 111, Lochcarron: County of Ross and Cromarty.
9. Proverb and translation provided by Scott Sutherland of Dualchas Building Design, Skye
10. Richard Ayton, *A Voyage Round Great Britain in the Summer of 1813* (London, 1815), p. 180.
11. Devine, *Clanship to Crofters' War*, p. 5.
12. Devine, *Clanship to Crofters' War*, p. 34.
13. John Macleod, 'Morvern Parish', *New Statistical Account of Scotland* (Edinburgh, 1843), p. 177.
14. Samuel Johnson, *A Journey to the Western Islands of Scotland in 1773* (London, 1775, reprint Edinburgh, 1996), pp. 88–9.
15. Peter Beacham (ed.), *Devon Buildings: an introduction to local traditions* (Exeter, 1995 second edition), pp. 47–59.
16. Ronald W. Brunskill, *Houses and Cottages of Britain: origins and development of traditional buildings* (London, 1997), p. 58.
17. S. J. Langdon, *The Native People of Alaska* (Anchorage, 2002), pp. 18–26.
18. Alexander Broadie, *The Scottish Enlightenment* (Edinburgh, 2001), p. 38

19. Henry Home, Lord Kames, *Elucidations respecting the Common and Statute Law of Scotland* (1777), new edn (Edinburgh, 1800), xiii (Preface); idem, *Law-Tracts*, p. 57. Cited in David Spadafora, *The Idea of Progress in Eighteenth-Century Britain* (New Haven, 1990) p. 302.
20. David Spadafora, *The Idea of Progress in Eighteenth-Century Britain*, p. 253
21. David Turnock, *The Making of the Scottish Rural Lanscape*, (Aldershot, 1995) p. 195.
22. Captain John Henderson, *A General View of the Agriculture of the County of Caithness, with observations on the means of its improvement, Drawn up for the Consideration of the Board of Agriculture and Internal Improvement. With an appendix including an account of the improvements carried on by Sir John Sinclair (founder and first president, of the Board of Agriculture) on his estates in Scotland* (London, 1812), p. 25.
23. Colin Kidd, *Subverting Scotland's Past; Scottish Whig historians and the creation of an Anglo-British identity, 1789–1830* (Cambridge, 1993), p. 164. Although a catalyst for agricultural economic improvement, Entail was considered by the English Establishment as one of the most outrageous examples of Scotland's legal backwardness. The local Sheriff Clerk registered all estates under entail, records of which can be found in the National Archives of Scotland.
24. SAS/vol. 2, p. 318, Cockpen: County of Edinburgh
25. SAS/vol. 3, p. 153–8, Bunkle and Preston: County of Berwick.
26. SAS/vol. 3, p. 158; vol. 3, p. 386: Channelkirk: County of Berwick
27. Devine, *Clanship to Crofters' War*, pp. 15–25.
28. SAS/vol. 6, p. 176, Ardchattan: County of Argyll
29. David Spadafora, *The Idea of Progress in Eighteenth-Century Britain*, p. 267.
30. Devine, *Clanship to Crofters' War*, p. 17.
31. Devine, *Clanship to Crofters' War*, p. 6.
32. Samuel Johnson, *A Journey to the Western Islands of Scotland*, p. 50.
33. Allan Macinnes, *Clanship, Commerce and the House of Stewart, 1603–1788* (East Linton, 1996) p. 195.
34. Macinnes, *Clanship and Commerce*, p.195.
35. A full account of works at Inveraray by a range of fashionable architects from John Adam to Robert Mylne can be found in Mary Cosh & Ian Lindsay, *Inveraray and the Dukes of Argyll* (Edinburgh, 1973).
36. Devine, *Clanship to Crofters' War*, p. 31.
37. Dodgshon, *From Chiefs to Landlords*, pp. 31–50.
38. Devine, *Clanship to Crofters' War*, pp. 26–7; Robert Clyde, *From Rebel to Hero: The Image of the Highlander, 1745–1830* (East Linton, 1995).
39. Dodgshon, *From Chiefs to Landlords*, p. 240.
40. Andrew Mackillop, *More Fruitful than the Soil: Army, Empire and the Scottish Highlands, 1715–1830* (East Linton, 2000), p. 192.
41. David Turnock, *The Making of the Rural Scottish Landscape*, p. 222.
42. Christopher Powell, *The British Building Industry since 1800: an economic history*, 2nd edn (London, 1996), p. 19.
43. John Muckarsie, Parish of Kirklistoun, County of Edinburgh, *Old Statistical Account* (Edinburgh, 1791–9), pp. 10, 71.
44. George Fraser, Parish of Monedie, County of Perth, *Old Statistical Account*, 3, p. 272.
45. National Monuments Record Service of Scotland/NG37SE.
46. David Jones, 'Living in Two Rooms in the Country', in Annette Carruthers (ed.), *The Scottish Home* (Edinburgh, 1996) p. 44.

Chapter 2

1. The Scottish Statutory Lists can provide historians with a panoramic sketch of historic building activity. There are some problems in the use of the Statutory Lists in this way but this is because they were instigated as a rapid geographical survey to flag buildings for certain treatment under the planning laws, not in order to create a catalogue as the basis of serious research projects. Historic Scotland's listed building criteria are:

   'All buildings erected prior to 1840 which are of any quality, even if plain, and survive in anything like their original form are listed . . . In choosing buildings, besides age, particular attention is paid to:

   i) the works of better known architects
   ii) the special value of particular building types
   iii) technological innovation or virtuosity
   iv) distinctive regional variation in design and use of materials
   v) significant association with well known persons
   vi) group value . . . townscapes and landscape value.'

   Planning (Listed Buildings and Conservation Areas)(Scotland) Act 1997. Historic Scotland, *Memorandum of Guidance on Listed Buildings and Conservation Areas* (Edinburgh, 1998), 1.8.

2. T. C. Smout, *A History of the Scottish People* (London, 1969), p. 272.

3. All information is based upon the statistical analysis of Historic Scotland's Statutory List and Supplementary Listed Building Descriptions. The survey incorporates all listed domestic architecture within the following Council districts as defined by Historic Scotland (2007): Highland (incorporating survey regions of Caithness, North Western and South Eastern Sutherland); Ross and Cromarty (incorporating Easter Ross and Cromarty and Wester Ross); Inverness (incorporating Eastern Inverness-shire and Western Inverness-shire including Skye and the Small Isles); Western Isles (incorporating Lewis, Harris, North Uist, South Uist, Barra and smaller isles); Argyll and Bute (incorporating Northern Argyll including Mull, Coll, Tiree and smaller isles and Southern Argyll and Bute including the Isle of Bute peninsula, Jura, Islay, Colonsay and Oronsay, Gigha and smaller isles). The Highlands also incorporates the western edge of Aberdeenshire and the northern region of Perthshire. However, these fringe areas are not included in the statistical survey data due to the inaccuracy of extrapolating sub-regional information from the regions of Perthshire and Aberdeenshire in their entirety and related problems in the comparison of fragmentary data to other Highland regions. The quantitative regional occurrences of specific building elements within each region are collated from the statutory listed building descriptions produced by Historic Scotland for each individual listed building. The resultant statistics cannot be definitive but serve as a useful indicator of regional building trends; listed building descriptions, ranging in date of listing from 1971 to 2005, contain a degree of variance in the detail provided, some buildings have not survived, and some extant buildings are not currently listed. The terms used for periods of construction are those used by Historic Scotland. The variety of overlapping terminology used for different periods requires that the statistics for each term must be recorded and then collated into wider time periods (for example, the terms later 18th, later 18th–early 19th and early 19th are taken together to broadly cover the period 1775–1825).

4. The survey evidence shows a distinction between houses of three bays or less and houses of more than three bays. In terms of building type this correlates to the maximum width of a typical improvement-era farmhouse of three bays and the

minimum width of a typical improvement era small-landowner's house of five bays. The clear social distinction evident between three and five bay houses relates to the eighteenth century notion of decorum discussed in chapter three.

5. Glen L. Pride, *Glossary of Scottish Building* (Edinburgh, 1975), p. 46.
6. Historic Scotland's listings do not regularly detail the type of stone used. This is because the prevalence of harling to buildings makes it impossible to ascertain without a detailed physical investigation.
7. Ingval Maxwell, *Building Materials of the Scottish Countryside*, SVBWG Regional and Thematic Studies No. 3 (Edinburgh, 1996), pp. 12–13.
8. John Dunbar, *The Historic Architecture of Scotland* (London, 1966), p. 241.
9. Mary Cosh and Ian Lindsay, *Inveraray and the Dukes of Argyll* (Edinburgh, 1973), pp. 100–35. For further information on steadings see J. Robinson, *Georgian Model Farms: a study of decorative and model farm buildings in the Age of Improvement, 1770–1846* (Oxford, 1983).
10. Bruce Walker, *Farm Buildings in the Grampian Region* (Aberdeen, 1978), p. 49.
11. NSA/ vol.14, p. 47: Resolis, County of Ross and Cromarty.
12. Information supplied to Historic Scotland by Camille Dresser, Isle of Eigg Archive Project, 1998.
13. Scheduled Monument (No 5872).
14. Colin McWilliam, *Scottish Townscape* (Edinburgh, 1975), p. 87. For further information on road building in the Highlands see A. R. B. Haldane, *New Ways Through the Glens* (London, 1962; reprinted 1995).
15. William Daniel, *A Voyage Round the Coast of Scotland and the Adjacent Islands* (London, 1817–22), p. 261.
16. NAS/SC29/64/1–2 pp. 132–85, 341–472.
17. Sir George Mackenzie, *A General View of the Agriculture of the Counties of Ross and Cromarty* (Edinburgh, 1820), p. 262.
18. NAS/GD9/3/144
19. RCAHMS, *Inventory of Argyll*, 7 (Edinburgh, 1994), p. 443.
20. Samuel Johnson, *A Journey to the Western Islands of Scotland* (London, 1775), p. 140.
21. NAS/GD9/3/553; NAS/GD9/4/248. An 1812 sketch of the harbour front at Tobermory by William Daniel shows the inn completed according to Mylne's design. However, the inn was subsequently extended and latterly converted into a supermarket.
22. James Loch, *An Account of the Improvements on the Estate of Lord Stafford* (Edinburgh, 1820), plate 5.
23. John Dunbar, *The Historic Architecture of Scotland* (London, 1966), pp. 87–8.
24. John Gifford, *Buildings of Scotland: Dumfries and Galloway* (London, 1996), p. 84.
25. Smout, *A History of the Scottish People*, p. 261.
26. Gifford, *Buildings of Scotland: Dumfries and Galloway*, p. 85.
27. Jane Geddes, *Deeside and the Mearns: An Illustrated Architectural Guide* (Edinburgh, 2001) 137; RCAHMS/NMRS/A16996.
28. RCAHMS/NMRS/NO11SW; NM62NE.
29. RCAHMS/NMRS/NG24NE; N2753.
30. Robert Naismith, *Buildings of the Scottish Countryside* (London, 1981), p. 28.
31. Sonia Hackett and Neal Livingston, 'Scottish Parliamentary Churches and their Manses', in David Breeze (ed.), *Studies in Scottish Antiquity* (Edinburgh, 1985), pp. 321–30. Other listed known Telford manses include: The White House, Berriedale, Latheron, Caithness; Kinlochbervie Manse, Eddrachillis, Sutherland; Ornsay House,

Ullapool, Wester Ross; Staffin Manse, Kilmuir, Ross and Cromarty; The Old Manse, Poolewe, Wester Ross, an example of the less common single-storey, H-plan design, 1826; Rothiemurchus Old Manse, Duthil and Rothiemurchus, 1830; Insh House, Kingussie and Insh, Inverness-shire, 1828. Telford's designs for the two types of manse were illustrated in the *Biographical Atlas to the Life of Thomas Telford* (London, 1838), p. 58–9.

32. For further reading on Wade see A. R. B. Haldane's classic *New Ways Through the Glens* (London, 1962), or, more recently, John L. Roberts, *The Jacobite Wars: Scotland and the Military Campaigns of 1715 and 1745* (Edinburgh, 2002).

33. Geoffrey Stell, *Ruthven Barracks* (HMSO, 1983).

34. From £450 contracted by the fish curer Roderick Morrison of Tanera for a two-storey dwelling on Lochbroom in 1789 to £792 for a two-storey dwelling house built on Mull by Stevensons of Oban, 1790 (NAS: GD9/3/630 & NAS/GD9/4/275).

35. NAS/CH2/361/442.

36. NSA/vol. 14, p. 47: Resolis, County of Ross and Cromarty. Sir George Mackenzie, *A General View of the Agriculture of the Counties of Ross and Cromarty* (Edinburgh, 1820), p. 72.

37. Deborah Howard (ed.), *The Architecture of the Scottish Renaissance* (Broxburn, 1990), p. 11.

38. Many well-known Scottish architects of the eighteenth century started their careers as master masons, including William Adam, John Adam, John Baxter, Robert Mylne and Thomas Telford.

39. David Stevenson, *The First Freemasons: Scotland's early Lodges and their members* (Aberdeen, 1988), preface iii–xii.

40. D. M. Lyon, *The History of the Lodge of Edinburgh (Mary's Chapel) No. 1: the Rise and Progress of Freemasonry in Scotland* (Edinburgh, 1900), p. 15.

41. J. S. Seggie and D. L. Turnbull, *Annals of the Lodge of Journeymen Masons No. 8* (Edinburgh, 1930), pp. 69–74.

42. Captain John Henderson, *A General View of the Agriculture of the County of Caithness* (Edinburgh, 1812), p. 28.

43. Elizabeth Beaton, *William Robertson, 1786–1841, 'Architect in Elgin'* (Inverness, 1984). Howard MColvin, *A Biographical Dictionary of British Architects 1600–1840*, 3rd edn (London, 1995), p. 824.

   Houses by William Robertson of Elgin include: Reelig House, Kirkhill, Ross and Cromarty, 1750 house remodelled 1837–8; Braelangwell, Resolis, Ross and Cromarty, late eighteenth-century house remodelled 1839–45; Holme Rose, Croy and Dalcross, Nairnshire, early nineteenth-century house fronting a mid-eighteenth-century core; Tomintoul House, Croachy, Daviot and Dunlichty, Inverness-shire, 1841; Dochfour House, Inverness and Bonar, Inverness-shire, a mid eighteenth-century house with extensive additions and alterations, 1839; Dochgarroch House, Inverness and Bonar, Inverness-shire, 1839.

44. W. Fraser, *The Chiefs Colquhoun and their Country* (Edinburgh, 1869), vol. 1, p. 374. Francis Hinde Groome, *Ordnance Gazetteer of Scotland* (London, 1882), vol. ?, p. 150. A. White and D. Macfarlan, *General View of the Agriculture of the County of Dumbarton* (Edinburgh, 1811), p. 26. Frank Walker and Fiona Sinclair, *North Clyde Estuary: an Illustrated architectural guide* (Edinburgh, 1992), pp. 52–3.

Chapter 3

1. NSA/vol. 14, p. 395, Avoch: County of Ross and Cromarty.
2. NSA/vol. 14, p. 464: Tarbat, County of Ross and Cromarty.
3. Sir George Mackenzie, *A General View of the Agriculture of the Counties of Ross and Cromarty* (Edinburgh, 1820), p. 91.
4. NSA/vol. 14, p. 238: Contin, County of Ross and Cromarty.
5. NSA/vol.14, p. 60: Kilmuir Wester and Suddy, County of Ross and Cromarty.
6. Tom M. Devine, *Scotland's Empire 1600–1815* (London, 2003), p. 68.
7. Andrew Mackillop, *More Fruitful than the Soil: Army, Empire and the Scottish Highlands, 1715–1830* (East Linton, 2000), p. 205.
8. NSA/vol. 7, pp. 71–6, Killbrandon and Killchattan, County of Argyll.
9. SAS/vol. 14, p. 157, Killbrandon and Killchattan, County of Argyll.
10. RCAHMS, *Inventory of Argyll*, vol. 3 (Edinburgh, 1980), p. 355.
11. SAS/vol. 6, p. 176, Archattan: County of Argyll.
12. Frank Walker and Fiona Sinclair, *North Clyde Estuary: an Illustrated architectural guide* (Edinburgh, 1992), p. 91. Francis Hinde Groome, *Ordnance Gazetteer of Scotland* (London, 1882), vol. 1, p. 63.
13. RCAHMS, *Inventory of Argyll*, vol. 5 (Edinburgh, 1984), p. 407.
14. Thomas Pennant, *Tour in Scotland*, 4th edn (London, 1776), p. 252.
15. RCAHMS, *Inventory of Argyll*, vol. 7 (Edinburgh, 1992), p. 342.
16. Thomas Pennant, *Tour in Scotland* (London, 1772), p. 255. RCAHMS, *Inventory of Argyll*, vol. 5 (Edinburgh, 1984) p. 410.
17. Philip Gaskell, *Morvern Transformed: a Highland Parish in the Nineteenth Century* (Cambridge, 1968), pp. 23–47.
18. RCAHMS, *Inventory of Argyll*, 3 (Edinburgh, 1980), pp. 37–9, 43.
19. Eric Cregeen, 'The Changing Role of the House of Argyll in the Scottish Highlands', in R. Mitchison and N. T. Philipson (eds), *Scotland in the Age of Improvement* (Edinburgh, 1970), p. 21.
20. Gaskell, *Morvern Transformed*, p. 244. NAS/RHP/3600. Map of Morvern illustrating Argyll-held farms, Argyll Sales, 1819.
21. While sheep farming persists in Movern, much of the land is now used for deer stalking and forestry.
22. Samuel Johnson, *A Journey to the Western Islands of Scotland*, p. 50.
23. Gaskell, *Morvern Transformed*, p. 244.
24. Eric Creegan, 'Argyll Estate Instructions: Mull, Morvern and Tiree, 1771–1805', *Proceedings Scottish History Society*, 17 (1964), p. 101.
25. The only surviving evidence of the character of the original Ardtornish House is a family photograph by Gertrude Smith, c. 1864, reprinted in Gaskell, *Morvern Transformed*, p. 259, pl. 12.
26. Gaskell, *Morvern Transformed*, p. 244.
27. NAS/RHP 3260. 'Map of Loch Sunart Surveyed for General Wade, 1733'.
28. Common to Edinburgh and the Lothians, raised stone skews are not usually found in West Highland buildings of this period. The exceptions prove the rule, for example, many of the older buildings in Ullapool, Loch Broom, feature skews, as masons were brought in from Dunbar by the British Fisheries Society, whereas at Tobermory they are largely absent as the principal contractors were Stevenson of Oban, with the exception of the inn, designed by Edinburgh-born Robert Mylne.
29. NAS/RHP 3260

30. The irregular ground plan of the present Beach House by the Ardtornish estate architect Samuel Barham can be seen in the first Edition OS map, 1872. I am grateful to Iain Thornber for information relating to the history of the existing houses from his own research.

31. Gaskell, *Morvern Transformed*, p. 259. Achranich was not an Argyll tack and was purchased by Macdonald of Borrodale from the Camerons of Dessary in 1775. The house was demolished in 1880. Achranich House would have been built in direct emulation of the neighbouring Argyll tacksmens' houses. Just as many improving Highland landowners took their lead and example from the Dukes of Argyll, so they took theirs from improving Lowland landowning peers such as Sir John Clerk of Pencuik.

32. Thomas A. Markus, *Order in Space and Society: Architectural Form and Its Context in the Scottish Enlightenment* (Edinburgh, 1982), pp. 10–25.

33. NSA, vol. 15, p. 62, Lairg: County of Sutherland.

34. David Macgibbon and Thomas Ross, *The Castelllated and Domestic Architecture of Scotland, from the twelfth to the eighteenth century*, vol. 4 (Edinburgh, 1887–92), pp. 372–3.

35. William Daniell, *A Voyage Round the Coast of Scotland* (London, 1815–22), p. 217.

36. SAS/vol. 3, p. 405, Kildonan: County of Sutherland.

37. NSA/vol. 15, p. 133, Kildonan: County of Sutherland.

38. Eric Richards, *The Highland Clearances* (Edinburgh, 2000), pp. 153-81.

39. James Loch, *An Account of the Improvements on the Estate of Lord Stafford* (Edinburgh, 1820), appendix p. 19.

40. Information supplied to Historic Scotland by Isle of Eigg Archive Project, 1998.

41. Daniell, *A Voyage Round the Coast of Scotland*, p. 164.

42. NSA, vol.14, p. 135: Glenelg, County of Inverness.

43. Daniell, *A Voyage Round the Coast of Scotland*, p. 208.

44. Sir George Mackenzie, *A General View of the Agriculture of the Counties of Ross and Cromarty* (Edinburgh, 1820), p. 258.

45. Also Dundonnell House, dated 1767, built by the Mackenzies of Lochbroom.

46. SAS/vol. 13, p. 551, Lochcarron: County of Ross and Cromarty.

47. SAS/vol. 7, p. 124, Glenshiel: County of Ross and Cromarty.

48. NSA/vol. 14, p. 181, Glenshiel: County of Ross and Cromarty.

49. SAS/ vol. 6, p. 242, Kintail: County of Ross and Cromarty.

50. NSA/vol. 14, p. 177, Kintail: County of Ross and Cromarty.

Chapter 4

1. S. J. Shennan (ed.), *Archaeological Approaches to Cultural Identity* (London, 1989), p. 5

2. Alfred Kroeber, *Style and Civilisations* (Cornell, 1957), p. 4

3. Helene Lipstadt, 'Sociology: Bourdieu's Bequest', *Journal of the Society of Architectural Historians*, 64:4 (2005), pp. 433–46, (pp. 434–5).

4. Nicholas Cooper, 'Display, status and the vernacular tradition', *Vernacular Architecture*, 33 (2002), pp. 28–33, (p. 31).

5. John Styles and Amanda Vickery (eds), *Gender, Taste and Material Culture in Britain and North America, 1700–1830* (New Haven, 2006) p. 14.

6. Styles and Vickery, *Gender, Taste and Material Culture*, p. 16.

7. Bernard L. Herman, 'Tabletop Conversations: Material Culture and Everyday Life in the Eighteenth-Century Atlantic World', in Styles and Vickery, *Gender, Taste and Material Culture*, p. 44.

8. SAS/vol. 6, p. 178, Archattan: County of Argyll.

9. Ross Noble, 'Turf-Walled Houses of the Central Highlands: An Experiment in Reconstruction', *Folk Life*, 22 (1983–4), pp. 68–83.

10. Styles and Vickery, *Gender, Taste and Material Culture*, p. 1

11. John Styles, 'Manufacturing, Consumption and Design in Eighteenth-century England', in John Brewer and Roy Porter (eds), *Consumption and the World of Goods* (London, 1993), p. 537.

12. Styles and Vickery, *Gender, Taste and Material Culture*, p. 18.

13. R. J. Finlay, 'Scottish Identity in the Eighteenth Century', in D. Broun, R. J. Finlay and M. Lynch (eds), *Image and Identity: The Making and Re-making of Scotland Through the Ages* (Edinburgh, 1998), p. 143.

14. Styles and Vickery, *Gender, Taste and Material Culture*, p. 17

15. Anon, 'The Builder's Dictionary', *Rudiments of Architecture* 2nd edn (Edinburgh, 1778; reprint 1992).

16. Anon, *The Complete English Farmer or A Practical System of Husbandry, founded upon Natural, certain, and obvious Principles; In which is comprised, A General View of the whole Art of Agriculture* (London, 1761), p. 25.

17. SAS/vol. 6, p. 178, Archattan: County of Argyll

18. Anon, 'Builder's Dictionary', p. 49.

19. Robert Naismith, *The Buildings of the Scottish Countryside* (London, 1989), pp. 139–40.

20. Elizabeth McKellar, Preface in Barbara Arciszewska and Elizabeth McKellar (eds), *Articulating British Classicism* (Aldershot, 2004), ix– xxv.

21. Cooper, *Display, Status and the Vernacular Tradition*, p. 30.

22. Anon, *The Complete Grazier: or, gentlemen and farmer's directory / written by a country gentleman, and originally designed for private use* (London, 1767).

23. Isaac Ware, *A Complete Body of Architecture* (London, 1756), p. 300.

24. William Halfpenny, *Six new designs for convenient farm houses . . . : adapted more particularly to the northern counties in England and all Scotland* (London, 1751); George Jameson's *Thirty-three Designs with the Orders of Architecture* (Edinburgh, 1765).

25. Batty Langley, *The builder's jewel or, The youth's instructor, and workman's remembrancer: Explaining short and easy rules, made familiar to the meanest capacity, for drawing and working* (Edinburgh, 1768).

26. David M. Walker suggests the *Rudiments of Architecture* is also by Jamieson in the preface to the 1992 reprint of *Rudiments of Architecture* (Edinburgh, 1992).

27. David Walker, *Rudiments of Architecture*, v.

28. Walker, *Rudiments of Architecture*, viii.

29. This is not the case in North America where the documented ownership of several British builders' manuals by American house builders has been proved by the historian Abbott Lowell Cummings.

Chapter 5

1. Nathaniel Kent, *Hints to Gentlemen of Landed Property: to which are added supplementary hints*, 2nd edn (London, 1799).

2. Sam Smiles, University of Plymouth, pers. comm. 2006.

3. John Ruskin, *The Poetry of Architecture* (London, 1837).

4. John Wood, *A Series of Plans for Cottages or Habitations of the Labourer* (London, 1781) preface.

5. Marc-Antoine Laugier, *Essai sur l'architecture* (Paris, 1753).

6. James Boswell, *The Journal of a Tour to the Hebrides with Samuel Johnson* (London, 1785) ed. I. McGowan (Edinburgh, 1996), p. 383.
7. John E. Crowley, 'In Happier Mansions, Warm, and Dry', The Invention of the Cottage as the Comfortable Anglo-American House', *Winterthur Portfolio*, 32:2 (1997), pp. 174–7.
8. Thomas Pennant, *A Tour in Scotland and Voyage to the Hebrides* (Chester, 1774), p. 216.
9. Certificate of Shipping, Dunbar Customs House, 8/6/1788: NAS/GD9/4/63.
10. NAS/GD9/4/63.
11. NAS/GD9/3/95.
12. Mull Museum Archive, British Fisheries Society Regulations, 1788 (on permanent display).

Chapter 6

1. Eric Richards, *The Highland Clearances: people, landlords and rural turmoil* (Edinburgh, 2000), p. 108.
2. Tom Devine, *Clanship to Crofters' War* (Manchester, 1994), p. 32; Allan Macinnes, *Clanship, Commerce and the House of Stewart 1603–1788* (East Linton, 1996), p. 14.
3. SAS/vol. 7, p. 124, Glenshiel: County of Ross and Cromarty.
4. 'A Survey and design for a Village at Ullapool', 1756, Annexed Estates Commission, NAS/RHP3400.
5. SAS/vol. 10, p. 461, Lochbroom: County of Ross and Cromarty.
6. SAS/ vol. 6. p. 537, Haddington: County of Haddington.
7. SAS/vol. 2, p. 336, Morham: County of Haddington.
8. Richards, *The Highland Clearances*, p. 48.
9. Rodger Dodgshon, *From Chiefs to Landlords: social and economic change in the Western Highlands, c.1493–1820* (Edinburgh, 1998), p. 240.
10. Devine, *Clanship to Crofters War*, p. 37; Andrew Mackillop, *More Fruitful than the Soil: Army, Empire and the Scottish Highlands, 1715–1830* (East Linton, 2000), p. 83.
11. Richards, *The Highland Clearances*, 43.
12. A. J. Youngson, *After The '45* (Edinburgh, 1973), p. 37.
13. David Turnock, *The Making of the Scottish Rural Landscape* (Aldershot, 1995), p. 229.
14. Colin McWilliam, *Scottish Townscape* (London, 1975), p. 94.
15. Douglas Lockhart, 'Planned Villages in North East Scotland, 1750–1860', in J. Frew and D. Jones (eds), *The New Town Phenomenon: the second generation*, St Andrews Studies in the History of Scottish Architecture and Design IV (St Andrews, 2000), p. 25.
16. Lockhart, 'Planned Village Development in Scotland and Ireland, 1700–1800', in T. M. Devine and D. Dickson (eds), *Ireland and Scotland 1600–1850* (Edinburgh, 1983), p. 133.
17. McWilliam, *Scottish Townscape*, p. 92.
18. RCAHMS, *Inventory of Argyll*, 7 (Edinburgh, 1992), p. 440.
19. Miles Glendinning, Ranald Macinnes and Aonghus Mackechnie, *A History of Scottish Architecture* (Edinburgh, 1996), p. 181.
20. Richard Reid, *The Georgian House and Its Details* (Bath, 1989), p. 75
21. Macinnes, *Clanship, Commerce and the House of Stewart*, p. 211.
22. Ian H. Adams, *Papers on Peter May, Land Surveyor, 1749–93* (Edinburgh, 1979), pp. 12–37.
23. Lockhart, *Planned Villages in North East Scotland*, pp. 25–7.
24. Macinnes, *Clanship, Commerce and the House of Stewart*, p. 211.

25. Adams, *Papers on Peter May, Land Surveyor*, pp. 12–37.

26. National Archives of Scotland (NAS)/GD248/242; Helen Woolmer, 'Grantown-on-Spey: an eighteenth century New Town', *Town Planning Review*, 41 (1970), p. 239.

27. Lockhart, *Planned Villages in North East Scotland*, pp. 30–1.

28. Sir John Sinclair, *Analysis of the Statistical Account of Scotland* (London, 1825), p. 179.

29. Spiro Kostof, *The City Shaped: urban patterns and meanings through history* (London, 1991), p. 15.

30. J. White, 'The Island of Easdale', *The Mining Journal, Railway and Commercial Gazette*, 34, 5 February, 1854.

31. M. Withall, 'How slate from a tiny Scots island helped roof the world', *Scottish Memories*, July 1993, pp. 13–17; RCAHMS, *Inventory of Argyll*, 2 (Edinburgh, 1976), p. 356; J. Hume, *The Industrial Archaeology of Scotland: Highlands and Islands* (Edinburgh, 1977), p. 167.

32. Macinnes, *Clanship, Commerce and the House of Stewart*, pp. 217–19.

33. Macinnes, *Clanship, Commerce and the House of Stewart*, pp. 218–20; John Knox, *A Discourse on the Expediency of Establishing Fishing Stations in the Highlands of Scotland* (Edinburgh1786); NAS: GD9/1/1.

34. Robert Clyde, *From Rebel to Hero: the image of the Highlander, 1745–1830* (East Linton, 1995), p. 23.

35. NAS/E730/32. Papers of the Board of Commissioners of Annexed and Forfeited Estates, 1771.

36. McWilliam, *Scottish Townscape*, p. 99. Nic Allen, 'Highland Planned Villages', *SVBWG Regional and Thematic Studies No 1* (Edinburgh, 1990), pp. 40–9.

37. NAS/RHP/2312; NAS/E777/313/290; McWilliam, *Scottish Townscape*, p. 99.

38. Edinburgh, NAS/RHP/2312/3; RHP/1056–71; GD/E732/18/2.

39. Annette Smith, *Jacobite Estates of the Forty Five* (Edinburgh, 1982), p. 148.

40. Smith, *Jacobite Estates*, p. 154.

41. NAS/RHP/2312; NAS/E777/313/290; McWilliam, *Scottish Townscape*, p. 99.

42. Andrew Mackillop, *More Fruitful Than the Soil*, pp. 190–5.

43. Clyde, *From Rebel to Hero*, p. 22.

44. Clyde, *From Rebel to Hero*, p. 17.

45. Macinnes, *Clanship, Commerce and the House of Stewart*, p. 195.

Chapter 7

1. The primary documentary sources for the British Fisheries Society are the British Fisheries Society Papers (NAS/GD9) held by the National Archives of Scotland (gifted by the Dukes of Argyll). A particular debt of gratitude is owed to Jean Dunlop's pioneering account of the political and economic history of the Society, *The British Fisheries Society, 1786–1893* (Edinburgh, 1978, repr. 2005).

2. James R. Coull, *The Sea Fisheries of Scotland: a Historical Geography* (Edinburgh, 1996), p. 3.

3. Coull, *The Sea Fisheries of Scotland*, p. 69.

4. Jean Dunlop, *The British Fisheries Society, 1786–1893* (Edinburgh, 1978), pp. 20–4.

5. Coull, *The Sea Fisheries of Scotland*, p. 75.

6. Andrew Mackillop, *More Fruitful than the Soil: Army, Empire and the Scottish Highlands, 1715–1830* (East Linton, 2000), pp. 190–5.

7. NAS/GD9/3/49.

8. NAS/GD9/3/28–30.

9. Dunlop, *The British Fisheries Society*, p. 89.

10. NAS/GD9/3/32.

11. NAS/GD9/3/200.

12. *Survey and Report on the Coasts and Central Highlands of Scotland. Made by the Command of the Right Honourable the Lords Commissioners of His Majesty's Treasury, in the Autumn of 1802*, Thomas Telford, Civil Engineer, Edin. FRS. Cited in Samuel Smiles, *The Life of Thomas Telford by Smiles* (London, 1867), p. 144.

13. NAS/GD9/3/20; Mull Museum Archive (MMA): *Edinburgh Evening Courant* 20 February and 6 March 1787; *Edinburgh Evening Courant, Caledonian Mercury* and *Glasgow Mercury*, February and March 1788.

14. NAS/GD9/3/95. Sir James Grant of Grant in a letter to the British Fisheries Society. Further information regarding the improving works of Sir James at Grantown-on-Spey can be found in Heather Woolmer, 'Grantown-on-Spey: An eighteenth century New Town', *Town Planning Review*, 41:3 (1970), pp. 238–45.

15. Elizabeth Beaton, 'Building Practices in Loch Broom and Gairloch Parishes', in John R. Baldwin (ed.), *People and Settlements in North West Ross* (Galloway, 1994), pp. 159–93; Jean Munro, 'Ullapool and the British Fisheries Society', *People and Settlements in North West Ross,* pp. 244–70; Elizabeth Beaton and Geoffrey Stell, 'Local Building Traditions in Ross and Cromarty', in Donald Omand (ed.), *The Ross and Cromarty Book* (Golspie, 1984), p. 207;. Beaton, *Caithness: an Illustrated Architectural Guide* (Edinburgh, 1996), pp. 36– 44; Munro, 'Pulteneytown and the Planned Villages of Caithness', in John R Baldwin (ed.), *Caithness a Cultural Crossroads* (Edinburgh, 1982). RCAHMS, *Inventory of Argyll*, vol. 3 (Edinburgh, 1980), p. 236; A. Whitaker, 'A Walk Around Tobermory', *Oban Times* (1988), p. 20.

16. The fifth Duke was chairman of the Society until 1800 but was relatively inactive after 1790 following the completion of the first two settlements.

17. Howard M. Colvin, *Autobiographical Dictionary of British Architects, 1600–1840*, 3rd edn (London, 1995), p. 684.

18. Jean Currie, *Mull: the Island and its People* (Edinburgh, 2000), p. 189.

19. Samuel Smiles, *The Life of Thomas Telford by Smiles* (London, 1861), p. 101.

20. Spiro Kostof, *The City Shaped: urban patterns and meanings through history* (London, 1991), p. 240.

21. NAS/GD9/3/95. Woolmer, *Grantown-on-Spey*, p. 239.

22. NAS/GD9/3/38; NAS/GD9/4/213; MMA/3/2/7.

23. MMA/ 3/2/2. RCAHMS, *Inventory of Argyll*, 3 (Edinburgh, 1980), p. 236.

24. Ian H. Adams, *Papers on Peter May, Land Surveyor, 1749–93* (Edinburgh, 1979), p. 18. Aitken rejected May's plan for Ullapool drawn up for the AEC (NAS/RHP/3400), *A Survey and design for a Village at Ullapool*, Peter May for the Annexed Estates Commission, 1756).

25. NAS/GD9/3/616.

26. NAS/GD9/3/617.

27. Nic Allen,'Highland Planned Villages', SVBWG *Regional and Thematic Studies No 1* (Edinburgh, 1990), pp. 40–9.

28. Other examples: Plockton, Lochalsh, Ross-shire founded by Mackenzie of Seaforth, 1801, plan by William Cumming; Poolewe, Gairloch, Ross-shire, founded by Mackenzie of Gairloch, 1808; Golspie, Sutherland, Duke of Sutherland, plan by David Wilson, 1805; and Helmsdale, Sutherland, Duke of Sutherland, plan by William Forbes, 1816.

29. NAS/GD9/3/448; NAS/GD9/3/553.

30. Thomas Telford, *Atlas to the Life of Thomas Telford by Himself* (London, 1838). None of Telford's subsequent biographies shed any light upon Telford's urban design and design influences. Samuel Smiles, *Life of Thomas Telford*; Alexander Gibbs, *The Story of Telford* (London, 1935); and L. T. C. Rolt, *Thomas Telford* (London, 1958). It has to be concluded that neither Telford in later life nor his biographers considered his town planning to be of much significance when set against his great civil engineering works.

31. David King, *The Complete Works of Robert and James Adam* (Oxford, 1991), p. 385. Planned villages incorporating crescents and semicircles had also been attempted in Scotland, such as Lord Garlies' crescent-plan for Garliestown, Wigtownshire, 1760.

32. Smiles, *The Life of Thomas Telford*, p. 113.

33. Damie Stilman, *English Neo-Classical Architecture* (London, 1988), p. 236.

34. Kerry Downes, *The Georgian Cities of Britain* (Oxford, 1979), p. 120.

35. NAS/GD9/7/264.

36. NAS/GD9/14/128/9/11/10.

37. Colvin, *Biographical Dictionary*, p. 97.

38. Smiles, *The Life of Thomas Telford*, p. 113.

39. Thomas Telford, letter to Andrew Little, 10 March 1793, cited in Rolt, *Thomas Telford*, (London, 1958) p. 24–5.

40. The industrial theme was lost when later changed to Saltoune Terrace, Telford St, and Burn St.

41. Telford, Atlas to the Life of *Thomas Telford by Himself*, pp. 115–20.

42. NAS/GD9/59; NAS/GD9/248/29/4/89; NAS/GD9/334/16/11/91.

43. NAS/GD9/3/183; GD9/8/119. Robert Melville was a bankrupt fishing agent from Dunbar, East Lothian who persuaded the Board of Directors to grant him the majority of the contracts for Ullapool. Melville employed James Miller, a minor Edinburgh architect, to produce the plans for his various contracted buildings at Ullapool. Anon, *Plan of Harbour and Breakwater*, 1854 (NAS:RHP/4286).

44. NAS/GD9/10, 45; NAS/GD9/1/164; NAS/GD9/21/28.5.92; NAS/GD9/9/13; NAS/GD9/22/9.5.01. William Mackenzie, *Sketch of the Pier at Stein in the Island of Skye*, 1807 (NAS: RHP/11800).

45. NAS/GD9/21/18.7.91.

46. Smiles, *The Life of Thomas Telford*, p. 154.

47. Telford, 'Harbours, Wharfs and Piers', *Thomas Telford by Himself*, RCAMHS/NMRS/XSD/158/1. Other examples of Highland Road and Bridge Commission harbours include: Avoch Harbour, Ballintraed Harbour, Banff Harbour, Burgh-Head Harbour, Channery Point Ferry Pier, Corran Ferry Pier, Cullen Harbour, Dornie Ferry, East Tarbet Harbour, Feoline Harbour, Fortrose Harbour, Fraserburgh Harbour, Gordon Harbour, Inverfarigaig Landing Pier, Invergordon Ferry Pier, Kirkwall Harbour, Kyle Ferry Pier, Nairn Harbour, Peterhead Harbour, Portmahomack Harbour, Portree Harbour, Small Isles Harbour, St. Catherine's Ferry Pier, and Tobermory Harbour Pier.

48. NAS/GD9/3/144.

49. Daniel Maudlin, 'Robert Mylne at Pitlour House', *Architectural Heritage*, 12 (2001), pp. 27–37.

50. NAS/ SRO/GD9/4/76.

51. NAS/GD9/3/140–7.

52. NAS/GD9/3/593; SRO/GD9/3/627.

53. NAS/GD9/3/144.
54. NAS/GD9/289/21.5.08.
55. NAS/GD9/289/14/05/08.
56. Several of the merchants and curers that took up leases at Pulteneytown were from Leith.
57. NAS/GD9/4/113.
58. NAS/GD9/3/177.
59. NAS/GD9/3/441.
60. NAS/GD9/3/57; NAS/GD9/3/553.
61. NAS/GD9/3/607.
62. John Hume, *The Industrial Archaeology of Scotland* (Edinburgh, 1977), p. 33.
63. Mark Girouard, *The English Town* (London, 1990), p. 94.
64. Daniel Maudlin, 'Regulating the Vernacular: the impact of building regulations in the eighteenth century planned village', *Vernacular Architecture*, 35 (2004), pp. 40–9.
65. Colvin, *Biographical Dictionary*, pp. 1072–5.
66. NAS/GD9/ 100/1/7/91.
67. King, *The Complete Works of Robert and James Adam*, p. 385.
68. NAS/RHP/ 11798.

Chapter 8

1. Tom M. Devine, 'Landlordism and Highland Emigration', in Tom M. Devine (ed.), *Scottish Emigration and Scottish Society* (Edinburgh, 1992), p. 84.
2. See David Dobson, *Scottish Emigration to Colonial America, 1607–1785* (Athens, Georgia, 1994).
3. Daniel Maudlin, 'Regulating the Vernacular: the impact of building regulations in the eighteenth century Highland planned village', *Vernacular Architecture*, 35 (2004), pp. 40–9; Eric Richards, 'Scotland and the Uses of the Atlantic Empire', in Bernard Bailyn and Philip D. Morgan (eds), *Strangers within the Realm: Cultural Margins of the First British Empire* (Williamsburg, 1991), pp. 67–115 (p. 92).
4. Richards, 'Scotland and the Uses of the Atlantic Empire', pp. 93–4.
5. Clearances continued through the nineteenth century, but later emigrants from across Scotland (and indeed Britain in general) set sail for Australia, New Zealand and South Africa, rather than for Canada.
6. A *tacksman* was the principal tenant of a clan chief, a figure of a certain wealth, status and authority within the clan system. Within the traditional social structure of the Highland clan, which survived into the mid or late eighteenth century, the position also involved a military role, roughly equivalent to that of a middle-ranking officer.
7. Marjory Harper and Michael E. Vance (eds), *Myth, Migration and the Making of Memory: Scotia and Nova Scotia, c.1700–1900* (Halifax, Nova Scotia, 1999), pp. 1–33 (p. 20).
8. Population statistics taken from James D. Kornwolf and Georgiana W. Kornwolf, *Architecture and Town Planning in Colonial North America* (Baltimore, 2002), pp. 13–33.
9. James Stuart Martell, *Immigration* (Halifax, Nova Scotia, 1942), p. 95.
10. Settlement in the Pictou area was divided into regular land grants initially laid out by the Philadelphia Grant Company, or by the British government in the case of military veterans. These land grants, each of about two hundred acres, were later subdivided by speculative grantees into lots of varying sizes.
11. Provincial Archives of Nova Scotia (PANS)/MFM/8154: Nova Scotia Gazette (25 November 1787), p. 3.

12. An investigation of all extant pre-1850 houses in Antigonish and Pictou counties was carried out, covering 529 houses distributed across 125 different settlements. No detailed study of the design, plan and elevation of the region's historic building stock had been undertaken previously; extensive recording and statistical analysis was therefore required in order to establish the dominant architectural characteristics and ethnic histories of farm ownership within the region, from which any conclusions concerning Scottish Gaelic settlement could be drawn. Photographic fieldwork surveys of both counties were conducted, 2002–5, using a modified form of Ronald Brunskill's extensive recording system, see Ronald Brunskill, *Vernacular Architecture: an illustrated handbook*, 4th edn (London, 2000). This extensive recording system establishes the dominant architectural character within a survey group, through the collation and analysis of comparative survey data of identifiable attributes such as form, materials and construction. Designed to highlight regional variations in building groups, the system is also remarkably effective for demonstrating uniformity. The survey group for Pictou and Antigonish counties was restricted to those extant buildings built between 1800 and 1850. The buildings' dates were established by using a combination of historical published sources, such as the *Illustrated Atlas of Pictou County* (Philadelphia, 1879) and the County Registry of Deeds, together with oral history. Histories of farm ownership are closely tied to the building of farmhouses. It was possible to establish the probable ethnicity of farm owners: at an individual level by name origins, and sometimes by explicit reference, through the Registry of Deeds and oral histories; and at a regional level, through analysis of census records. The whole project was greatly assisted by research into 'heritage houses' and family histories carried out by volunteers at the Antigonish Museum and Pictou Heritage Centre in 1985 as part of a wider initiative undertaken by the Nova Scotia department of Culture, Fitness and Recreation. The identification and characterisation of buildings within the survey group cannot be completely without error as many buildings have been destroyed and many more heavily altered or entirely rebuilt even within the historic period of the survey (1800–50).

13. In each case the current building is not necessarily the original one on its site, as in some cases subsequent generations had replaced this with a larger structure, within the survey period (1800–50).

14. Access to house interiors was restricted, so that the analysis of interiors has had to be based upon a small sample group, and therefore does not constitute a full empirical survey.

15. L. B. Jenson, *Wood and Stone: Pictou, Nova Scotia* (Pictou, Nova Scotia, 1972), pp. 1–2.

16. William Cameron, 'Drummer on Foot', *The Casket* (January 1914), p. 4.

17. Pers. comm. Mary Fraser, Rosemary Maclean and Frances Dunn, Antigonish Historical Society.

18. Pictou Heritage Centre (PHC): Registry of Deeds; Jenson, *Wood and Stone*, pp. 17–18.

19. PHC: Registry of Deeds; Jenson, *Wood and Stone*, pp. 7–8; supplementary information provided by St Clair Prest, Director, Pictou Heritage Centre.

20. Information provided by David Jones, University of St Andrews.

21. Information provided by Wayde Brown, University of Georgia, Athens, Georgia.

22. Karen E. Mackay, *1838 Census of Pictou County* (Halifax, Nova Scotia, 1995), pp. 176–9 (transcribed from: PANS/RG1/vol. 449/166a–166f).

23. PHC: Registry of Deeds; Jenson, *Wood and Stone*, pp. 13–14.

24. PANS/MFM/4693: *Colonial Patriot* (18 June 1831), p. 5; Elizabeth Tratt, 'A Survey and

Listing of Nova Scotia Newspapers, 1752–1957',unpublished PhD thesis, Dalhousie University, 1979, pp. 2–3.

25. Mackay, *1838 Census of Pictou County*, pp. 176–9; Karen E Mackay, *1838 Census of Shelburne and Yarmouth Counties* (Halifax, Nova Scotia, 2002), pp. 170–83.

26. Information supplied by the Nova Scotia Museum, Halifax, Nova Scotia.

27. Alan Gowan, 'New England Architecture in Nova Scotia', *Art Quarterly*, 25 (Spring 1962), pp. 24– 36 (p. 30).

28. Peter Ennals and Deryck Holdsworth, *Homeplace: the making of the Canadian dwelling over three centuries* (Toronto, 1998), pp. 76–9.

29. Information supplied by the Chester Municipal Heritage Society.

30. Amir H. Ameri, 'Housing Ideologies in the New England and Chesapeake Bay Colonies, c. 1650–1700', *Journal of the Society of Architectural Historians,* 56:1 (1997), pp. 6–15 (p. 6); Nora Pat Small, 'New England Farmhouses in the Early Republic: Rhetoric and Reality', in Carol L. Hudgins and Elizabeth Collins (eds), *Shaping Communities: Perspectives in Vernacular Architecture VI* Cromley (Knoxville, Tennessee, 1997), pp. 33– 45 (p. 36).

31. The low number of extant pattern books may suggest that the printed sources were less influential in the dissemination of architecture than the migration and the passing on of knowledge through the apprentice system (pers. comm. Jeffrey Cohen, Brynmar College).

32. Abbot Lowell Cummings, 'The Availability of Architectural Books in Eighteenth-century New England', in Kenneth Hafertepe and James F. O'Gorman (eds), *American Architects and their Books to 1848* (Amherst, 2001), pp. 1–16 (p. 1).

33. Cummings, 'The Availability of Architectural books', pp. 5–8.

34. PANS/MFM/8154: *Nova Scotia Gazette,* 14 July 1772, p. 2.

35. PANS/MEM/8158: *Halifax Gazette,* 9 June 1753, p. 5.

36. PANS/MEM/8158: *Halifax Gazette,* 18 April 1752, p. 6.

37. John Clive and Bernard Bailyn, 'England's Cultural Provinces: Scotland and America', *The William and Mary Quarterly*, 11:2 (1954), pp. 200–13 (p. 207).

38. Fiona A. Black, 'Advent'rous Merchants and Atlantic Waves: A Preliminary Study of the Scottish Contribution to Book Availability in Halifax, 1752–1810', in Harper and Vance, *Myth, Migration and the Making of Memory,* pp. 157–189 (p. 161).

39. Bernard Bailyn, *To Begin The World Anew: the genius and ambiguities of the American founders* (New York, 2003); Bailyn and Morgan, *Strangers within the Realm*; Nicholas Canny and Anthony Pagden (eds), *Colonial Identity in the Atlantic World, 1500–1800* (Princeton, 1987); Jack P. Greene and J. R. Pole (eds), *Colonial British America: essays in the new history of the early modern era* (Baltimore, 1984).

40. *Strangers within the Realm*, pp. 1–33, (p. 1).

41. James T. Lemon, 'Spatial Order: Households in Local Communities and Regions', in *Colonial British America*, pp. 86–123 (p. 86).

42. Ennals and Holdsworth, *Homeplace,* pp. 76–9.

43. Richard MacKinnon, 'Log Architecture on Cape Breton Island, Nova Scotia: Cultural Borrowing and Adaptation', *Material Culture*, 24:3 (1992), pp. 1–18 (p. 6).

44. James Symonds, 'Surveying the Remains of a Highland Myth', in Harper and Vance, *Myth, Migration and the Making of Memory*, pp. 73–89 (84–5).

45. Ameri, 'Housing Ideologies in the New England and Chesapeake Bay Colonies', p. 73.

46. Symonds, 'Surveying the Remains of a Highland Myth', p. 86.

47. Harper and Vance, *Myth, Migration and the Making of Memory,* pp. 14–49, (p. 33).

48. To those not familiar with the culture of traditional Highland society and the history of the suppressed Jacobite Rebellion, the Gaels' subsequent monarchism and support of the British government in the late eighteenth century was, and still is, baffling. The Gaels were zealous monarchists. It was the House of Hanover to whom they objected, and against whom they rebelled, in support of the House of Stewart, the true line of kingship. By the late eighteenth century, when the Hanoverian ascendancy was clearly a permanent fixture, most Highlanders transferred their monarchist loyalties to the House of Hanover. This cleared the path for the successful careers of Highlands Scots throughout the British Empire in the nineteenth century (notably as pioneer farmers and trained professionals, such as soldiers, doctors, lawyers, teachers and ministers).

49. See Nora Pat Small, *Beauty and Convenience: architecture and order in the new republic* (Knoxville, Tennessee, 2003).

50. Nicholas Cooper, 'Display, Status and the Vernacular Tradition', *Vernacular Architecture*, 33 (2002), pp. 28–33 (p. 31).

51. Saint Clair Prest, *Nineteenth Century Pictou County Furniture* (Pictou, Nova Scotia, 1977). The 1838 census shows four joiners and eight cabinetmakers active in Pictou town. In the 1870s, the Scots-owned firm of Dewar Bros. ran a large sawmill and furniture factory on Barney's River, Pictou. See Mackay, *1838 Census of Pictou County* (transcribed from: PANS/RG1/vol. 449/166a–166f). 'Dewar Bros. Builders & Manufacturers, Barneys River, Pictou Co. N.S.', illustrated in Sir John Douglas Sutherland Campbell, *Illustrated Historical Atlas of Pictou County, Nova Scotia* (Philadelphia, 1879).

Appendix 3

1. The primary manuscript sources relating to the British Fisheries Society are the papers of the British Fisheries Society held by the National Archives of Scotland (NAS/GD9). Within this extensive archive collection the key folios relating to the Society's foundation and building works are: Letter Books of the British Fisheries Society, 1787–1845; Minutes of the Board of Directors, 1787–1845; and Letter Books of Thomas Telford, 1790–97(NAS/GD9/ 1–4; GD9/4–259; NAS/GD9/32; NAS/GD9/32; NAS/GD9/39). Maps and Plans from the British Fisheries Society papers are held separately at Register House Papers (RHP). Other useful archives are the National Monuments Record Service of the Royal Commission on Ancient and Historic Monuments of Scotland (RCAHMS), and the Mull Museum Archives (MMA).
   MMA: 3/2/7. NAS:GD9/4/213. James Maxwell, *Sketch of Port and Village of Tobermory*, 1790. RCAHMS: AGD/483/5). James Maxwell, *Sketch of Shore and Bank*, Tobermory, 1789 (RCAHMS: AGD/537/1). William Daniell, *Tobermory* (watercolour sketch), 1815 (RCAHMS: AGD/483/3). *Aerial Photograph of Tobermory*, 1978 (RCAHMS: AG/9046).

2. NAS/GD9/59; GD9/248/29/4/89; GD9/334/16/11/91.

3. NAS/GD9/4/275. Robert Mylne, *Plans and Elevation for an Inn at Tobermory*, 1790 (RCAHMS: AGD/535/1)

4. J. Dunlop, *The British Fisheries Society* (Edinburgh, 1978), 150. NAS: GD9/4/113; GD9/3/441.

5. NAS/GD9/3/399; GD9/4/313.

6. NAS/GD9/4/459. William Daniell, *Bridge and Harbour at Tobermory* (watercolour sketch), 1815 (RCAHMS: AGD/483/1).

7. NAS/GD9/3/379.

8. NAS/GD9/186; GD9/4/207. Thomas Telford, *Plan of a Boatbuilder's Shed to be Built at Tobermory*, 1790 (RCAHMS: AGD/536/1).

9. NAS:GD9/3/616. Donald Macleod of Geanies, *Sketch plan of Ullapool*, 1789 (NAS/GD9/3/617).

10. NAS:GD9/3/183; GD9/8/119. Robert Melville was a bankrupt fishing agent from Dunbar, East Lothian who remarkably persuaded the Board of Directors to grant him the majority of the contracts for Ullapool. Melville employed James Miller, a minor Edinburgh architect, to produce the plans for his various contracted buildings at Ullapool. Anon, *Plan of Harbour and Breakwater*, 1854 (NAS:RHP/4286).

11. NAS/GD9/4/76; GD9/3/630; GD9/3/140–7.

12. NAS/GD9/3/615. *Photograph of Great Storehouse, Shore St, Ullapool*, 1968 (RCAHMS: RC/579).

13. NAS/GD9/4/107. The high cost of building timber, as natural scarcity required the import of deal from Scandinavia, lead to many improving landlords, including the Society at Ullapool and their Lochbroom neighbour, Kenneth Mackenzie of Dundonnel, setting aside land for fir plantations. See, E. Beaton, 'Building Traditions in Lochbroom and Gairloch Parishes', in *People and Settlements in North West Ross,* J R Baldwin (ed), Scottish Society for Northern Studies (Newton Stewart, 1994), 171.

14. NAS/GD9/4/29. *Photograph of Red Herring House, Shore St, Ullapool*, 1968 (RCAHMS: RC/581)

15. NAS/GD9/111.

16. NAS/GD9/3/132; GD9/111.Thomas Telford, 'Highland Church and Manse: Plans and Elevations', *Atlas to the Life of Thomas Telford* (London, 1838) plate 59.

17. NAS/GD9/3/106

18. NAS/GD9/ 35/2/10/90. Thomas Telford, *Plan of the Town and Quay for the Society's Settlement at Lochbay*, 1790 (NAS/RHP/11786). Thomas Telford, *The General Plan of Lochbay in the Island of Sky*, 1791 (NAS: RHP/11791). Anon, *Road Survey Map of Skye Showing the Village of Stein* (detail), 19th century (NAS:RHP/11673).

19. NAS/GD9/10, 45; GD9/1/164; GD9/21/28.5.92; GD9/9/13; GD9/22/9.5.01. William Mackenzie, *Sketch of the Pier at Stein in the Island of Skye*, 1807 (NAS/RHP/11800).

20. NAS/GD9/82/15.9.90; GD9/22/24.6.01; RHP/11787; GD9/1/73.

21. NAS/GD9/21/15.12.94; GD9/34/13; GD9/191.

22. NAS/GD9/9/225. Thomas Telford, 'Highland Church and Manse: Plans and Elevations', *Atlas*, plate 59.

23. NAS/GD9/10/222.

24. NAS/GD9/155; GD9/189.

25. NAS/GD9/189.

26. NAS/GD9/14/218. *Aerial Photograph of Pulteneytown*, 1991 (RCAHMS: B49611). Thomas Telford, *Plan for a Village and Habour at Pulteneytown*, 1807 (NAS/GD9/7/264).

27. NAS/GD9/263/16.6.03.

28. NAS/GD9/289/21.5.08; GD9/289/14/05/08

29. NAS/GD9/3/30.

30. NAS/GD9/294.

31. NAS/GD9/5/85; GD9/282/160; GD9/282/150.

32. NAS/GD9/311/27.2.09; GD9/289/21.5.08.

33. NAS/GD9/273; GD9/294; GD9/289/6.5.08; RHP/11801.

Bibliography

Primary Sources

Papers of the British Fisheries Society (NAS/GD9)
Papers of the Board of Commissioners of Annexed and Forfeited Estates (NAS/E730)
Ullapool (Lochbroom) Parish Records and Photographic Archive (UMA)
Mull Museum Records and Photographic Archive (MMA)
Wick Burgh Records and Historical Archive (WHC)
Registry of Deeds, Pictou and Antigonish County Records (PHC)
Inventory of Historic Buildings, Pictou and Antigonish Counties, Nova Scotia (NSDTC)

Printed Primary Sources

Adam, William. *Vitruvius Scoticus . . . : Principally from the Designs of the Late William Adam* (Edinburgh, 1750)
Anon. *The Complete English Farmer . . . In which is Comprised, A General View of the whole Art of Agriculture* (London, 1761)
Anon. *The Complete Grazier* (London, 1767)
Anon. *Rudiments of Architecture* (Edinburgh, 2nd edn 1778, reprint 1992)
Asher, Benjamin. *The Country Builder's Assistant* (Boston, 1798)
Ayton, Richard. *A Voyage Round Great Britain in the Summer of 1813* (London, 1815)
Boswell, James. *The Journal of a Tour to the Hebrides with Samuel Johnson* (London, 1785)
Burt, Edmund. *Letters from a Gentleman in the North of Scotland* (London, 1724–28)
Crunden, John. *Convenient and Ornamental Architecture* (London, 1791)
Daniell, William. *A Voyage Round the Coast of Scotland and the Adjacent Islands* (London, 1815–22)
Garnett, Thomas. *Observations on a Tour through the Highlands and Part of the Western Isles of Scotland* (London, 1800)
General Assembly of the Church of Scotland (eds). *New Statistical Account of Scotland* (Edinburgh, 1834–45)
Halfpenny, William. *Six New Designs for Convenient Farm-houses . . . : Adapted more particularly to the Northern Counties in England and all Scotland* (London, 1751)
Henderson, John. *A General View of the Agriculture of the County of Caithness* (Edinburgh, 1812)
Hogg, James. *A Tour of the Highlands* (Edinburgh, 1803)
Jameson, George. *Thirty-three Designs with the Orders of Architecture* (Edinburgh, 1765)
Johnson, Samuel. *A Journey to the Western Islands of Scotland* (London, 1775)
Kent, Nathaniel. *Hints to Gentlemen of Landed Property* (London, 1799)

Knox, John. *A Discourse on the Expediency of Establishing Fishing Stations in the Highlands of Scotland* (Edinburgh, 1786)

Langley, Batty. *The Builder's Jewel* (Edinburgh, 1768)

Lightoler, Thomas. *The Gentleman and Farmer's Architect* (London, 1762)

Loch, James. *An Account of the Improvements on the Estate of Lord Stafford* (Edinburgh, 1820)

Lugar, Robert. *Plans and Views of Buildings* (London, 1811)

Lugar, Robert. *The Country Gentleman's Architect* (London, 1823)

MacDougall, Robert. *The Emigrants Guide to North America* (Edinburgh, 1841, Thompson, E. (ed.) 1998 reprint).

Mackenzie, George. *A General View of the Agriculture of the Counties of Ross and Cromarty* (Edinburgh, 1820)

Moxon, Joseph. *Mechanick Exercises* (London, 1678)

Nicholson, Peter. *The Carpenter's New Guide* (London, 1793)

Pain, William. *The Practical House Carpenter* (Boston, 1796)

Pennant, Thomas. *A Tour in Scotland and Voyage to the Hebrides*, 4th edn (London, 1776)

Plaw, John. *Sketches for Country Houses* (London, 1800)

Price, Francis. *The British Carpenter* (London, 1753)

Salmon, William. *Palladio Londinensis* (London, 1737)

Sinclair, John (ed.). *Statistical Account of Scotland* (Edinburgh, 1791–99)

Spurrier, J. *The Practical Farmer . . . Adapted to the Different Soils and Climates of America* (Delaware, 1793)

Telford, Thomas. *A Biographical Atlas to the Life of Thomas Telford by Himself* (London, 1838)

Ware, Isaac. *A Complete Body of Architecture* (London, 1756)

Wood, John. *A Series of Plans for Cottages or Habitations of the Labourer* (London, 1781)

Secondary Sources

Adams, I. H. *Papers on Peter May, Land Surveyor, 1749–93* (Edinburgh, 1979)

Arciszewska, B. and McKellar, E. *Articulating British Classicism: New Approaches to Eighteenth-Century Architecture* (Aldershot, 2004)

Armitage. D. and Braddick, M. J. *The British Atlantic World 1500–1800* (London, 2002)

Ayres, P. J. *Classical Culture and the Idea of Rome in Eighteenth-Century England* (Cambridge, 1997)

Bailyn, B. and Morgan, P. D. (eds) *Strangers within the Realm; Cultural Margins of the First British Empire* (Williamsburg, 1991)

Bailyn, B. *To Begin The World Anew: The Genius and Ambiguities of the American Founders* (New York, 2003)

Baldwin, J. R. (ed.) *People and Settlements in North West Ross* (Galloway, 1994)

Baldwin, J. R (ed.) *Caithness: A Cultural Crossroads* (Edinburgh, 1982)

Beaton, E. *Caithness: An Illustrated Architectural Guide* (Edinburgh, 1996)

Beaton, E. *William Robertson, 1786–1841, 'Architect in Elgin'* (Inverness, 1984)

Black, J. *Culture in Eighteenth-Century England: A Subject for Taste* (London, 2005)

Brewer, J and Porter, R. (eds) *Consumption and the World of Goods* (London, 1993)

Broun, D., Finlay, R. J. and Lynch, M. (eds) *Image and Identity: The Making and Re-making of Scotland through the Ages* (Edinburgh, 1998).

Brown, W. *N. S. Vernacular* (Halifax, 1986)

Brunskill, R. W. *Vernacular Architecture: an Illustrated Handbook*, 4th edn (London, 2000)

Bumstead, J. M. *The People's Clearance: Highland Emigration to British North America 1770–1815* (Edinburgh, 1982)

Burton, A. *Thomas Telford* (London, 1999)

Canny, N. and Pagden, A. *Colonial Identity in the Atlantic World, 1500–1800* (Princeton, 1987)

Carruthers, A (ed.) *The Scottish Home* (Edinburgh, 1996)

Christie, C. *The British Country House in the Eighteenth Century* (Manchester, 2000)

Clyde, R. *From Rebel to Hero: The Image of the Highlander, 1745–1830* (East Linton, 1995)

Colley, L. *Britons: forging the Nation, 1707–1837* (London, 1992)

Colvin, H. M. *Biographical Dictionary of British Architects, 1600–1840* (London, 1995, third edition)

Cosh, M. and Lindsay, I.G. *Inveraray and the Dukes of Argyll* (Edinburgh, 1973)

Coull, J. R. *The Sea Fisheries of Scotland: A Historical Geography* (Edinburgh, 1996)

Crowley, J. E. *The Invention of Comfort: Sensibilities and Design in Early Modern Britain and Early America* (Baltimore, 2001)

Cruft, K. and Fraser, A. *James Craig, 1774–1795* (Edinburgh, 1995)

Cummings, A. L. *The Framed Houses of Massachusetts Bay, 1625–1725* (Cambridge, 1979)

Currie, J. *Mull: The Island and its People* (Edinburgh, 2000)

Devine, T. M. *Scotland's Empire, 1600–1815* (London, 2003)

Devine, T. M. *Clanship to Crofters' War: The Social Transformation of the Scottish Highlands* (Manchester, 1994)

Devine, T. M. (ed.) *Scottish Emigration and Scottish Society* (Edinburgh, 1992)

Devine, T. M. (ed.) *Improvement and Enlightenment* (Edinburgh, 1989)

Devine, T. M. and Dickson, D. (eds) *Ireland and Scotland 1600–1850* (Edinburgh, 1983)

Dobson, D. *Scottish Emigration to Colonial America, 1607–1785* (Athens, Georgia, 1994)

Dodghson, R. A. *From Chiefs to Landlords: Social and Economic Change in the Western Highlands, c. 1493–1820* (Edinburgh, 1998)

Donovan, K. (ed.) *The Island: New Perspectives on Cape Breton's History, 1713–1990* (Cape Breton, 1990)

Dunbar, J. G. *The Historic Architecture of Scotland* (London, 1966)

Dunlop, J. *The British Fisheries Society, 1786–1893* (Edinburgh, 1978)

Ennals, P. and Holdsworth, D. *Homeplace: The Making of the Canadian Dwelling over Three Centuries* (Toronto, 1998)

Fenton, A. (ed.) *Highland Vernacular Architecture*, SVBWG (Edinburgh, 1989)

Fenton, A. and Walker, B. *The Rural Architecture of Scotland* (Edinburgh, 1981)

Frew, J. and Jones, D. (eds) *The New Town Phenomenon: The Second Generation* (St Andrews, 2000)

Gaynor, J. M. and Hagedorn, N. L. *Tools: Working Wood in the Eighteenth Century* (Williamsburg, 1993)

Gaskell, P. *Morvern Transformed: A Highland Parish in the Nineteenth Century* (Cambridge, 1968)

Geddes, J. *Deeside and the Mearns: An Illustrated Architectural Guide* (Edinburgh, 2001)

Gibbs, A. *The Story of Telford* (London, 1935)

Gifford, J. *Buildings of Scotland: Highlands and Islands* (London, 1992)

Gifford, J. *Buildings of Scotland: Dumfries and Galloway* (London, 1996)

Glendinning, M., Macinnes, R. and Mackechnie, A. *A History of Scottish Architecture* (Edinburgh, 1996)

Grant, I. F. *Highland Folk Ways* (Edinburgh, 1961, reprinted 1995)

Greene, J. P. and Pole, J. R. *Colonial British America: essays in the new history of the early modern era* (Baltimore, 1984)

Hafertepe, K. and O'Gorman, J. F. *American Architects and their Books to 1848* (Amherst, 2001)

Haldane, A. R. B. *New Ways Through the Glens* (London, 1962, reprinted 1995)

Harper, M. and Vance, M. E. (eds) *Myth, Migration and the Making of Memory: Scotia and Nova Scotia c.1700–1900* (Halifax, 1999)

Harris, E. *British Architectural Books and Writers, 1556–1785* (London, 1990)

Haynes, N. *Perth and Kinross: An Illustrated Architectural Guide* (Edinburgh, 2000)

Hudgins, C. L. and Cromley, E. C. *Shaping Communities: Perspectives in Vernacular Architecture* VI (Knoxville, 1997)

Hume, J. *The Industrial Archaeology of Scotland: Highlands and Islands* (London, 1977)

Hunter, J. *A Dance Called America: the Scottish Highlands, the United States and Canada* (Edinburgh, 1994)

Kidd, C. *Subverting Scotland's Past: Scottish Whig Historians and the Creation of an Anglo-British Identity, 1789–1830* (Cambridge, 1993)

King, D. *The Complete Works of Robert and James Adam* (Oxford, 1991)

Kornwolf, J. D. *Architecture and Town Planning in Colonial North America* (Baltimore, 2002)

Kostof, S. *The City Shaped: Urban Patterns and Meanings through History* (London, 1991)

Kroeber, A. L. *Style and Civilisations* (Cornell, 1957)

McAlester, L. and McAlester, V. *A Field Guide to American Houses* (New York, 2003)

McKean, C. *The Scottish Chateau: The Country House of Renaissance Scotland* (Stroud, 2001)

McWilliam, C. *Scottish Townscape* (London, 1975)

Mays, D. (ed.) *The Architecture of Scottish Cities* (East Linton, 1997)

Macaulay, J. *The Classical Country House in Scotland, 1660–1800* (London, 1987)

Macinnes, A. *Clanship, Commerce and the House of Stewart, 1603–1788* (East Linton, 1996)

Mackillop, A. *More Fruitful than the Soil: Army, Empire and the Scottish Highlands, 1715–1830* (East Linton, 2000)

Mancke, E. and Shammas, C. (eds) *The Creation of the British Atlantic World* (Baltimore, 2005)

Markus, T. (ed.) *Order in Space and Society: Architectural Form and its Context in the Scottish Enlightenment* (Edinburgh, 1982)

Maxwell, I. (ed.) *Building Materials of the Scottish Farmstead*, SVBWG (Edinburgh, 1996)

Mitchison, R. and Philipson, N. T. (eds) *Scotland in the Age of Improvement* (Edinburgh, 1970)

Murdoch, A. *British History 1660–1832: National Identity and Local Culture* (London, 1998)

Naismith, R. *Buildings of the Scottish Countryside* (London, 1989)

Nasson, B. *Britannia's Empire: Making a British World* (Stroud, 2004)

Olwell, R. and Tully, A. *Cultures and Identities in Colonial British America* (Baltimore, 2006)

Omand, D. (ed.) *The Ross and Cromarty Book* (Golspie, 1984)

Pictou Heritage Society, *Century Buildings of Rural Pictou County* (Pictou, Nova Scotia, 1973)

Powell, C. *The British Building Industry Since 1800: An economic history*, 2nd edn (London, 1996)

Prest, S. C. *Nineteenth Century Pictou County Furniture* (Pictou, Nova Scotia, 1977)

Pride, G. L. *Glossary of Scottish Building* (Edinburgh, 1975)

Reid, R. *The Georgian House and Its Details* (Bath, 1989)

Richards, E. *The Highland Clearances* (Edinburgh, 2000)

Riches, A. and Stell, G. (eds) *Materials and Traditions in Scottish Building: essays in memory of Sonia Hackett* (Edinburgh, 1992)

Roberts, J. L. *The Jacobite Wars: Scotland and the Military Campaigns of 1715 and 1745* (Edinburgh, 2002)

Rolt, L. T. C. *Thomas Telford* (London, 1958)

RCAHMS. *Scottish Farm Buildings Survey. 1 East Central Scotland* (Edinburgh, 1998)

RCAHMS. *Scottish Farm Buildings Survey. 3 Sutherland* (Edinburgh, 1999)

RCAHMS. *Inventory of Argyll,* 3 (Edinburgh, 1980)

RCAHMS. *Inventory of Argyll,* 5 (Edinburgh, 1984)

RCAHMS. *Inventory of Argyll,* 7 (Edinburgh, 1992)

Shennan, S. J. (ed.) *Archaeological Approaches to Cultural Identity* (London, 1989)

Small, N. P. *Beauty and Convenience: Architecture and Order in the New Republic* (Knoxville, 2003)

Smiles, S. *The Life of Thomas Telford by Smiles* (London, 1861)

Smith, A. *Jacobite Estates of the Forty Five* (Edinburgh, 1982)

Smout, T. C. *A History of the Scottish People, 1560–1830* (London, 1969)

Spadafora, D. *The Idea of Progress in Eighteenth-Century Britain* (New Haven, 1990)

Stevenson, D. *The First Freemasons: Scotland's Early Lodges and their Members* (Aberdeen, 1988)

Stilman, D. *English Neo-Classical Architecture* (London, 1988)

Styles, J. and Vickery, A. (eds) *Gender, Taste, and Material Culture in Britain and North America, 1700–1830* (New Haven, 2006)

Taylor, A. *American Colonies: The Settling of North America* (New York, 2001)

Turnock, D. *The Making of the Scottish Rural Landscape* (Aldershot, 1995)

Whatley, C. A. *Scottish Society, 1707–1830: Beyond Jacobites, towards industrialisation* (Manchester, 2000)

Wade Martins, S. *Farmers, Landlords and Landscapes: Rural Britain 1720 to 1870* (Macclesfield, 2004)

Walker, B. *Farm Buildings in the Grampian Region* (Aberdeen, 1978)

Walker, F. and Sinclair, F. *North Clyde Estuary: an Illustrated architectural guide* (Edinburgh, 1992)

Wahrman, D. *The Making of the Modern Self: Identity and Culture in Eighteenth-Century England* (New Haven, 2004)

Womack, P. *Improvement and Romance: Constructing the Myth of the Highlands* (London, 1989)

Worsley, G. *Classical Architecture in Britain: The Heroic Age* (London, 1995)

Youngson, A. J. *After the '45* (Edinburgh, 1973)

Index